CASTORIADIS AND AUTONOMY IN THE TWENTY-FIRST CENTURY

ALSO AVAILABLE FROM BLOOMSBURY

Cornelius Castoriadis: Key Concepts, ed. Suzi Adams
Postscript on Insignificance: Dialogues with Cornelius Castoriadis, Cornelius Castoriadis (trans. Gabriel Rockhill and John V. Garner)
Castoriadis, Foucault, and Autonomy: New Approaches to Subjectivity, Society, and Social Change, Marcela Tovar-Restrepo
Contemporary Cosmopolitanism, Angela Taraborrelli

CASTORIADIS AND AUTONOMY IN THE TWENTY-FIRST CENTURY

ALEXANDROS SCHISMENOS, NIKOS IOANNOU, AND CHRIS SPANNOS

BLOOMSBURY ACADEMIC
LONDON • NEW YORK • OXFORD • NEW DELHI • SYDNEY

BLOOMSBURY ACADEMIC
Bloomsbury Publishing Plc
50 Bedford Square, London, WC1B 3DP, UK
1385 Broadway, New York, NY 10018, USA
29 Earlsfort Terrace, Dublin 2, Ireland

BLOOMSBURY, BLOOMSBURY ACADEMIC and the Diana logo are trademarks of
Bloomsbury Publishing Plc

First published in Great Britain 2021
This paperback edition published in 2022

Copyright © Alexandros Schismenos, Nikos Ioannou, and Chris Spannos, 2021

Alexandros Schismenos, Nikos Ioannou, and Chris Spannos have asserted
their right under the Copyright, Designs and Patents Act, 1988, to be
identified as Authors of this work.

For legal purposes the Acknowledgments on p. vii constitute an extension of this
copyright page.

Cover design by Charlotte Daniels
Cover image © Jason Chu / Getty Images

All rights reserved. No part of this publication may be reproduced or transmitted
in any form or by any means, electronic or mechanical, including photocopying,
recording, or any information storage or retrieval system, without prior
permission in writing from the publishers.

Bloomsbury Publishing Plc does not have any control over, or responsibility for, any
third-party websites referred to or in this book. All internet addresses given in this
book were correct at the time of going to press. The author and publisher regret
any inconvenience caused if addresses have changed or sites have ceased to
exist, but can accept no responsibility for any such changes.

A catalogue record for this book is available from the British Library.

A catalog record for this book is available from the Library of Congress.

ISBN: HB: 978-1-3501-2337-3
PB: 978-1-3501-9928-6
ePDF: 978-1-3501-2338-0
eBook: 978-1-3501-2339-7

Typeset by Deanta Global Publishing Services, Chennai, India

To find out more about our authors and books visit www.bloomsbury.com and
sign up for our newsletters.

CONTENTS

Acknowledgments vii

PART ONE Toward a Critical Reflection on the West 1

1 Our Decisive Moment 3

2 The Project of Autonomy 24

3 Eurocentric Visions of Modern Greece 41

PART TWO Past—Time and Politics 49

4 Cornelius Castoriadis: A Brief Biography 51

5 The Social-historical Dimension of Time 62

PART THREE Present—Politics and Crisis 83

6 Crisis and Insignificance 85

7 The Invisible Subject 110

8 Power, Authority, and Freedom 126

9 The Ontological Revolution of the Internet 137

PART FOUR Future—Autonomy, Direct Democracy, and Limited Economy 153

10 The Collapse of the Old and the Emergence of New Significations 155

11 New Forms of Social Networking and Local Autonomy 176

Notes 205
References 210
List of Contributors 219
Index 220

ACKNOWLEDGMENTS

In December 2008 a social uprising occurred in Greece, kicking off a dialogue about Cornelius Castoriadis and the project of autonomy between the three of us—Alexandros Schismenos, Nikos Ioannou and Chris Spannos—that has been evolving ever since. That uprising has had a formidable influence on the text that you are about to read. We began to collaborate on this book in 2015, building upon work that each of us had been developing independently. Since coming together, we have conceptualized, re-conceptualized, written, and rewritten this text, with feedback from friends, family, conferences, social movement participants, and anonymous reviewers. Thus, this work has grown beyond the work of the three of us combined. As Aristotle has stated, the whole is greater than the sum of its parts.

We would like to thank Liza Thompson in particular at Bloomsbury for taking on this project, as well as Lisa Goodrum and Lucy Russell for helping us see it through. Bloomsbury has a strong record of publishing exceptional titles about Castoriadis. We are thrilled to have found a home for our book with a publisher that recognizes the importance of Castoriadis's work, and which has enabled us to contribute to his legacy.

After thanking everyone, authors typically assert their own responsibility for any remaining blemishes. We are no different. Any shortcomings are evidence of our own doggedness in the face of generous suggestions on sources, structure, and conceptualizations from friends, family, colleagues, comrades and reviewers. In the end, we only hope to have made original contributions to advance the project of autonomy and to keep the dialogue with Castoriadis open and progressing.

In friendship and freedom,
Chris Spannos, Alexandros Schismenos, and Nikos Ioannou

PART ONE

TOWARD A CRITICAL REFLECTION ON THE WEST

1

Our Decisive Moment

We may now be witnessing the beginning of the end of history. Not because liberal "democracy," "freedom," and markets are emerging to define the modern global order (Fukuyama 1992), no—they are not. But because for nearly three centuries, since "the Age of Enlightenment," the West has pursued a relentless project of conquest and unlimited growth which today threatens the planet's survival. The end of history can make way for a variety of new ways of being, ranging from forms of barbarism, such as fascism and neo-fascism, to forms of autonomy, including collective self-reflection and direct democracy. This book explores the prospects for autonomy as it was proposed by Greek-French philosopher Cornelius Castoriadis, drawing heavily from reflections of practicing direct democracy in social movement spaces in Greece since 2011. In his life, which spanned most of the twentieth century, Castoriadis sought to interpret the world through his philosophy of autonomy while drawing from individual and social struggles to develop his ideas into practical actions aimed at improving lives and deepening democracy. Our book attempts to follow in his footsteps, but in our period, in the twenty-first century. In this opening chapter, we contextualize our lessons within a broader moment that we define as our *decisive moment*. A moment in which we must choose the liberatory potential of autonomy over the deepening barbarism of our times.

The Western project of violent dispossession and accumulation (of people, land, and resources) kicked off in the fifteenth century, evolved in the mid-eighteenth century, and has gained remarkable momentum since the mid-twentieth century. Now, numerous indicators suggest that we are living through a *decisive moment*. In 2005, scientists first used the term "Great Acceleration"[1] to describe the era since the Second World War when humanity's relationship with the natural world embarked upon the most dramatic and rapid transformation "in the history of humankind."[2] This transformation has been so extreme that it has caused scientists to warn that if we want to increase our chances of averting global climate catastrophe, we must act now to decrease our greenhouse gas emissions.[3] But climate change is just one among numerous combined threats that have pushed the planet as close to self-destruction as during the height of Cold War tensions. When the Soviet bloc fell in 1991, scientists set the Doomsday Clock—a symbol of proximity to global catastrophe—to "seventeen minutes to midnight." In this century, numerous threats such as climate change, nuclear weapon proliferation, and information warfare have grown giving scientists reasons to push the clock closer to midnight, closer to self-annihilation.[4] In 2020, the clock inched forward to 100 seconds to midnight. That was before the global Coronavirus pandemic spread, causing millions of people to struggle with Covid-19 symptoms (the disease caused by the virus), resulting in hundreds of thousands of deaths by the Spring of 2020. As the world faces simultaneous existential dangers, mortality casts its dark shadow over our collective future.

In this *decisive moment*, we may, however, also be witnessing the emergence of new history in creation. This is not because governments, corporations, or the market are able to solve the problems of our era. No, in fact, they are often at the root of heartbreaking oppressions.[5] Instead, it is because social movements of the twenty-first century have begun to shake the yoke of what Castoriadis (1997b: 32–43) called the "retreat into conformism"—the decline of social, political, and ideological conflict that has characterized the West since the mid-twentieth century. In the first decade of this century, the West's cynical global "War on Terror" chilled critical self-reflection, as the predominant bipolar view that "you are either with us or against us" divided the world into two camps, "Us and Them," which framed anti-war critics and activists as extremists. Authorities resuscitated this bipolar framing in 2020 when, in May, police murdered George Floyd in the US city of Minneapolis,[6] sparking national outrage against persistent racism across the country in what may have been the largest protests in US history.[7] They categorized those revolting as "extremists" and "terrorists."[8] But times have changed since the Twin Towers collapsed in 2001 and social movements have continued to confront old oppressions that manifest in new ways.

One after another, social movements and uprisings around the world have been challenging the conformism that characterized the early part of this century. Among recent examples, in the early days of the Coronavirus pandemic, thousands of mutual aid groups, involving hundreds of thousands of people,[9] mobilized around the world to support marginalized communities. The virus exposed neoliberalism's underfunding of public health and social safety systems, the ways in which extreme events highlight existing inequities, and—in some countries— the risks that states were willing to take with exposing residents to the virus in order to maintain economic activity. In the UK, the Conservative government had reduced the stock of available emergency personal protective equipment allocated for a possible epidemic by 40 percent.[10] When Covid-19 spread through the UK, some nurses were forced to wear trash bags instead of protective gear, exposing key care providers to heightened risks of catching the virus.[11]

In the months leading up to the Coronavirus crisis protests against neoliberalism rocked countries in 2019's "Autumn of Discontent," from Latin America—Chile, Honduras, and Haiti—to the Middle East—Iraq, Egypt, and Lebanon. Social movements in Hong Kong and Sudan fought authoritarian regimes for deeper democratic participation. Extinction Rebellion championed quick decarbonization, raising concerns long voiced by indigenous peoples, not least with Idle No More in Canada and Standing Rock in the Midwestern US state of South Dakota. Black Lives Matter, Trans Lives Matter, and the #MeToo movements each exposed the violence of racism, gender binaries, and sexism that punctuate everyday life in the West. Omnipresent and intersecting oppressions abound, women and girls led protests against sexism and xenophobia in India, while freedom struggles in Western Sahara, West Papua, Palestine, and elsewhere continued. Earlier in the decade, the Movement of the Squares across Europe, the Occupy movement globally, as well as the Arab Spring demonstrated the power of using public space for civic reflection and deliberation. These and other social movements aim to confront the dangers threatening the world. They inspire hope that the reign of conformity to oppressive ways of being and organizing societies is declining. In this regard, we draw from the reservoir of direct democracy as contemporary social movements have experienced it, but we situate these experiences within the broader political and philosophical project of autonomy that Castoriadis proposed.

Our *decisive moment* at the onset of the twenty-first century is defined by the vibrance of today's global social movements, the presence of deepening ideological conflict, the escalating threats to human and ecological survival, and by the increasing difficulty that society's dominant social imaginary significations (defined in this chapter) face in reproducing themselves. A crescendo of global actors resist conforming to the institutions of power that aim to limit what we can be, in order to institute new forms of direct democracy and self-organization as approaches to collective life that proximate autonomy. To understand our crucial moment, our *kairos*, the work of Castoriadis is important. The extreme precariousness of our planet urgently demands the type of self-limiting response that he advocated within his exploration of autonomy. The rise of global and local social movements that reclaim public space, deliberate, and, in the process, create a public time consistent with the objective of social and individual freedom present new horizons for the project of autonomy, not as a fully defined or complete model, but as the open-ended, self-reflective, directly democratic, and uncertain project that Castoriadis intended. This project is the opposite of heteronomy, which is defined as the unreflective and deterministic rule by an external force.

In this book, our contribution is the application of Castoriadis's philosophy to the world as we experience it in the early twenty-first century. We apply his thinking to the West, broadly defined as the Anglosphere and Europe, but more specifically as it exposes the global crisis in heteronomous social imaginary significations currently affecting the United States, the United Kingdom, and the European Union and as it reveals modern tendencies toward the project of autonomy.

The Social Imaginary Significations of Capitalism

The concept of social imaginary significations is one that we apply throughout this book. In simplifying for brevity here, it conveys the process through which society institutes (creates itself in the first instance) its own world of significations. These become instituted and amount to preconditions and sources of meanings which influence individual and social perceptions of the relationship between society and the individual, between the social-historical constructions of our current lives and the horizons of what is possible. In this way, social imaginary significations are an ensemble, shaping the mode of being in an ontological sense. Castoriadis often used language as an example, given that languages, regardless of origin, rely upon the significations embedded in them for the purposes of communication (Castoriadis 1987: 359; Castoriadis 2002: 64–70; Arnason 2014: 31). It is important to note that social imaginary significations can support both autonomous and heteronomous projects and that these projects are deeply related; however, they are not causal. A main thread in the argument that we weave throughout this book is that, on the one hand, the twenty-first century is experiencing a collapse of the predominant social imaginary significations across the multiplicity of economic, political, and cultural heteronomous forms. These significations include the universally accepted goal of economic growth, but also the ubiquitous objectives of unlimited expansion and rational mastery over nature that drives modernism. Our discussion of the crisis of capitalism's social imaginary significations in this chapter, the Greek crisis in Chapter 3, and Chinese and other capitalisms in Chapter 10 each illustrate how these objectives manifest in our modern world. On the other hand, there has been a simultaneous emergence of new social imaginary significations from below, in the articulation, assertion, and action of public space and public time by social movements. Just as twenty-first-century Greece provides a central reference point for how we perceive capitalism's diverse heteronomous forms, similarly, we draw from the modern Greek experience of social uprisings and autonomous forms of struggle as our main reference point because it is our own experience, even as we identify diverse and equally important manifestations of autonomy, be they in southeast Mexico or northern Syria. Ancient Greece, specifically ancient Athens,[12] is critically referenced for contrasting modern democratic forms, no matter their electoral and representational variety. Our intent is to explore these examples, not as historical or sociological analyses, but to highlight how the philosophical concepts of autonomy and heteronomy manifest, and to give examples of the more recent Greek social imaginary significations that allow people to traverse the distance between them.

With respect to the heteronomous social imaginary significations of capitalism, our analysis is concerned with how

1. economic significations dominate over other spheres of social life. Five centuries of capitalist expansion has resulted in the displacement of the totality of prior social imaginary significations to the extent that economic significations have assumed unprecedented importance.

2. capitalism produces its own temporality that supports the significations of indefinite progress, unlimited growth, accumulation, and the pursuit of exact knowledge for the conquest of nature in our time. Capitalist temporality institutes chronometric time, calibrated in hours, minutes, and seconds, allowing for the organized discipline of society, such as production and consumption, for example.

3. capitalist consumption operates to perpetuate a semblance of meaning through the use of economic incentives to learn, train, work, obey, produce and reproduce capitalism (Smith 2014: 160–5).

We explore these themes throughout the book. One observation, in short, is that, for the vast majority capitalism appears to be the only "rational" economic system (Straume 2011: 27–50). The problem is not simply that there is no alternative, as Margaret Thatcher infamously declared. The problem, as it was considered by cultural theorist Fredric Jameson, can be glimpsed by admitting that it is easier to imagine the end of the world than the end of capitalism.[13] That is because the ideologies rationalizing capitalism's existence, from its inception, had been working to establish capitalism as an object occupying a place in the natural order of history and society, emerging from and operating on "natural laws" (Mirowski 1992).[14] Its "naturalization" has contributed to it being a dominant signification to such an extent that capitalism appears as a "total social fact" (Mauss 2002: 100–2). In this sense, it is worse than Jameson suggests because the underlying, yet unstated, problem is really that capitalism is assumed to be eternal.

When the Eternal Trembles

The various forms of society that we have known throughout history are, as Castoriadis proposed, in essence defined by imaginary creation. This does not mean that societies are a figment of the imagination, but that they create their own forms, and that these forms bring into being their own world by constituting networks of norms, institutions, and values that shape orientations and goals for collective and individual life (Castoriadis 1987: 117, 146–7, 160; Castoriadis 1993: 102–29; Arnason 2014: 34). We mentioned language as one example before, but religion is another example of a social imaginary signification. When these created norms, values, institutions, and their outcomes begin to fail systematically, there is a crisis in the reproduction of the social imaginary. The failure of the West to reproduce its social imaginary, and the consequences for the project of autonomy, is introduced in the chapters that make up Part One of the book, while the remaining parts explore these aspects in more depth. It is our view that this crisis can help clarify the possibilities for the contestation of significations that define and dominate societies. Or to put it another way, the crisis can open new opportunities for the project of autonomy.

Long before the 2007 global financial crisis, positive attitudes toward capitalism began falling in the United States. In 2002, four out of five people in the United States (80 percent) viewed capitalism as the best economic system for the future.[15] By 2014, people living in China, India, South Korea, and Vietnam all held stronger positive beliefs in capitalism than the US public.[16] Since then, perceptions in the United States have continued to fall so that, by 2018, only a slight majority (56 percent) held a positive view of capitalism.[17] Polls in early 2020 found that public perception of capitalism as a system changed very little in the United States.[18] This trend also appears elsewhere in the West. For instance, a 2016 poll showed that in Britain 39 percent viewed capitalism unfavorably (*versus* 33 percent favorably).[19] This shift occurred in parallel to rising global social movements challenging extreme inequalities—not least the European Squares and Occupy movements already mentioned. But economic crisis combined with a decade of sluggish recovery, growing concentrations of wealth, the increasing potential for the impending global economic crisis to be worse than that of 2007, burgeoning understandings that factors beyond our control—like our place of birth or residence, the wealth we are born into, gender, race, sexual orientation, age, or ability—impact upon our freedoms, are compounded by environmental, climate, biodiversity, and health crises—including the Coronavirus pandemic—stoking anxieties and fears across the political spectrum.

Ideological Conflict

Neoliberalism may have enforced the dominance of economy over all spheres of social life, imposing the prisms of calculation and rational mastery over everything. Yet the crisis in social imaginary significations of capitalism has opened the way for new manifestations of ideological tensions—not visibly present since the conflicts between liberalism, socialism, and fascism that defined most of the twentieth century. These tensions emerge as new generations of fascists and leftists vie to take power. Actors on the political right have grown more ambitious in the first two decades of this century, from first proposing cuts to taxes and welfare to graduated attacks on women's rights, migrants, people of color, science, and LGBTQI+ communities. The convergence of the center-and far-right has grown in strength and size, encompassing so-called center-right parties as well as white supremacists, fascists, and neo-Nazis (Renton 2019). The victories of conservative parties in 2016, when the Brexit referendum took place in the UK and when Donald Trump was elected president in the United States, are illustrative. The right made the Brexit vote possible by curating British concerns for armies of immigrants "invading" the UK to take healthcare, pensions, and benefits away from worthy domestic citizens. These are the same fears that Boris Johnson rode onto prime ministerial power with, in December 2019. Similar scapegoating, rails against women's liberation, promises to build a US/Mexico border wall to keep migrants out, enabled Trump. Shortly after taking office Trump enacted his visa ban on seven majority Muslim countries. A right-wing offensive has been successful and continues to creatively mutate and adapt. In the UK, the Labour Party's 2019—ostensibly popular[20]—promises to nationalize key sectors of the economy, support the national healthcare system, and implement a "Green Industrial Revolution" and other social welfare benefits were not sufficient to stem the rising right.

The convergence of the far-right in the West is more than the simple amalgamation and concentration of previously disparate forces. It is the manifestation of a social-historical form. For Castoriadis, the social-historical is the idea that society and history are one and the same; that is because they are both comprised of time. This notion is a radical departure from traditional reflections on history and society which has situated them "on the terrain and within the boundaries of inherited logic and ontology" (Castoriadis 1987: 168). The inherited view of history and society is the sum and sequence (conscious or not) of a multitude of subjects which are determined by necessary relations and by which a system of ideas either is embodied in an ensemble of things or reflects it. Through its determinism, traditional ontology prejudices being in a way that excludes the essential elements of society and history, namely their creation, self-creation, and comparative indeterminacy (Klooger 2014: 108). This is crucial for Castoriadis's theory of social-historical creation because he views human beings themselves as not being defined by reason, but by radical imagination (Castoriadis 2007: 179). It is through the radical imagination's negotiation with society as a whole—the social, historical, and institutional fabrics comprised of time and networks of social imaginary significations—that human beings proximate autonomy to alter their own societies. We consider the social-historical dimension of time in Chapter 5 and, more deeply, the creation of the state and power in Chapter 6, but for our purposes here, it is enough to say that the state apparatus defines society's significations by providing legitimacy and normalization to these far-right ideologies, their convergences, networks, and emerging norms as they cut across and share overlapping ideological values and goals. For example, Trump's placement of right, far-right, and fascist figures in top positions in his administration provided a parallax view where formerly politically distinct elements were brought together in ways that not only unified and normalized emergent extreme-right networks and cultures but also created a context enabling obscene abuses of power, such as Trump's family separation policy, which forcefully and systematically removed thousands of immigrant children from their parents, placed them in separate detention centers, held them in unhealthy conditions, refused them access to medical treatment, forced children including toddlers (unaccompanied by the carers they traveled with) into courtrooms, and even arbitrarily placed released children into new care settings. His initial chief strategist Steve Bannon, arrested and charged with fraud in August 2020, is a celebrity figure in the global alt-right. His former press secretary Sean Spicer denied—in the White House press room—that Hitler gassed millions of Jews during the holocaust.[21] That these figures are no longer part of the Trump administration notwithstanding, the state as a social-historical form has legitimized right-wing extremism in a country that political theory considers the pinnacle of modern democracy (Wagner 2007). Around the world, autocratic, authoritarian, fascist, and crypto-fascist states—from India to Turkey, Saudi Arabia to the Philippines, Brazil to Greece—are following suit.

The right's weaponization of digital technologies to wage ideological war is characteristic of this new conflict. From tracking user's mobile devices while they attend political rallies and church to knowing their Netflix preferences, violations of privacy, exploitation of data, and social engineering are being used to sway major electoral outcomes.[22] The case of Cambridge Analytica and its influence on both the UK Brexit vote (to leave the EU) and the election of Donald Trump are emblematic.[23] Before joining Trump's campaign in 2016, Steve Bannon served as vice-president of Cambridge Analytica for two years. There, he intended to suppress black people from voting in the 2016 US elections, exploit racial tensions, and promote a "cultural war."[24] Cambridge Analytica rehearsed the impact of targeted messaging in Malaysia, Kenya, and Brazil. They harvested the profiles of more than 50 million Facebook users for a social engineering strategy to achieve the ends of their right-wing clients. While it is difficult to know the extent to which Cambridge Analytica's strategy contributed to either the Brexit vote or Trump's electoral success, these examples highlight how the right has leveraged digital technology to its advantage in the ideological conflict.[25] And this is just a glimpse of what is to come. Modern far-right strategies in the West rely less on building traditional parties and organizations—which can be disbanded, discredited, and outlawed—and more on unaccountable talking head figures who use social media platforms to build followings and amplify calls for extreme violence, leaving individuals to either act as "lone wolfs," as numerous mass shooters have done, or loosely mobilize networks, gatherings, and events as the talking heads remain unaccountable.[26] Far-right extremists, for example, created

125 Facebook groups representing, as of April 2020, 72,686 members. These new groups' mission is to mobilize for "boogaloo," a term the far-right uses to call for civil war. Following Donald Trump's tweets calling for people in the United States to "liberate themselves" from Coronavirus lockdown, far-right groups strategized on the ways to leverage the president's call to promote civil war.[27] Rather than being an isolated feature of our times, however, this example is one of many which together illustrate a dangerous dimension of our digital era. The internet, which provides opportunities for freedom and autonomy, is itself a site of ideological contestation and is at risk of being turned into an anti-human platform. Chapter 9 is dedicated to the ontological problems and opportunities that the internet presents for the project of autonomy.

On the left of the political spectrum, the struggle of significations of capitalism to reproduce themselves has accompanied a simultaneous rise in positive attitudes toward "socialism." In the United States, an upward trend of "socialist-curious" young adults occurred from 2010, when 51 percent of millennials held a positive view of "socialism," climbing to 56 percent in 2016. These views held a steady baseline at 51 percent in 2018, with many millennials willing to describe themselves as "democratic socialist." This trend has coincided with the rise of Democratic Socialists in the United States, with new members swelling the ranks of the Democratic Socialists of America (DSA). Within just two years, the DSA's membership grew from 6,000 members to more than 50,000, which makes it the largest socialist organization in the United States since the 1940s, when the Communist Party had about 100,000 members.[28] Before curiosity about socialism increased, the meteoric rise of figures such as Bernie Sanders and Alexandria Ocasio-Cortez, who have become household names and challenging figures opposing dominant policy approaches, was practically unimaginable in the United States. Similarly, despite the UK Labour Party's defeat in December 2019, public support for nationalization of major sectors of the economy grew substantially[29] and a broader left resurgence transformed the neoliberal Blairite Labour Party into a more explicitly left-leaning party, however temporarily, promoting a strong program of revitalizing the welfare state and nationalization with a view to placing the well-being of people and communities at the center of their program.[30] These developments, including policy proposals in the United States such as the "70 percent top marginal tax rate" and the "Green New Deal," have been hotly contested in the ideological arena, putting elites on the defensive and reclaiming the notion that economies and policies can be directed to addressing inequities as well as responding justly to climate, biodiversity, and health emergencies. Whereas previously capitalism was surreptitiously woven into the inevitably unseen but all-encompassing fabric of life, not to be mentioned but painfully experienced by the majority, in 2017, the then British prime minister, Theresa May, was forced, in Bank of England speech, to defend free market capitalism explicitly. A rupture challenging the eternal status of capitalism. In the United States, Donald Trump's Council of Economic Advisers produced their 2018 report, "The Opportunity Costs of Socialism," which expressed worry that socialist policies in Congress were gaining support, particularly among younger voters.

Come 2020, the global Coronavirus pandemic flung the curtains open to cast a challenging critical light on previously held economic orthodoxies. In the UK, parents stopped sending their children to school while the government stalled in its response. Then, tens of thousands of former healthcare workers returned to the National Health Care service to provide critical support to victims of the disease. More than 750,000 members of the public offered to aid the fight as volunteers. Speaking from a self-isolation bunker, the then Covid-19–infected prime minister Boris Johnson, due to the public response, was forced to contradict a central tenet of Thatcherism when he admitted that "there really is such a thing as society."[31] The Conservative government enacted an unprecedented yet temporary 80 percent wage subsidy for workers facing temporary layoffs (furloughs). More widely, the concept of a European financial transaction tax is gaining traction among powerful EU countries.[32] While airline levies and progressive tax suggestions abound, so do more radical ideas to nationalize fossil fuel emitting and financing industries in order to engage in just transitions moving us toward decarbonized, democratic, and renewable energy systems, high levels of energy efficiency, sustainable agriculture and transport, and protecting ocean and biodiversity for nature-based solutions to climate change and health risks. Demands that factors which increase exposure to poor health outcomes (poverty; hunger; crowded, unsafe, and inconsistent housing; differentiated access to healthcare services; and exposure to precarious or onerous work, for example) be systematically addressed have also increased as Covid-19 disproportionately impacts people of color in both the United States and the United Kingdom.[33] These demands, however, can be sharply contrasted to those protesting Covid-19 social distancing measures, backed by a loose coalition of Conservative groups affiliated with Trump's White House,[34] often armed and calling for liberation with signs like "This 'Cure' Is Deadlier Than Covid" and confederate flags. This hastening gap also defines our time.

Further defining this ideological conflict, twenty-first-century social movements have critically challenged institutions and social relations perpetuating authoritarianism, oppression, white supremacy, sexism, and inequality. They have opened public debate in ways that rightly challenge Western identity and supremacy. For many in the West, it is no longer acceptable to speak, for example, of democracy, development, and human rights without also accepting the West's legacy of slavery, colonialism, imperialism, preemptive war, and its numerous disastrous attempts at "promoting democracy" violently and, often, even undemocratically. Movements to decolonize the university, such as "Rhodes Must Fall"—spanning from the University of Cape Town in South Africa to the University of Oxford in the UK—are conscious of the legacies of apartheid and racism as well as their role in perpetuating these problems in academia today (Bhambra, Gebrial, and Nişancıoğlu 2018). We are living through an age that is more self-reflexive and more aware of the legacies of colonialism and slavery that persist through inequities today. Increasingly, Western values, norms, and identity cannot be approached from a position of ideological neutrality (Whitmarsh and Thomson 2013). At the same time, nationalism has increasingly defined political rhetoric—again, highlighting deepening divides in ideological positionings.

The Radical Imaginary *versus* Inherited Ontology

Ideological schisms have created a cleavage between the right and traditional left from which a radical autonomous imaginary could emerge, but both the manifestation and direction are uncertain. The crisis of legitimacy that capitalism presently faces impacts the vast majority of people, regardless of whether and how they vote. Everyone that does not own significant amounts of capital seems to be searching for something new. While the right is reconfiguring old narratives to stoke hatred and fear in order to scapegoat the traditionally marginalized and build their base, they are doing so in new ways. The left, on the other hand, is attempting to revitalize the project of "socialism" without fully reckoning with the problems of socialism's past. This has taken various forms, including "democratic socialist" visions of more democracy (however stopping far short of direct democracy), co-ops, and markets,[35] as well as post-capitalist (Mason 2016) and post-work (Srnicek and Williams 2016) imaginaries which mobilize Soviet-era science fiction, automation (Bastani 2019), and universal basic income for versions of modernism and growth inherited from the West's Enlightenment project of unlimited expansion and rational mastery.

The debates about the Green New Deal—and whether it should be growth-driven precisely when numerous indicators suggest that we have pushed our planet's scarce resources to the precipice—highlight the precarious position of the radical imagination. Left proposals for a Green New Deal, such as Robert Pollin's, argue that a higher economic growth rate will "accelerate the rate at which clean energy supplants fossil fuels, since higher levels of GDP will correspondingly mean a higher level of investment being channeled into clean-energy projects."[36] For Pollin, neoliberalism—which became the dominant economic policy when fascist Augusto Pinochet overthrew Chile's moderate president Salvador Allende in a 1973 coup—warps economic growth in negative ways. In his view, neoliberalism evangelizes the real religion of "maximizing profits for business in order to deliver maximum incomes and wealth for the rich," but growth per se, is not itself a bad thing. Certainly not "green" growth. This understanding contrasts sharply with Castoriadis who saw economic growth emerging from the early "critical" period of modernity (1750–1950), which gave rise to capitalism and accumulation, not just for accumulation's sake but for the "relentless transformation of the conditions and the means of accumulation, the incessant revolutionizing of production, commerce, finance, and consumption." Growth embodies a new social imaginary signification: the unlimited expansion of "rational-mastery." In this view, growth is a germ that sprouted from traditional Western logic and ontology and reflects the negative side of modernity, which poses dire consequences for the planet. The concept of green growth should not complicate this. To be against growth is not to reject projects for clean energy or green jobs, increased energy savings, sustainable agriculture and transport, universal childcare, or more leisure time. Rather, it is to be for these things but question who will pay for them and how the costs and benefits will be distributed globally to avoid a colonizing Green New Deal that promotes renewable energy in the rich West through the devastating extraction of the necessary mineral and metal resources from the global south.[37] To elaborate, growth is a social imaginary signification that actively operates against the need for critical reflection and self-limitation precisely when the world needs such reflection and boundaries. Ingerid Straume's (2011) thought experiment illustrates the problem:

> Let us try to imagine an economic theory whose principle is de-growth, lessened consumption, production, transportation, and which, above all, is based on leaving all earth's remaining minerals in the ground—forever. In the light of the current economic doctrine, such ideas are plainly absurd. In light of resource ecology and planetary sustainability, it is perfectly logical. As this thought experiment shows, it is very hard, if not impossible, to think wholly "outside capitalism." The significations of capitalism—instrumentalism, consumerism, rational control, computation, etc.—are

deeply rooted in the social world, and therefore in the socialized psyche of all individuals in capitalist societies.

In our *decisive moment*, however, climate change requires a rupture away from the predominant ideas, norms, and practices. As economic anthropologist Jason Hickel has stated, it is theoretically possible to achieve a good life for all within planetary boundaries by adopting fairer distributive policies. However, this requires rich nations—predominantly of the West—to dramatically reduce their biophysical footprints by 40–50 percent. Hickel concludes that rich nations need to abandon growth as a policy objective and shift to post-capitalist economic models in order for them to fit within the boundaries of a safe and just space of policy making that protects us from climate change breakdown.[38]

As Covid-19 related social distancing measures lift in the Spring of 2020, government concerns for kickstarting the economy are preeminent despite public worries[39] and scientific concerns[40] about the virus spreading. The social imaginary signification of growth—in the face of our ocean and biodiversity losses, climate and health crises, and continuing economic inequities—will hasten global emergencies.

The Hold of Inherited Ontology

Highlighting the depth and dominance of the significations of capitalism exposes obstacles for the radical imagination to overcome. But there is another set of problems for those who have already traveled far enough to critically understand capitalism's many problems and are now open to consider alternatives, including those who are willing to identify themselves as "socialist" or "democratic socialist." The return to socialism coincides with a revitalization of the Marxist Imaginary: "the entire range of socio-cognitive creations instituted in ways shaped by the sedimented history of that tradition" (Hastings-King 2014: 5, 303). And, this is not without its problems.

The Marxist Imaginary was the primary reservoir from which were drawn the dominant critiques of capitalism and historical understandings of change during the period of industrialization spanning the nineteenth and twentieth centuries. But Marx's absolutist view promoting historical and social determinism,[41] his reduction of alienation to the sphere of production, his affirmation of the naturalization of capitalism (through forcefully asserting its supposed "natural laws"), and his conviction that capitalist growth would serve the masses are untenable with regard to the goals of social-historical change as the project of self-emancipation (most certainly characterized by free-association, direct democracy, freedom from oppression, classlessness, well-being, and ecological sustainability). We are not inevitably traveling toward utopia. In heteronomous societies, such as those which manifest in diverse forms throughout history, where the social imaginary significations are attributed to an external source rather than posited explicitly as self-made human creation, alienation from history and society exist across all spheres of human life. Capitalism adapts quickly and morphs as required for the interests of the most wealthy and powerful. Limitless growth—which is making the planet uninhabitable for so many already experiencing the impacts of unequal trade relations and climate change (as well as for future generations)—was never possible in a world with finite resources. Harking back to the legacy of Marxism—regardless of technological upgrades or moonshot bets on asteroid mining and colonizing Mars—is to risk further failure in our *decisive moment*. The Marxist Imaginary will not be the source of a new radical imaginary in the West.

Autonomy or Barbarism

Our *decisive moment* emerges from the "retreat into conformism" mentioned earlier, in which depoliticization—characterized as cynicism and lack of meaning, or "insignificance" in Castoriadis's terminology—in the West collapsed in on itself and gave rise to reactionary and scapegoating movements. As this chapter lays out, this new phase is characterized by the combined weakening significations of capitalism, the urgency of multifold planetary crisis threatening nature and society, the rise of new ideological conflicts, and openings for the radical imagination required to advance the project of autonomy today. Our present period is not a determined or successive phase of history or society. Heightened social and environmental precariousness, amplified by technological innovation, threaten the possibilities of lapsing back into a closed society and tearing ourselves apart. These problems characterize what Castoriadis defined as barbarism. They emerge when a society is no longer able to critically self-reflect, the problem which Part One of this book aims to address.

It is urgent that the radical social imaginary activates in ways that transcend the dominant, heteronomous, social imaginary significations. In this, Castoriadis's thought is helpful. According to him, the rejuvenation of the radical social imaginary does not necessarily depend on ideological conflict and, fortunately, nothing requires that it emerge from pre-existing modes of thinking and being, what Castoriadis called creation *ex nihilo* (Mouzakitis 2014: 53–63), creation from nothing. Revolt, rebellion, and revolution can occur from within any sphere of human life, beyond simply the economic. For that to occur, however, a consciousness that we create society and history—wherever we are—and that we can place limits on our own excesses will have to emerge. This is the project of autonomy, which challenges head-on the modern ethos of growth, indefinite progress, unlimited expansion, and rational mastery which are typically placed beyond question or doubt. Our *decisive moment*, therefore, brings us closer to the choice between autonomy or barbarism.

Moving Forward

In Chapter 1, we introduced forthcoming parts of this book as well as key ideas (such as social imaginary significations and the social-historical) to argue that a new social imaginary consistent with the project of autonomy must overtake the social imaginary that defines heteronomous rule. While heteronomy is rule by the other—an external force such as a god, feudal lord, president, capital, or some perceived natural force such as Marx's "economic law of motion of modern society," for example—the project of autonomy places human creative imagination at the center of societal transformation and overthrows historical, social, and cultural determinisms that historically have acted as obstacles to self-rule. Chapter 2 introduces the concept of autonomy, both its meanings and ancient origins, laying the ground for a new ecology of critical self-reflection and collective decision-making as a radical break from the modern ethos. We take note of the important role that civic time and space played in ancient autonomy because we argue that public time and space is similarly important for modern movements. We contrast the strengths and weaknesses between the ancient form of direct democracy in Athens with modern representative democracy in the West. While the Western Imaginary draws from ancient Greek sources to support its own claims to modernity, Chapter 3 surveys recent history from the creation of modern Greece in the early nineteenth century to the economic crisis that rocked the country in the early twenty-first century. We explore this example as an illustration of how the heteronomy of modern capitalism in the West enforces a Eurocentric notion of modernity back onto Greece, the source of its imaginary, in order to advance the project of modernity that further abstracts away notions of direct democracy and autonomy. We elucidate these notions, as they appear in modern Greece, in later chapters. Before doing so, however, we take a step back. Chapter 4 provides a short biographical account of Castoriadis's life which offers a window to glimpse the tumultuous and revolutionary history and politics of Europe in the twentieth century that both shaped and was shaped by him through his militant and intellectual contributions across the realms of politics, philosophy, economics, and psychoanalysis. From this summary of Castoriadis's life and thought, Chapter 5 proceeds to further elucidate important concepts in his ontology and political theory. In Chapter 6, we apply key concepts to history, including major events in the twentieth century such as the Second World War and the Cold War, and to early twenty-first century history such as corporate globalization and economic crisis. This is done to frame our discussion of the state as a social-historical form and emergent social movements. Chapter 7 interrogates the various concepts of revolutionary subject in relation to the project of autonomy and direct democracy, drawing from the example of Greek social unrest since 2008. Chapter 8 looks at the process of the imaginary institution of society and Chapter 9 turns to explore dimensions of cyberspace as a nexus of social representations of individual identity that forms a new sphere of being. Turning to look more broadly at the global crisis in heteronomous significations, Chapter 10 assesses how capitalism produces significations consistent with commodification of public and private space in China, Africa, Latin America, and Europe, with attention paid to Greece, and assesses the impact on the crisis of significations in the West. Finally, Chapter 11 reflects on how autonomous individuals and communities find meaning in global culture and how these new meanings advance the project of autonomy in the twenty-first century.

2

The Project of Autonomy

As a collective and as individuals, we both make and are made by society. Thus, for Castoriadis, autonomy corresponds to a partial-determinist ontology, one which allows for both the determinate *instituted* and the collective-self-creating *instituting*. Castoriadis posits direct democratic forms of self-organization as approaches to collective life that most closely approximate autonomy. In this way both the ancient Athenian and modern experiences of democracy are two instances of the project of autonomy (Straume 2014: 191–204). This chapter focuses on the link between autonomy and direct democracy, first by outlining the essence of autonomy and how it manifested in ancient democratic practices, then by contrasting it against modern representative forms of democracy in order to flesh out the differences and expand on the meaning of autonomy.

Ancient Athens features heavily in Castoriadis' thinking on direct democracy and autonomy. To help understand his views on the relationship between autonomy and ancient Athenian democracy, let's consider recent work by historian and classical political theorist Josiah Ober, as it provides a good comparison. Ober draws from the ancient experience of Athenian democracy to highlight how direct democracy could operate in the modern world as a "plausible regime" on a scale larger than the city-state. He argues that direct democracy is possible in "a complex society far larger than the tiny, face-to-face foraging communities in which participatory self-government was first practiced" (Ober 2017: 59). His model is designed to answer the question of how a human community can gain the benefits arising from social cooperation despite imperfect human beings and without relying on a master (Ober 2017: 34).

In sharp contrast with Castoriadis's understanding, the example of ancient Athens as a model of democracy is simply a "germ" from which our modern societies evolved and mutated. It is not to be considered as an "eternal model, prototype, or paradigm" nor, in the study of cultures, is it to be examined relatively, as "one specimen among others" (1997c). It is not even a "regime" in the traditional sense of the word. For Castoriadis, no law or set of laws designed to model a utopian society could ever encompass all aspects of human activity. That is not to say that it is worthless to design models. Ober's work forcefully argues that direct democracy is not only possible, because it existed for nearly 200 years, but also scalable and does not depend on ideal subjects.

But Castoriadis suggests something different. He argues that the gap between law and reality which makes such models impossible is not accidental but essential. This is because "No regulation will ever be able to get a tight grip upon the perpetual alteration of social and historical reality. At the very most, such a regulation can try to kill this alteration. But then, in killing it, it kills the social-historical; it kills its subject and its object" (Castoriadis 2002: 30–1). This killing of the subject and object occurs through the institution of heteronomy—the established denial that we create our own institutions and the attribution of this creation to an external force such as god or some immutable laws imposing progressive stages of history. When the institution of heteronomous forms occurs, it means that these forms—institutions, cultures, laws, norms, networks, etc.—break with their makers, those who created them, and establish alienation. The social imaginary significations of the new heteronomous forms present new ways of being. These new heteronomous forms become instituting, or self-creating, and they institute the types of social individuals that sustain them through the creation of new forms of education, training, cultures, networks, incentives, and more. Thus we aim at changing the relationship between the instituting society and the instituted society (the dominant order) in which participating in street and community level decision-making is considered fanciful while forms of representative democracy that elect to power leaders with limited public support is celebrated. The relationship between the instituted and the emerging instituting society is one of a continuous interaction through the collective self-creation of collectivities and the social-historical environments highlighted in a struggle for a more self-reflective and equitable way of organizing decision-making.

For example, Chapter 3 illustrates the tense relationship between instituting and instituted forms in modern Greece, between perceived past and present, as capitalism attempts to institute new forms of financial dominance advancing the Western Imaginary. And Chapter 6 provides an overview of the modern social movement institution of autonomous forms, specifically through the creation of a new public space and time. These latter forms suggest a society that "once and for all condemns the reign of the instituted and seeks the correct relationship, the just relationship between the instituting and the instituted" (Castoriadis 2002: 31). Democracy, in the autonomous sense, is the pursuit of this relationship through praxis because it "is the self-institution of the collectivity by the collectivity, and it is this self-institution as movement . . . facilitated by determinate institutions, but also by the knowledge, *spread out among the collectivity, that our laws have been made by us and that we can change them*" (Castoriadis 1996: 122, emphasis added). It is this collective knowledge combined with the practice of self-institution which opens the gateway to autonomy as a historical project that transcends models.

Defining Autonomy

In the social-historical sense, autonomy is an unfinished project of modernity. According to Castoriadis, pseudo-rational mastery, the state, and capitalism are just one side of modernity, currently the dominant heteronomous side. On the other side, however, are the emancipatory social movements of past and present—those struggling for autonomy, self-governance, and direct democracy. The co-birth of philosophy and politics found in the emergent democratic project of Athens, created in the sixth and fifth centuries BCE and spanning nearly two centuries, helped give rise to these struggles. Events occurring between 510–506 BCE which resulted in the revolutionary reorganization of Athens into ten tribes, thus breaking tyrannical rule, led to temporalities of popular governance that came to self-define ancient Athens. Debates about whether the practice of self-government was instantiated by the reforms of Cleisthenes, a politician of aristocratic origins who is well positioned to play the role needed for "The Great Man Theory" of history, or through a revolutionary period and popular uprising that sustained these reforms through a wider and deeper process of self-institution are not our focus (Curtis in Lévêque and Vidal-Naquet 1996; Ober 1996; and Cartledge 2016). We are interested, instead, in the instantiation of, ultimately, a secular civic space and time that was separate from religious space and time (Lévêque and Vidal-Naquet 1996). A moment which enabled the collectivity to interrogate its own past and grasp possibilities for future autonomous horizons (Castoriadis 1997: 281). A time which allowed for the self-institution of directly democratic forms of self-governance so that the demos could appeal "against itself in front of itself" (Castoriadis 1997: 283). This is the essence of the project of autonomy that concerns us. In this chapter, we introduce the project of autonomy by exploring features of the ancient example. Then, to further clarify what autonomy means, we compare it to contemporary democratic systems, cultures, and attitudes.

Autonomy, in Castoriadis's terms, does not mean the type of individual freedom that classical liberalism proposes (Karagiannis and Wagner 2013). Rather, it is a sociopolitical project aspiring for the creation of a self-limiting society. The importance of reflectively arrived at but collectively agreed limits contrasts sharply with our modern world. The project of autonomy forcefully challenges notions of growth, indefinite progress, unlimited expansion, and rational mastery inherited from the traditional logic and ontology of modernism, which adherents across the political spectrum uphold religiously, for example, when maintaining mantras that data, artificial intelligence, markets, the state, perceived natural laws, or god(s) always know more than human beings.

While we have outlined the essence of autonomy in this chapter, dictionary definitions of the word "Autonomous" explain that "Auto" + "Nom(os)" is, of course, derived from the Greek. Auto meaning "self," "same," and "spontaneous," and nomos meaning "law" or "custom," as in, "one who gives oneself his or her own law is practicing the act of self-governance." This is in sharp contrast to heteronomy which, as mentioned, is rule by an external other. Castoriadis goes further by explaining that the creation of an autonomous society is the historical creation of individuals "who have internalized both the necessity of laws and the possibility of putting the laws into question."

The "Accusation of Unlawfulness"

One of the ways that autonomy manifested in the ancient Athenian experience was through the "accusation of unlawfulness." This procedure could be invoked when an Athenian citizen made a proposal to the democratic assembly and the assembly voted for it. Another citizen could accuse the proposer of inducing the people to vote for an "unlawful law." In this case, the proposer could be acquitted or convicted. A popular court of 1,001 to 1,501, drawn by lot, would decide to uphold the law if the proposer was acquitted or annulled if convicted. What made this aspect important, according to Castoriadis, was that the demos was appealing against itself in front of itself. The "appeal was from the whole body of citizens (or whichever part of it was present when the proposal in question was adopted) to a huge random sample of the same body sitting after passions had calmed, listening again to contradictory arguments and assessing the matter from a relative distance" (Castoriadis 1997: 283–4).

Tragedy

For Castoriadis, an autonomous society enables a collective of individuals who are at once "capable of interrogation, reflectiveness, and deliberation" and of individuals "loving freedom and accepting responsibility" (Castoriadis 1991: 173–4). Autonomy, in this context, is more than the simple specification of rules and procedures, their functions, and outcomes. It is a new constellation of meaning, relationships, history, and creation. It aspires to bring "to light society's instituting power" and render it "explicit in reflection." This process requires what Castoriadis described as "perpetual interrogativity" (Castoriadis 2002: 49). Among the other ancient forms that enabled this was a sixth-century cultural breakthrough that we know of as tragic drama. Tragedy at this moment represented a "fruitful clash between the old, myth-based explanation of both the natural world and of human society and the new, revolutionary, human-centered view of the world" (Cartledge 2016: 64). Thus, tragedy was not simply a literary form or religious practice. It was an institution facilitating the process of creative self-limitation in that it exposed the dangers of hubris. This danger was exemplified, according to Castoriadis, by the fall of Athenian democracy. Athens' defeat in the Peloponnesian War was the result of the hubris of the Athenians where "'limits' were transgressed which were nowhere defined" (Castoriadis 1997: 282).

Tragedy reflected these risks of self-limitation as a political dimension through an ontological chaos, such that "being is chaos." Chaos is understood here as the absence of order or "order through catastrophe." Tragedy does not express this through reasoning, but rather makes it visible so that the audience can feel it (Klimis 2014). For Castoriadis, the play that effectively illustrates this political dimension of tragedy, this "ontological chaos," is Antigone (442 BCE). In the play Creon, king of Thebes, condemns Polyneices's corpse to rot on the battlefield as lawful punishment for treason. Yet, Polyneices's sister Antigone seeks a burial for him consistent with the gods' wishes, thus placing divine law over human law. For Castoriadis, the play illustrates how justice of the gods does not suffice any more than do the laws of the land suffice. In obeying these laws, people must know that they do not define exclusively what is permitted and that they do not exhaust, either, what is forbidden (Castoriadis 2007: 13–19). The paradox is that by insisting on this punishment for Polyneices, Creon, who upholds the city's laws, demonstrates his willingness to be alone in thinking that he is right. As such, he transgresses collective wisdom and becomes a man without a city. But Antigone is also without a city as she flouts the city's laws to champion divine laws. In these ways, both Creon and Antigone commit hubris. The play exhibits the uncertainty pervading political action and democratic frameworks as it "sketches the impurity of motives" and "exposes the inconclusive character of the reasoning upon which we base our decisions" (Castoriadis 1997: 286). The ancient role of tragedy served to illuminate that human intentions, as causes, are unable to guarantee the production of positive and corresponding outcomes. This is especially pertinent for individuals who are alone in thinking they are right. For, tragedy shows "not only that we are not masters of the consequences of our actions but that we are not even masters of their *meaning*" (Castoriadis 1997: 284; emphasis in original). Thus, aside from exposing the dangers of hubris, tragedy also exposed the need for collective wisdom (Klimis 2014), a key characteristic of creative self-institution, however uncertain the outcomes of the autonomous project may be.

Reabsorbing Explicit Power Back into Politics

Thus, tragedy and the "unlawful law" are both examples of how ancient direct democracy reabsorbed the political as explicit power back into politics "as the lucid and deliberate activity whose object is the explicit institution of society" (Castoriadis 1991: 174). Institution, in this sense, is used as a verb and includes directly democratic creation without representation in legislation, jurisdiction, and law but also encompasses the totality of social institutions generally. The self-instituted society deliberately proposes to itself to fulfill common objectives and public endeavors and is the opposite of the closed society that is no longer critically self-reflective and becomes stagnant or self-destructive.

Ancient Lessons, Modern Illuminations

To further elucidate autonomy, it is important to specify that, for Castoriadis, the project of autonomy is orthogonal to modern democratic forms, which we will shortly explain and, through doing so, expose to critique. Certainly, those living in modern democracies would find very little that is familiar in the ancient Athenian democratic experience (Arnason, Raaflaub, and Wagner 2013). Likewise, ancient Greeks would not recognize much, if anything at all, from their system in ours today. They likely did not think about democracy in the way that the West has come to think about it (Karagiannis and Wagner 2013). Thought experiments designed "to show how people might solve the puzzle of masterless cooperation without the special conditions of culture and scale that pertained in ancient Greece" (Ober 2017: 36) illustrate that, despite its role in the Western Imaginary, we cannot attribute our modern understanding of democracy to understandings that ancient Athenians put forward.

Representation

Castoriadis's analysis of ancient Greek democratic forms contrasts sharply with modern Western forms. In the ancient period, he explains, the relationship between society as a collective and power was crucial. Democracy in its ancient form was direct whereas its modern form is representative. The significance of this difference, Castoriadis underscores, can be measured by noting that ancient Greek public law had no conception of representation and that the idea was unknown, whereas modern political systems enshrine representation in their very foundations. Occasionally, when people do seize power directly in the modern world, in popular assemblies and councils for instance, the seizure is a rupture in modern systems where the alienation from representation is, subsequently, exposed. The public assemblies of the global Occupy movements, for instance, illustrate this rupture, as the occupations opened spaces for public deliberation and reflection. The exceptions in the ancient world include magistrates, who were elected based on expertise, such as military strategists (other magistrates were selected by lot or rotation), but it is important to note that among the *polis* all were considered to be equally knowledgeable about political affairs, that politics was a matter of *doxa* (common sense), and that representation was unnecessary. In contrast, in the modern world every politician is assumed to be an expert in some specialization and the citizen must defer their decision-making abilities to the expert. However, this assumption is based on a deep tradition in Western political thought and ideology that is anti-democratic, in that it assumes that people are unable to govern themselves.

Until the early nineteenth century, the West held the authoritarian and totalitarian regimes of ancient Sparta in high esteem. But the rise of modern forms of representative democracy in the United States and Britain, as well as the newly established Greek state in 1830, enabled the reconfiguration of the West's political imaginary to better situate the more democratic ancient Athenian experience within its ancestral constellation as the supposed progenitor of today's democratic systems (Cartledge 2009: 89–90). But there are fundamental differences, as we have explained earlier in this chapter, between those aspects of the ancient directly democratic forms offering self-reflection for self-institution and those liberal representative forms of politics, which Castoriadis understood to be "liberal oligarchies" and thus not democratic in the deep, direct, autonomous sense. The ancient experience of democracy, however, predates the philosophical expression of liberalism as a body of thought and politics. Even so, the ancient experience stirred hatred among its contemporary critics who have supplied modern liberal oligarchies with philosophical reasoning for representative rule that dismisses popular self-governance.

One of the ancient critics to provide this reasoning was Plato, as exemplified by his dialogue translated into English as *Statesman*. This translation has enshrined a concept of representative rule into the Western Imaginary even though there was no state apparatus that was separate from the *polis* in ancient

Athens, and the concept of "statesman" likewise did not exist at the time. As translator David Ames Curtis noted (Castoriadis 2002: *xxvii*), it is not possible to accurately describe the person who participated in self-governing the *polis* as a "statesman." The Greek translation of this title as *Politikos* as well as the Latin translation as *Le Politique* are less suggestive. Nevertheless, this insertion of the statesman into the Western Imaginary has enabled Plato's anti-democratic message to be cemented into our conception of democracy as the rationalization for liberal oligarchy. That message included the argument that the statesman possesses true knowledge and that it is his task to prescribe to each individual who participates in society, each citizen, to follow what the statesman believes is the just thing to do. The underlying assumption being that the individuals who make up society are incapable of running their own lives (Castoriadis 2002: 32–3). This is complementary to modern democratic systems described earlier in this chapter, where every politician is assumed to be an expert in some specialization, but it is also consistent with the basis for state socialist (bureaucratic capitalist) and totalitarian domination, from the factory floor to the public square. The statesmen know what is best. In terms of the Western Imaginary, Castoriadis saw Plato as a great philosopher but ultimately working to stop and suppress self-institution. Plato, in this sense, represented "everything reactionary and pro-establishment; everything opposed to the democratic movement . . . found among the Romans, among the first Christians, during the Middle Ages, and in modern times" (Castoriadis 2002: 5).

Modern liberal democracies have taken the idea of "knowing what is best" and have applied it to institute many anti-democratic and authoritarian forms of decision-making both at home and abroad. Take US influence in Greece in the twentieth century, for example. Following the end of the Second World War, on March 12, 1947, US president Harry Truman addressed a special joint session of Congress, in which he articulated what became known as "The Truman Doctrine," a Cold War strategy aimed at affecting the balance of power in favor of the United States. Through the Truman Doctrine, the United

States began to support authoritarian regimes in Greece and other countries to ensure that these states did not fall under Soviet influence. Fearing the spread of a leftist contagion in countries surrounding Greece, the United States and British helped to brutally defeat the Greek Communist Party. The CIA began working closely with the Greek military in the early 1950s, including supporting those that would later carry out the coup to bring the Regime of the Colonels to power, instantiating an authoritarian period in the country. Following the Second World War, Greece entered into a civil war that lasted from 1946 to 1949. The United States and Britain supported the Greek government and army—which included many former Nazis—against the Greek Communist Party. The post-civil war years in Greece were characterized by social and material crisis. The Truman Doctrine sought to contain leftist forces and exacerbate political polarization in the Mediterranean country. On May 22, 1963, two far-right extremists assassinated left-wing politician and peace activist Grigoris Lambrakis. They murdered Lambrakis publicly after he had delivered the keynote speech at an anti-war meeting in Thessaloniki, Greece's second largest city.[1] On April 21, 1967, with the intention of allying Greece with NATO to combat "communist influence," Greek right-wing army officers led by Colonel George Papadopoulos, who *The Observer* described as "the first CIA agent to become premier of a European country,"[2] executed a coup. Thus, began the reign of the Regime of the Colonels in Greece from 1967 to 1974. In the following chapter, we situate this history within the broader context of the institution of heteronomous forms, since the origins of the Greek state in the late nineteenth century, to support the Western Imaginary of liberal democracy and superiority. But the role that the United States played in Greece is emblematic of US intervention to instantiate forms of liberal oligarchy and authoritarianism around the world, for example in China (1949 to early 1960s), Iran (1953), East Germany (1954), Egypt (1957), Congo (1960), Chile (1964–73), Afghanistan (1980s), Iraq (2003), Haiti (2004), Somalia (2007), Honduras (2009) to name but a few.[3] Carrying forward Plato's ethos, the West knows best, for other countries. More recently, the administration of then president Barack Obama carried out, from the White House, drone killings of non-state combatants or "suspected terrorists" in Yemen and Somalia between 2011 and 2012.[4] Such extra-judicial executions have been decried for their lack of due process.

Peaceful and democratic domestic resistance has also been quelled. The United States's FBI COINTELPRO program enacted covert, violent, and illegal actions against its domestic population—such as indigenous, black, student, and anti-war groups—struggling for economic, social and cultural rights between 1956 and 1971. More recently, following the September 11, 2001, terror attacks, New York City police systematically, disproportionately, and without due process surveilled Muslims. In 2015, the FBI surveilled the Black Lives Matter movement in Baltimore following the suspected police execution of a 25-year-old black man, Freddie Gray, from the west side of the city in April that year. In 2016, they surveilled indigenous communities defending Standing Rock, in North Dakota, working to stop the construction of an oil pipeline through their reservation. During his eight-year term, then president Obama persecuted more whistleblowers under the 1917 Espionage Act than all previous presidents combined. These anti-democratic trends prevail under US president Donald Trump, who has continued to surveil mosques and has continuously threatened journalists and the freedom of the press.[5] Simultaneously, the right has weaponized digital technology, outlined in Chapter 1, to wage ideological war and suppress the nonwhite vote.

Social imaginary significations embodying these systems expand the established forms of voting and representation in ways that move decision-making power further away from the population. The Electoral College system can decide the president of the United States regardless of popular opinion. Such was the case in 2000 when the Electoral College made George W. Bush US president despite Al Gore winning the popular vote by a margin of more than 500,000. The Electoral College again overruled the popular vote in 2016, when it elected Donald Trump president despite him polling close to three million fewer votes than his opponent Hillary Clinton. Heteronomous forms of representative democracy aspire to reproduce themselves in ways that further enhance anti-democratic outcomes. That a person's vote may not really matter, that the people they vote for do not represent their own or the majority of people's interests, that issues they are voting on mostly don't affect their lives, all could be reasons contributing to voter apathy in liberal democracies like the United States, where voter turnout ranging from 40 to 50 percent is considered a good outcome.[6] With such high levels of voter apathy, it is no wonder that many hold skeptical views about the liberal democratic system.

This skepticism is healthy. Liberalism has been violently opposed to meaningful democratic engagement at home and abroad. At the same time, much of our media has—far too often—aligned itself with those in power, rather than critically engage with why economic, social, and cultural disparities exist locally and globally. It could play a powerful role in enabling discursive informed decision-making but fails to do so. Edward Bernays—nephew of psychoanalysis pioneer Sigmund Freud, but father of "public relations" (more honestly known as "propaganda" during his time)—understood that in being consumed by material objects and/or fear—the US public could be easily manipulated through the media. He was transparent about the "need" to "engineer the truth" enabling economic and political elites to maintain control, while maintaining the facade of democracy. Internationally, Bernays also played a role in the June 1954 ouster of democratically elected president of Guatemala, Colonel Jacobo Árbenz Guzman, working with the United Fruit Company and the CIA to foment public sentiment against President Árbenz, laying the groundwork for a military coup against him. He did this by exploiting the anti-communist sentiment gripping the United States at the time. Fake news is not new. Whether it is the lack of weapons of mass destruction in Iraq (and much of liberal media's reluctance to question assertions as to their existence) or the lack of coverage about inadequate labor, environmental, air and water pollution or housing regulations, our media has failed to empower citizens with the information needed to critically evaluate politicians that are supposed to represent them.

Sovereignty

Ancient and modern social imaginary significations of democracy diverge on the relationship between people and political institutions as well. Castoriadis distinguished between the ancient awareness of the collectivity as the source of political institutions and modern sovereignty of the people *from* political institutions. For example, Castoriadis points out that Athenian laws always began with the preamble that "it appeared (it seemed) good to the Council and to the people, that . . ." and in this way the collective source of the law is made explicit. It is rooted in the people themselves. In the modern West, however, sovereignty of the people has emerged (between 1776 and 1789) which proposes that political institutions are rooted in something other than the people, such as reason, natural law, rationality, or history (Karagiannis and Wagner 2013). For Athens in the fifth century BCE, the collectivity was seen as a set of individuals reared by the *paideia* (broadly meaning education) and the common works of the city, as noted by Pericles in his "Funeral Oration." Modern social contract theory, however, posits that the individual shapes society (i.e., Rawls's "Veil of Ignorance" [1971]). Whereas the objective of ancient political activity was to reinforce political collectivity, the modern objective of politics is to defend private, group, or class interests, as well as the interests of the state.

Rights and Political Participation

On the issue of political participation—where matters concerning private property and the family were considered beyond reach—the ancient Athenians excluded women, slaves, and migrants from political activity, while the modern West has adopted universal human rights standards. These rights have come, however belabored, from protracted social struggles of the disenfranchised, such as the suffragettes who fought for the women's right to vote in public elections. Even so, many human rights—as individual rights but not collective rights—enshrined in law remain abstract aspirations as states are simultaneously responsible for upholding, promoting, and protecting human rights, while also being the violators of human rights. However, on the right of political participation, Castoriadis recognized the failure of ancient direct democracy to universalize and expand the right of citizenship to every person as the ultimate reason for its collapse.

The Strong Do What They Will . . .

While modern politics has surpassed the ancients in some ways, the West has also carried forward aspects of the ancient's cold brutality, for example, by the modern adoption of the ancient maxim "the strong do what they will, the weak suffer what they must." Athens used this maxim to justify its decimation of the entire population of the island of Melos (416 BCE)—killing the men and enslaving the women and children—because they refused to renounce their allegiance to Sparta during the Peloponnesian War. Modern Western political realism in the realm of international relations expresses this ancient ethos when it executes "preemptive wars" and "democracy promotion."

Happiness, Mortality, and Immortality

Beyond political activity were the objectives of human activity more broadly. For example, Pericles described the way of living in and through the love of beauty and of wisdom;[7] this objective was fulfilled through the *paideia* that the city offered. In contrast, the proclaimed modern objective is the pursuit of individual happiness and the sum of individual happiness, universal happiness, manifested through the acquisition of property, money, and power. Castoriadis argued that behind this is a deeper difference between the stratums of ancient and modern social imaginaries which is the difference between mortality and immortality. Ancient mortality was closely associated with self-limitation, in that while one was alive they could commit hubris, or excess, and that this could tarnish their reputation. However, it was only when one was dead that they became free from the possibility of hubris and thus became happy. Immortality in the West, however, manifests itself in the modern ethos of indefinite progress, unlimited expansion, and rational mastery. Finally, the ancient Greek perception of mortality was rooted in an ontology found in the oppositions of chaos and cosmos and nature and law, which meant that it provided a sense of indeterminacy. This is the consequential difference between ancient and modern ontologies, whereas the modern ontology relies upon determinism, such as *Cogito, ergo sum* (Descartes). This deterministic ontology has its roots in Plato and has been expressed theologically in the Hebraic-Christian idea of a Promised Land which, Castoriadis proposes, ultimately transferred to the Western notion of "Progress."

Beyond Ancient and Modern

The purpose of this brief summary of differences between ancient and modern experiences is not to argue for a return to the ancient social-historical forms or its social imaginary. On the contrary, it is to elucidate these forms and their imaginary in order to deepen our understanding of autonomy and to enable a radical critique of the West and modernity. The point is to go further, beyond both the ancient Greeks and the moderns. More precisely, to *instaturate* (create original forms in their first instance) genuine democracy under contemporary conditions, to universalize the project of autonomy where each society faces their own unique set of *problématiques* (Wagner 2010: 53–60).[8] For Castoriadis, this is only possible by demolishing the dominance of the economic sphere in the modern world (neoliberalism)—the heteronomous belief that capitalism is eternal and that markets know more than people—and by trying to create a new ethos connected at its center to humanity's essential mortality (Castoriadis 1993: 102–29). While Chapter 1 argued that the *decisive moment* we are now living in makes this project all the more urgent, Chapter 2 offered a definition of autonomy and sought to compare it with the modern democratic experience to further illuminate what makes autonomy distinct and how it fits into our modern world. We turn now, in Chapter 3, to explore how the Western Imaginary has imposed economic dominance and liberal oligarchy on modern Greece, and how the social imaginary significations of capitalism struggle to maintain their dominance, in order to demonstrate how Castoriadis's philosophy can be applied as critical reflection on the West.

3

Eurocentric Visions of Modern Greece

The concept of modernity reproduces many problematic tropes. It presents clear demarcations between those who are forward looking and those who are backward looking, between progress and tradition, between extroversion and introversion, between those who are for freedom, democracy, and human rights and those who are against. It drives wedges between those who apply rationality and scientific enquiry on the one side and those who consult religion and superstition on the other. Because modernity has historically been associated with Western Enlightenment, it has been used to rationalize Eurocentrism, Western exceptionalism, colonialism, imperialism, and extreme polarities between "East and West" and "Us and Them." In these ways, modern Greece finds itself occupying a paradoxical location—geographically, socially, culturally, historically, politically, and economically—in the Western Imaginary.

Cultural Dualism

The West has appropriated notions of ancient Greek civilization to support its own claim to modernity while also abstracting away the most democratic and self-reflective aspects of this ancient experience. By this we mean the view that "Greek civilization gave birth to democracy—indeed, the world—as we know it" while simultaneously minimizing those important aspects outlined in the previous chapter which precisely call into question our modern notions of democracy. More, as this chapter exposes, the West has forcefully projected its own Eurocentric notion of modernity back onto Greece, the source of its imaginary. For us, this experience is emblematic of the problems of global capitalism as it highlights how capitalism aspires to maintain the dominance of its social imaginary significations over all spheres of social life—to project its eternal status—regardless of social or cultural history, hopes, and influences. This dominance has created a devastating social-historical feedback loop in Greece, described later in this chapter, wreaking havoc on the imaginary of Greek society ever since its modern foundation. The thesis of "cultural dualism" by Nikiforos Diamandouros[1] (1994, 2013) has been an important reference point for debates about Greece in relation to Western modernity and illustrates its many problems. The thesis has been used to interpret the crisis of Greek identity and explain the unfolding of national history, since 1974 (the post-authoritarian period) up to today, as a conflict between tradition and modernity.[2] On the one side is the "underdog culture," which emerged after the fall of the military dictatorship. This culture, according to Diamandouros, evolved with significant influence from the Byzantine and Ottoman empires on Greece. It is characterized by traditionalism and introversion; it contains pre-democratic traits and nationalism, and it favors clientelist networks of power and is heavily influenced by the Orthodox Church. The underdog culture promotes a skeptical attitude toward outside influences on Greek society and perceives capitalism and the free market as ambiguous forces. In contrast, modern culture is inspired by the European Enlightenment and promotes rationalization, secularism, republicanism, and free markets. This culture is characterized as extroverted and aspires to advance social, political, and economic reform in order to uphold Greece's continued integration into the European Union and international system more broadly.

Cultural dualism, according to Diamandouros, has plagued Greek society since the creation of its modern state in 1830, after 450 years of Ottoman rule. At that time, the country was still figuring out what version of the Greek language to speak. Author Vassilis Vassilikos suggested that this contributed to a "national schizophrenia" (Marker 1989). Greek identity, Vassilikos proposed, is the basic problem that torments Greeks. All countries have this problem. However, the many waves of invasions, occupations, and human migrations to, through, and from the country—which makes any direct genetic connection between the ancient and modern Greeks unlikely—compound it. It contributes to an ontological chaos, described in the previous chapter. Chaos, such that "being is chaos" or the absence of order through catastrophe. Nevertheless, from the beginning of the creation of the Greek state, the West sought to incorporate an ancient Greek Imaginary, particularly the ancient Athenian experience of democracy, into the Western Imaginary. This incorporation of ancient Greek democracy into the Western Imaginary coincided with the rise of modern representative democracy, particularly in the United States and Britain (Cartledge 2009: 89). The Great Powers imposed Western statecraft and institutions derived from an enlightenment ethos and sought to advance European modernization. However, Greece was a largely precapitalist and agrarian country so was unable to fulfill the goals of the West's modernization project.

The cultural dualism thesis further defines the period from the 1920s to 1967–74 as divided between the liberal forces of the left and center left on one side and the right on the other. This is reflected in the conflicts between the monarchy and Eleftherios Venizelos and his Liberal Party. The transition to a republic, which followed the abolition of the monarchy and the downfall of the Regime of the Colonels' dictatorship in 1974 (see Chapter 2), was characterized by the institution of parliamentary democracy which, along with other modernizing reforms and an emergent public discourse on equal opportunity and political rights, helped minimize the deep political and ideological divisions that had persisted from the civil war period (from

1945 to 1948). It was after the dictatorship, in the post-authoritarian era, in which Diamandouros identifies the emergence of the underdog culture and which has since been responsible for supposedly impeding the progress of the country. From 2009, for example, the underdog culture was faulted nationally and internationally for bringing Greece to the brink of political and economic bankruptcy. A modernization project—driven by European Union, European Central Bank, and International Monetary Fund austerity plans—would rescue Greece and provide salvation (Triandafyllidou, Gropas, and Kouki 2013: 15).

Imperial Modernism

The Western project of modernizing Greece—imposed from its origins through to today—can be described as the subjugation of Greece. This occurs through the West's selective appropriation of ancient Greek history, philosophy, and culture in order to fulfill its own modern social imaginary of an ideal democracy as liberal oligarchy. This imaginary is made possible precisely by the belief that the ancient Greek experience belongs within the Western tradition and that this Western tradition is superior. This superiority is expressed as the final end state of history or as the West being the only culture capable of attaining enlightenment. This imaginary is projected as "imperial modernism." As Peter Wagner (2007) defined it, imperial modernism is the assumption in political theory, made since the end of the Second World War and especially since the end of the Cold War, that there is a single model of "modern society" to which "all societies will eventually converge because of the higher rationality of its institutional arrangements." This single institutional model is based on electoral representative democracy and a set of basic individual rights. The United States and United Kingdom (although to a lesser degree) represent the ideal of this model while the rest of the world struggles to catch up.

The Heteronomy of Neoliberal Economics

The subjugation of Greece was given special impetus with the 2007 financial crisis, known simply in Greece as "the crisis."[3] The crisis is a dramatic example of the dominance of the economic sphere in the modern world, as it highlights the heteronomous significations that underpin

1. the assumption that capitalism is eternal;
2. the religious belief that markets know more than people;
3. the determination that societies can be managed with calculation and economic precision;
4. the tendency of capitalism to reorganize society to perpetuate itself and its own objectives.

The crisis was an opportunity, according to the cultural dualism thesis, to implement structural reforms that could help dismantle the underdog culture (those "lazy Greeks" that the media, operating on capitalist temporality, reported pejoratively about despite data showing they have been among the hardest working people over the past two decades[4]) and finally put to rest the legacy of cultural dualism. The crisis was a painful struggle between old and new, instituting heteronomous forms. As such, it was an opportunity to modernize and to advance the enlightenment project of Europeanization, to bring Greece in line historically and ideologically. This would entail breaking with the legacy of Greece's "Ottoman" and "oriental" past, to finally extricate "Islamic barbarism" from Greek society (Triandafyllidou, Gropas, and Kouki 2013). Greece would have to adopt political, constitutional, and legal arrangements enabling the country to transition to a modern, legal, rational state and to take a decisive step forward in its long, tortuous, and frustratingly protracted transition to modernity (Diamandouros 2013: 218). In other words, it was a chance to advance imperial modernism. In the words of Diamandouros (2013: 227):

[S]tructural reform lies ahead, not behind, for Greece. And the efforts to attain substantive results on this front will need to overcome the stiff and determined resistance that will be strenuously mounted by those adherents of the underdog coalition who, at present, constitute the primary beneficiaries of existing labour market arrangements, that is, the widespread social strata currently in control of the trade unions and of state structures, including the public administration.

The Big "No"

Two years later, "the stiff and determined resistance" to the structural reforms included 61 percent of the Greek public. On July 5, 2015, Greece held a referendum on whether or not to accept further conditions that the European Commission, European Central Bank, and the International Monetary Fund were imposing. On a podium in Syntagma Square in Athens, the new Prime Minister Alexis Tsipras called on Greeks to "say a big 'no' to ultimatums, 'no' to blackmail," and to "Turn your back on those who would terrorize you." While thousands clamored in support, a resounding 61 percent of the Greek electorate voted *Oxi* (No) to the Troika conditions.[5] For all the ambiguity and uncertainty that the *Oxi* vote represented,[6] much like the ancient forms of autonomy outlined in Chapter 2—the "accusation of unlawfulness" and tragedy—this referendum was an opportunity for Greek society to reabsorb this political expression as an explicit power into politics, to deepen democracy formally. But this was denied, and liberal oligarchy reigned. Seven days after the referendum Tsipras signed the very measures that most had voted against, such as an increase in VAT, sweeping privatizations, cuts to public-sector pay, and phasing out early retirement.

This subjugation meant nothing less than the total reorganization of Greek society. In this sense, the "modernists" inside and outside Greece took advantage of the crisis to advance the organizational and methodological, indeed the relentless, transformation of the conditions and means of accumulation across production, commerce, finance, and consumption. Micro- and macro-level structural transformations—in agriculture, tourism, shipping, energy, public administration, health, education, the environment, and more—were oriented to stimulate "growth" through the prism of rational mastery and instrumentalism. This shattered the collective forms of Greek society—family, kinship, health, education, and community—and imposed the society of the individual instead. This individual, "seen as an atom linked to other human beings only through instrumental rationality, is at the center of imperial modernism" (Wagner 2007).

Conclusion

So long as Greece strives to catch up with the modernization project of the West its subjugation will continue. While the answer is obviously not to turn back to replicate the ancient experience—as impossible or undesirable as that option may be—a contemporary alternative to imperial modernism is necessary. We explore emergent alternatives in chapters to come. The chapters that comprised Part One offered "launching pads" for critical reflection on the West. We introduced our *decisive moment* as a social-historical moment characterizing the West, defined autonomy and juxtaposed it against modern forms of heteronomy, such as how the West projects its own imaginary back onto its supposed progenitor. In Chapter 6, we analyze modern Greek social movement struggles since the 2008 uprising to create new forms of autonomous space and time. And we assess the imposition of "the society of the individual," within the broader context of the global crisis of imaginary significations of capitalism, more extensively in Chapter 10. These chapters highlight the tumultuous tensions between the instituting and instituted forms, between autonomy and heteronomy. But first, in order to lay a foundation which helps understand Castoriadis's philosophical framework, particularly its development, we provide a biographical sketch of his life and work.

PART TWO

PAST—TIME AND POLITICS

4

Cornelius Castoriadis
A Brief Biography

The life and work of Cornelius Castoriadis, from 1922 to 1997, spanned some of the most turbulent years of the twentieth century in Europe. This chapter takes a new direction, to look at this great polymath, who remains virtually unknown, neglected, or misunderstood. This brief biographical detour helps elucidate the ways in which Castoriadis developed the project of autonomy, how the events in his personal and political life helped shape its formation, and how Castoriadis uniquely advanced this project.

The Paradoxical Life

Castoriadis's French biographer described his life as a paradox (Dosse 2014). For how can one explain the neglect of an intellectual of such a magnitude? Despite dedicating a great deal of his life's work to studying the deep relationship between philosophy and politics, he was perceived in the English-speaking world, where a rigid distinction separates these domains, as too political for philosophy and too philosophical for politics (Hastings-King 2014: 2). Unlike many of his more well-known intellectual peers in the mid to late twentieth century, Castoriadis stands out for his elaborate ideas, political experience, and militancy (Tovar-Restrepo 2012). He did not try to position himself within academia or meet academic expectations. Instead, as a life-long-revolutionary, his political life was deeply related to his intellectual life. Engaged in a wide array of struggles, he grappled with ideas and sought to advance his thinking (Tovar-Restrepo 2012).

Magmatic Origins

Born in March 1922 in the Ottoman city of Constantinople (today Istanbul, Turkey), Castoriadis was raised in Athens, Greece, where his family emigrated when he was just three months old. Athens became Castoriadis's new cradle. As he grew up, the city offered him an education in art, politics, law, sociology, and philosophy, which would mark him for the rest of his life. Far from experiencing an idyllic childhood, however, at the age of eight he tried to commit suicide by electrocution in order to avoid corporal punishment from his school master. At the young age of 16 he cared for his dying mother who, having contracted syphilis from his father, was bedridden, suffered from incontinence, and often plunged into madness. This also left its mark, not least his resentment toward his father, but physically too as he became a victim to a spectacular form of alopecia, which killed his hair follicle system and caused the loss of all his bodily hair (Dosse 2014: 14-15).

Most of his creative years were spent in Paris, where he fled to in 1945, at the age of 23 due to the civil war. A brutal struggle for power and subsequent civil war between the communists and the Western-backed nationalists between 1946 and 1949 tore Greece apart, setting the stage for the Cold War.[1] The threat of political violence from all sides forced him into hiding. With other Greek students, artists, journalists, and scholars Castoriadis sought to escape his shattered country. In December 1945, he left the cellar where he had been hiding for nearly four months. The now famous *Mataroa* had finally arrived in the port of Piraeus (Dosse 2014: 37). With only a bag of clothes in his hand, Paris offered a new beginning.

During the Nazi occupation of Greece from 1941 to 1945, Castoriadis was a member of the Trotskyist resistance group led by Agis Stinas (revolutionary pseudonym of Spyros Priftis, the legendary co-founder of the Greek Communist Party) that insisted on an internationalist approach to the war, proposing the transformation of a national war to a class war by the self-organization and solidarity of workers internationally (Castoriadis 2014: 59). Trapped on all sides, its members found themselves under threat of death by both the patriotic Stalinist Communist Party, which was then the backbone of the resistance movement, and the Nazi Occupation forces and their extreme-right collaborators. From the right, Castoriadis narrowly escaped a violent fate when the Gestapo searched a bus he was riding and then again when they raided an apartment he was living in. From the left, according to the testimony of one journalist, the United Panhellenic Organization of Youth (the youth wing of the left National Liberation Front (EAM)) had placed Castoriadis at the top of their enemy kill list (Dosse 2014: 28). Two of Castoriadis's comrades were not so lucky and were killed because of their political actions. Castoriadis's escape to the West undoubtedly saved his life and liberated his thought, since he was deeply shocked by the experience of the 1944 December riots in Athens. The month-long battle between the British military forces, who were encouraged by Winston Churchill to treat Greece as an "occupied country," and the forces of EAM ended with hundreds of dead communists. Castoriadis was shocked to realize that the people of Athens were ready to sacrifice themselves blindly following either the orders of a Stalinist party aspiring for absolute authority or the old politicians eager to receive support from Nazi collaborators.

Subterranean in Paris, France

Castoriadis's arrival in Paris brought him in direct contact with the critical political questions and tensions that rose, not only in France but also in post-war Europe generally. His brief participation in the Trotskyist party of France ended in 1949, when he co-founded, together with French philosopher and activist Claude Lefort, the leftist revolutionary group Socialisme ou Barbarie,[2] which published the homonymous journal of social and political critique from 1949 to 1965. The group had emerged among very few other groups of that period which shared a similar understanding of socialism being rooted in direct democracy, emerging from the praxis of revolutionary organization, theory, and new forms of autonomous worker action. Castoriadis had already been[3] in contact with formations such as the Johnson-Forest Tendency in the United States—comprised of C. L. R. James, Raya Dunayevskaya (Trotsky's secretary while exiled in Mexico), and Grace Lee Boggs. Later, *Socialisme ou Barbarie*'s collaborations with the Detroit-based *Correspondence* collective resulted in mutual translations and dialogues to enable, despite differences, shared learning and political development (Hasting-Kings 2014). Similarly, in the early 1950s, Castoriadis engaged in a series of friendly exchanges with Dutch astronomer and leading council communist Anton Pannekoek in which they agreed on the importance of workers' control.[4] Notwithstanding these initial international connections, the group remained small. In France, however, the journal had a significant impact in French radical thought, particularly in their rejection of Stalinism, Trotskyism, and embrace of workers' councils and self-management, with contributors such as philosopher Jean-Francois Lyotard and theorist Guy Debord. This influence would manifest in the May 1968 uprising in France which had a profound social-historical impact, nationally and internationally, in ways that reverberate today.

Moving beyond Marx to Remain Revolutionary

Through his writing and political activity, Castoriadis quickly distanced himself from the Trotskyist conception of the Soviet Union as a "degenerated workers' state" to demonstrate that the Soviet regime was defined by the emergence of a new ruling class, state bureaucracy, founded on the most ferocious oppression of society by a rigid, monolithic, militarized party-state government. Leading up to the 1950s, Castoriadis gradually deepened his critique of the widely held philosophical system of Karl Marx until, in the early 1960s, he wholly denounced Marxism. In the core of Marxian philosophy Castoriadis uncovered a conservative, dogmatic side, manifested in the key concepts of historical necessity, theoretical orthodoxy, and historical materialism which, he said, suppressed its initial revolutionary aspiration to change the world through the self-liberation of humanity. Marxism could not be salvaged through revisions, he argued. There had to be a complete break.

Castoriadis's critique of Marxism began in 1953, when he criticized the economic system that Marxism proposed. The social reality in the Soviet Union proved that exploitation and inequality can persist even if the owners of the means of production change. He arrived at this understanding by observing that the extreme concentration of the forces of production in the Soviet system operated as an advanced phase of monopoly capitalism which evolved around the intermingling between the most powerful stratum of finance capital and the concentration of state and labor bureaucracies. He labeled this mode of exploitation "bureaucratic capitalism." In this sense, Soviet "socialism" was a more advanced form of bureaucratic capitalism, toward which the West was also progressing. In this framework, capitalism exploits workers up to the limits of laws regulating the rate of surplus value and up to the value of labor power while Soviet socialism—unhindered by any such limitations and emboldened by total ownership and control over the productive forces—exploited workers up to the point where only worker resistance was able to impede exploitation. The 1953 East Berlin "June Days," a mass uprising against the government's attempt to "increase productivity" is an example of the latter while the August 1953 French general strike against attempts to cut public-sector workers' salaries and retirement benefits is an example of the former (Hastings-King 2014).

The 1956 worker uprisings in Hungary and Poland against Soviet domination inspired Castoriadis to study workers' councils and self-management

(Castoriadis 1957). And he developed his analysis, critiquing Tito's "self-managed market socialism" in Yugoslavia. In 1957, Castoriadis refuted Marx's idea of the primacy of production in social life as well as the labor theory of value which, he argued, objectifies workers' power as a commodity. He continued developing his critique of Marxism and in 1959 questioned Marx's conception of the capitalist crisis and argued that the real antithesis within the system is the division between directors and executants, those who decide and those who are just instruments, and that the true crisis lies in the paradox of capitalism's tendency to objectify workers while being utterly dependent on the workers' human caring and readiness to correct systemic dysfunctions. In 1960, Castoriadis proceeded to refute the Marxian philosophy of history and the theory of historical materialism. Was the class struggle between those who sold their labor and those who owned the means of production, in the orthodox Marxian two-class model, the driving force of history? Were people only workers acting out their roles on the grand historical stage in a predetermined play? Castoriadis demonstrated that, like every rationalist theory, this too confined human action to abstract metaphysical laws. Consequentially, Marxism became a supplement for state authorities and served the division between the oppressed and the oppressors, rationalizing oppression in the name of scientific politics, which is in itself a negation of politics. Castoriadis accused Marx of adopting basic capitalist ideas and significations—essential elements of the dominant capitalist worldview—like scientific dogmatism, the predominance of economy, dominance over nature, and exponential production growth and transplanting them within the revolutionary movement. Castoriadis undertook the task of combining action and theory within the praxis of autonomy beyond Marxist dialectics when he declared, "Starting from revolutionary Marxism, we have arrived at the point where we have to choose between remaining Marxist and remaining revolutionaries" (Castoriadis 1987: 14).

At this stage in his political and philosophical development, Castoriadis's break with Marxism began to inspire other groups in the West who had become similarly disenchanted with the legacy of Marxism, Leninism, Trotskyism, and "actually existing socialism." In Britain, the distinguished neurologist Christopher Agamemnon Pallis[5] translated many original and popular works of Castoriadis. Along with industrial organizer Ken Weller, Pallis co-founded the London Solidarity group, which organized to agitate for a libertarian socialist vision of autonomy and direct democracy in deep collaboration with Castoriadis and *Socialisme ou Barbarie*. Spanning the years from 1960 to 1992, the Solidarity group had a significant impact on housing movements in the UK, as well as on industrial disputes, antifascist organizing, and organizing for peace, particularly through the industrial subcommittee of the Committee of 100. At their peak, Solidarity had approximately 30 chapters and 100 members across the UK. Back in France, Castoriadis's ideas had a significant influence on those tumultuous and historic events of May '68, as many have admitted (Hastings-King 2014: 2, footnote 3). But his influence can also be seen in one of Pallis's best writings for Solidarity, his May 1968 diary documenting the explosive student and worker uprising (Brinton 1968).

The Imaginary Institution of Society

Castoriadis continued to develop his philosophy and moved on to study the emergence of democracy throughout history, alongside broader studies in philosophy, ontology, and the natural sciences. He discussed ontological issues[6] beyond the individualism of phenomenology or the objectifications of science, by proposing the concept of a magmatic temporal reality, where being is time, where society and history appear unified within the social-historical stratum, created by human interference and activity. He stressed the importance of social imaginary significations, the "pre-eminent element in and through which the social-historical unfolds" (Castoriadis 1997: 201) and argued that we cannot understand society without acknowledging the imaginary element that constitutes social meaning:

> We cannot understand a society outside of a unifying factor that provides a signified content and weaves it with the symbolic structures. This factor is not simple "reality"; every society has constituted its reality (we are not bothering to specify here that this constitution is never completely arbitrary). Nor is it the "rational," as the most summary inspection of history suffices to show, for if it were, history would not have been genuinely history but the instantaneous access to a rational order, or, at most, a pure progress in rationality. Although history indisputably contains progress in rationality [. . .] it cannot be reduced to this. A meaning appears here from the very start, one that is not a meaning of the real (referring to what is perceived), one that is neither strictly rational nor positively irrational, neither true nor false and yet that does belong to the order of signification and that is the imaginary creation proper to history, that in and through which history constitutes itself to begin with. (Castoriadis 1987: 160)

Castoriadis published his early works, until 1970, under various pseudonyms, such as Paul Cardan and Pierre Chaulieu, because he was not a full French citizen. We might as well call his work before his radical breach with Marxian thought the "Cardanian" (or "Chaulieuan") period, when he still supported the idea of a central structure of political power as the regulator of workers' self-government and the Marxist idea of the primacy of economic structures. In the years following 1960, and especially after the publication of his magnum opus *The Imaginary Institution of Society* (1987), he began the mature period of his philosophy, his "Castoriadean" period, when he passionately supported direct democracy and broadened his vision of self-government to the whole of society, rejecting any central state. Instead, he proposed a network of autonomous communities connected by democratic institutions of public decision and social action, based not on authority, but on the instituting power of society to proximate autonomy.

Psychoanalysis

Special mention should be made of Castoriadis's involvement with psychology and psychoanalysis from the early 1960s onward, which put him in contact with the theories of Sigmund Freud and the school of Jacques Lacan, whom Castoriadis later criticized.[7] Lacan based his analysis on the imposition of a triangular pattern on the psychic, formulated as the triad of the symbolic, the imaginary, and the real, the Symbolic being prior as the primal imposition of social stereotypes on imagination and the conception of reality. Castoriadis pointed out that social symbolisms and ideas are also formulated by the imaginary function of the social whole that cannot be attributed to the individual. He refuted the Lacanian triangle for being too formative and, instead, insisted on the primacy of the imaginary through its dual manifestation, as individual imagination and as social imaginary.

After ending a long career as a professional economist for the OECD from the post-war period till 1970, Castoriadis began working as a psychoanalyst. In 1973, he formulated his theory of the psyche, placing radical imagination as the creative source of all unconscious images, desires, and feelings, where memories are withdrawn and transformed. During the process of socialization, through language and education, this psyche becomes a functional individual, in accordance to the dominant social images and significations. These are the creation of another psychic pole, the anonymous social imaginary, transmitted through language, custom and social behavior. The central set of dominant social significations constitutes a stable dominant world-image that justifies the dominant social structure and authority. The social imaginary is responsible for providing reality with a coherent meaning available to the individual psyche, in order to reconcile the break-up of the monadic core of the primal subject.

The psyche is formed into a functional individual through the process of socialization that is carried out by language and human interaction. For Castoriadis, it is through the contact with the Other that we formulate our conscious Self. Therefore, our own conscious Ego includes elements of what others have taught us and we are, in our consciousness, a bridge between society and the psyche. The human individual is a social individual that can become an autonomous human subjectivity, but only if society provides the conception of autonomy. This is individual autonomy, which corresponds to social autonomy, the collective, public, deliberate, and equalitarian self-positing of laws and self-governance based on the recognition that every individual is autonomous. Direct democracy is the political condition of social autonomy.

The Project of Autonomy

Every society is self-instituted as a proper world, a nexus of meanings that constitutes its own semantic ecosystem and its distinguished mode-of-being, its own history. Most societies attribute their self-institution to metaphysical beings like god, in order to sanctify their customs. Central institutions and authorities are presented as sacred, are attributed to divine inspiration or divine mandate and are placed beyond doubt or questioning. Medieval theocratic monarchy is an example. This is what Castoriadis calls heteronomy, and it resembles a state of societal cognitive enclosure. Heteronomy is the way in which most societies protect themselves from other societies, the future and their own citizens. However, the exception to the rule of heteronomy appeared in human history with the emergence of democracy and philosophy in ancient Asia Minor and Greece. Both represent revolutions of autonomy in the fields of political action and contemplative theory, respectively. Both resisted oligarchical and clerical authority to create a self-governed community and to publicize the great questions of existence, ethics, and power. Both recognize the individual as a distinct subjectivity, a free agent with responsibility and society as a plane of intersubjective relations. As defined in Chapter 2, autonomy means the condition when a society not only posits its own laws freely but also explicitly recognizes itself as the only source of those laws. An autonomous society is a self-governed community, constituted by autonomous individuals, that is, a society without separate authority mechanisms, where every citizen participates equally and publicly in governance and law-making. In the next chapter we dig deeper into the subterranean ontology and political theory of autonomy. We should stress the relationality in Castoriadis' view. Since society is self-instituted, there is no universal essence of an ideal society the horizon of which we approach. Thus, heteronomy and autonomy, more than collective relations to the schematic underpinnings of the social-historical world, are also ways of organizing and instituting the individual's relation to reality according to the dominant social significations. That is to say, heteronomy and autonomy are juxtaposed both as conceptual formations of social-historical being and as contents of value, embracing opposing significations.

Castoriadis traces the project of autonomy throughout history, from ancient and late-medieval democratic movements and autonomous cities to the modern workers' movement and contemporary social movements. He expands the concept of revolution, asserting that a social revolution could begin from a crisis in any social sphere, not just economy, since every social establishment is empowered by a core of meanings and significations, rather than raw functionality. Revolution does not imply a heroic, bloody (or bloodless) coup d'état against the Winter Palace, but rather the radical transformation of society through the rational activity of the people toward direct democracy and autonomy.

Castoriadis died on December 26, 1997, in Paris. He loved jazz and played the piano. At his funeral, a Greek musician played a lamentation with a clarinet.

5

The Social-historical Dimension of Time

Castoriadis challenged the Western conception of ontology of being as a fixed state. We are—as individuals and societies—constantly changed and changing. Castoriadis's insistence on this demands that we leave behind the imaginaries that embolden heteronomous significations, ways of being, and institutions. We are not essentially any one thing, and certainly not necessarily brutish, power hungry, and afraid. That our institutions may encourage this has been instituted, which gives us the agency to create something new. In our *decisive moment* (Chapter 1) the understanding of our individual and collective agency (instituting capacities to create something new) and the imaginaries, institutions, and actors that aim to limit it (the instituted heteronomous order) (Chapter 2) is crucial to empower actions that aim to proximate autonomy even as those actions bound up against the existing order (Chapter 3).

In this chapter, we outline key concepts in Castoriadis's ontology and political theory, such as the "*ensemblistic-identitary*," "imaginary," "ontological creativity," and the "poietic." These terms provide a base for understanding Castoriadis's concept of "magma," as well as for subjective and objective interpretations of time. We outline Castoriadis's radical positions on the philosophy of time and society and clarify basic concepts of his ontology that emphasize the creative and indeterminate aspects of human activity and history. These understandings help us interpret social movements in the twenty-first century, particularly those in Greece, as they use social time and social space, which are key to advancing the modern project of autonomy.

The Enigma of Time

Poetry often succeeds in expressing that which is ineffable or, at least, *ought to be ineffable* according to the final proposition of Ludwig Wittgenstein's *Tractatus Logico-Philosophicus* (1974): "Whereof one cannot speak, thereof one must remain silent." However, in his *Four Quartets* (1943), T. S. Eliot discusses something that philosophy, being the matrix of sciences, must take into consideration, the enigma of time. The image that he presents does not depict time as we experience it empirically. On the contrary, it is an image of Eternity, an image of a spatialized temporality, time objectified in eternal stasis, like a gem that reflects different colors on every cut and surface but exists simultaneously as a form of unified space. "What might have been and what has been, point to one end, which is always present," Eliot wrote. It is a theological vision that corresponds with the image of an eternal omnipotent being, namely god, who exists outside and beyond time. "He" can thus intervene or observe from above, rendering, by "his" presence, our world of phenomena a mere shadow of an eternal, immortal, and unchangeable substance. The Roman Catholic Eliot seems to suggest that the enigma of time can only be resolved as a *theological* problem, reducing time to an attribute of a finite, illusionary world, which needs to be ontologically supported by an infinite, transcendental will. The deduction of eternity from temporality is at once a reduction of temporality to the illusory randomness of a semblance. The veil of words hides time behind an image of a metaphysical sanctity. We must take our distance from this solution which tries not to resolve, but instead conceals, the existential problem.

But, if the enigma of time is not the question of immortality, then it must be the question of mortality, the problem of death. And as such it is an issue equally personal and social, the only fundamental existential issue of both the individual and society. Moreover, it is a social issue in the sense that mortality is a truth that we learn by others, by society, by family, since, without contact with other people, the individuals cannot apprehend their birth nor their impending death, the two marginal points that define individual time. Even the price and value of labor, the most important equation in capitalist society, is measured by, ultimately arbitrary, time-units (working hours). The phrase "time is money," besides being a cliché, indicates this unbreakable connection between social temporality and the capitalistic structures of production and distribution. The division and management of social and public time is a primary function of instituted authority. Therefore, the question of time is also a deeply political issue, a question that underlines every political theory and a question that every critical social theory must consider.

Traditional Ontology and Logic as *Ensemblistic-identitary*

Castoriadis asserted that "being is time—and not in the horizon of time" (2008: 258) and correlated history to society and being to temporality within the social-historical stratum, the ontological plane created by human existence where "existence is signification." This concept of the social-historical, encompassing all human activities, places the notion of time in the center of both Castoriadean ontology and political theory. Time, is the self-generation of absolute otherness, the emergence of new forms of a magmatic reality, layered with non-regular stratification, where the social-historical manifests as human action that creates social sub-realities, in the manner of social imaginary significations:

> What is is not ensemble or system of ensembles. What is is not fully determined. What is is Chaos, or Abyss, or Groundlessness. What is is

Chaos with non-regular stratification. What is bears with it [*comporte*] an *ensemblistic-identitary* dimension—or an *ensemblistic-identitary* part everywhere dense.

Question: Does it bear this dimension with it or do we impose this dimension on it? The response (to be done with constructivism, reflections and *tabulae rasae*) is as follows: For the "near-perfect" observer, the question of knowing, in an ultimate sense, what comes from the observer and what comes from the observed is undecidable. (Nothing absolutely chaotic is observable. No absolutely unorganized observer can exist. The observation is a not fully decomposable coproduct.) (Castoriadis 1997: 307–8)

This concept of temporality is accompanied by a profound criticism of traditional rationalistic philosophy, the ontological base of Western philosophy, to which Castoriadis assigns the name "*ensemblistic-identitary*" (Castoriadis 1987: 175). Castoriadis uses this concept to describe the traditional ontology and logic that is based on the axiom of the absolute identity of a being with its determinate definition (a=a), which considers being as being determined. On that theoretical ground, rationalistic or tautological philosophical systems are constructed. For example, we may ask: *Who am I?* Traditional rationalistic ontology and logic would demand a strict definition of myself that would remain constant and valid in any given time and place. Of course, there is no such definition, since the passage of time and the physical procedure of aging constantly changes my body, not to mention the psychic transformations in knowledge, attitude, memory, and experience. A strict *ensemblistic-identitary* response would be that, I either never actually changed from before birth to beyond death, since my essence remains the same or I never actually existed, since I am constantly changing, and my own presence in reality is but a temporary phenomenon.[1] Both answers are absurd.

Instead, Castoriadis argues that every individual is already a social institution, a psyche informed by society through education. Both are subjected to time, so my own self is intermingled with official social time, society's present, historical past, and aspirations for the future. Both my self and society are subjected to natural time as well as the public time informed by my personal relations with other individuals and our social relations with other societies. My presence is dynamic within the social-historical, even when I am passive, since my attitudes are what realize society's dominant significations. Consequently, human subjectivity and individuality are, for Castoriadis, historical categories and not anthropological constants. In simpler words, the concept of the free, autonomous individual does not appear in *any* society, but in a society that recognizes the concept of a free, autonomous community. Individuality and human subjectivity are significations that have risen from the struggle against heteronomy and absolute authority.

Since everything is subjected to time and change, to Becoming, which implies non-being, traditional rationalistic philosophy leaves little space for empirical truth. Instead, it disconnects contemplation from the real world in the search for mathematical abstractions and eternal truths. This metaphysical road leads to the abandonment of the practical and critical aspects of philosophical inquiry, downgrading philosophy to theology. From Parmenides to Plato to Christianity, it quickly became the mainstream philosophical attitude, with a strong tradition and a lasting influence. Human history and action were downgraded to deterministic manifestations of metaphysical eternal laws. Castoriadis argues that since Parmenides, traditional philosophy has never managed to escape the confines of *ensemblistic-identitary* logic.

Ensemblistic-identitary is the logic that focuses exclusively on the mathematical and quantifiable dimension of human thought, which corresponds to the mathematical and quantifiable dimension of reality. *Ensemblistic-identitary* logic is the logic of identity, which is based on the axioms of identity, non-contradiction, and the exclusion of the third. Mathematics, beyond their axiomatic principles, is by definition a tautological system, based on fixed points and equivalences. Modern set theory is the most precise example of this logic, which grasps one fragment of reality, just to abandon the rest. In the beginning of the twentieth century, Kurt Gödel

(1931) demonstrated, by his incompleteness theorems (1931), that no logical or mathematical system could prove its own consistency, since it must necessarily contain axioms that are true, but unprovable. Castoriadis argued that the *ensemblistic-identitary* dimension of mathematics does not include the basic mathematical axioms, which are imaginary creations. There is an immanent *ensemblistic-identitary* dimension of being, which, however, cannot include the totality of beings. Nevertheless, this does not affect the influence that mathematical logic exercises on modern society. The theoretical ambition to completely and definitively explain everything, for supposed "rational mastery," is deeply linked with the human psychic need for a coherent meaning but this is an impossible task that leads to the denial of reality and dogmatism. The world itself has no inherent meaning.

Ontological Creativity: The Poietic Dimension

What traditional (*ensemblistic-identitary*) logic fails to consider is the poietic dimension of reality, the immanence of ontological creativity, which is densely interwoven with the (*ensemblistic-identitary*) tautological dimension of reality. For instance, ontological multiplicity exists both in the manner of difference, which is the arithmetic multiplicity of numbers, quantity, *ensemblistic-identitary* multiplicity, *and* in the manner of alterity, which is the multiplicity of forms, quality, and poietic multiplicity. Both are interwoven within time and space. For Castoriadis, difference is defined as the differentiation between an object and other similar objects, the arithmetic multiplicity of distinct points and the algebraic multiplicity of determinate relations, the multiplicity of the individual particulars of a generic kind. These notions of difference and identity include both differences of degree and differences of nature, because, in order for a point to be considered different from another point, in order for it to receive a different truth value according to its position in a sequence or a level, it should first be considered as identical to itself. On the other hand, o*therness/alterity* is defined as the emergence of irregular, new forms that are irreducible to prior definitions and to one another, like the living being is irreducible to inorganic matter or any person is irreducible to another. Alterity is the heterogeneous multiplicity of diverse beings.

In the *Imaginary Institution of Society* Castoriadis (1987) draws a sharp distinction between space and time based on the distinction between difference and alterity, whereas later, in his essay "Time and Creation" (1997b), he modifies this initial schema with the incorporation of the horizon of space into the horizon of time. He also expresses his disagreement with Bergson's identification of abstract space with "space *tout court*," pointing out that mathematical space is an abstraction of real space, and that real space always appears within time. In reality, there is not one straight line, nor a perfect circle in the universe. However, a perfect circle is thinkable, as a perfect image of eternity, of a time in stasis and unchangeable, a spatial time that is the radical negation of time-in-itself, since the fundamental attributes of the latter is motion and change. Should we accept such an image of eternity as the pure being, then all Becoming and time itself are reduced to secondary representations or illusions. Time is the emergence, creation, and destruction of new, irreducible forms. A creation of the new that happens *ex nihilo* but not *cum nihilo* or *in nihilo*. "Something is new when it is the positi[ng] of a form neither producible nor deducible from other forms. Something being new means, therefore: something is the positi[ng] of new determinations, of new laws" (Castoriadis 1997b: 382). In that manner, creation is the action of bringing non-being into being.

Magma

Ontological creativity is the reason of historical relativity. History is the creation of human action, determined by human action within a social scope in correspondence with the natural environment. Without the acknowledgment of the social-historical we cannot comprehend the interaction between the tautological and the imaginary that localizes and unifies the myriad magmatic temporal formations. Without the acknowledgment of ontological creativity and historical relativity, we cannot understand how human activity transforms the world and how society creates its own history.

The concept that Castoriadis adopts from mathematics to describe ontological multiplicity is the *magma*.[2] Castoriadis writes (1987: 343), "A magma is that from which one can extract (or in which one can construct) an indefinite number of *ensemblist* organizations but which can never be reconstituted (ideally) by a (finite or infinite) *ensemblist* composition of these organizations." The notion of the magma allows Castoriadis to escape the confines of *ensemblistic-identitary* logic without resorting to the chaos of pure indetermination. He observes that there are enduring, *ensemblistic* forms within the magma of significations that formulate each society:

> We are positing that everything that can actually be given—representation, nature, signification—is according to the mode of being of the magma, that the social-historical institution of the world, of things and individuals, considered as the institution of *legein* [language] and *teukhein* [technique], is always the institution of *identitary* logic as well and hence the imposition of an *ensemblist* organization on an initial stratum of the given which unceasingly lends itself to this. But we are also positing that it is never and can never be simply that— that it is always at the same time necessarily the institution of a magma of social imaginary significations, and, finally, that the relation between *legein* and *teukhein* and the magma of social imaginary significations cannot be thought in terms of the *identitary* and *ensemblist* grid. (Castoriadis 1987: 344).

The Being-For-Itself

As an example of the creative dimension of reality, Castoriadis (1997b: 145) considers the being-for-Itself, the being that creates itself and whose finality refers to itself. Such is any living being, from the simplest to the most complex species. Every animal or plant has the purpose of conserving and reproducing its own self and its own kind, and every biological function serves that purpose. Every living being is a being-for-itself in the sense that its end *is* its own existence. Every lifeform is characterized by self-finality, intention, and action oriented by passion toward that finality. Purpose and meaning are attributes of life. Non-living beings and natural procedures, the birth and death of stars and galaxies, no matter how beautiful or terrifying to us, are actually purposeless activities, without intention or passion.

The living being creates a plexus of assessments of its environment and informs its proper world according to its own senses.³ We could describe this function as the cognitive and evaluative function, schematically articulated in three instances—cognition, passion, and intention—all relevant to reproduction and conservation. The living being creates and organizes a system of inclusions and exclusions that complements and constructs broader ontological ecosystems. The creation of a proper world means the creation of a proper time in the sense of both duration and bio-chronical orientation. These temporalities have to not only be both distinct and complementary but also correspond to natural time and above all, time in-itself, while differentiating in rhythm, duration, or entropy. For example, from the perspective of life, entropy is negative and tends to order, from the simpler form to the complex, in direct contrast to thermodynamic or natural positive entropy that tends to chaos.

The human psyche and the human society are other examples of the being-for-itself, the non-individual, since the individual is more than the psyche but less than society. Subjectivity is an attribute of the individual human being, but only finality is the attribute of every being-for-itself. The distinction between any other living being and humanity, according to Castoriadis (1997: 328), is that humans bear a defunctionalization of imagination which creates a constant flux of psychic images that generate urges aiming to ends other than the basic biological purpose of self-preservation. Imagination is immanent transcendence, the ability to present that which is not present, to create representations of the un-presented and to formulate chaos into a world. Psychic intention is arbitrary, its content is imaginary, its passion illogical. Human psyche is a distinct being-for-itself whose sufficient and necessary condition for survival is society, which creates an imaginary social world to provide existence with meaning.

Castoriadis agrees with Freud that the emergence of the psyche creates a proto-image of completeness and timeliness, of the Self as the Whole, which is shattered upon contact with the outside world. However, the vision of this lost omnipotence and immortality remains as a psychic ghost, the repulsion of which generates the unconscious part of the psyche, the Id that remains inaccessible to the conscious mind. This unconscious ghost guides the urges and desires of each person and socialization is the only way to formulate that person into an individual. This means that these urges and desires must invest in the relevant social significations and dominant attitudes, so that the individual can satisfy the quest for meaning by resuming a social role. However, the psychic thirst for meaning is almost insatiable and, more often than not, the social significations fail to control the restiveness of human imagination.

Individual and Social Time

Bearing upon the relationship between subjective and objective dimensions, Castoriadis, following Paul Ricoeur's analysis of the narrative representations of time (Ricoeur 1985), identifies two traditional approaches to the issue of time. One is the *objective or cosmological* approach, presented in Aristotle's *Physics*, which considers time an objective attribute of reality, the "number of motion in respect of 'before' and 'after.'"[4] The other is the *subjective or phenomenological* approach, presented in St. Augustine's *Confessions*, which considers time a subjective phenomenon, the internal rhythm of personal experience and existential anxiety. Both approaches fail to address the question of *time* per se, time in-itself which lies above subjective experience, and beyond measurement, encompassing and unifying them. Both approaches propose a rigid division between subjectivity and objectivity, ignoring society, where *time is history*, where subjects and objects are represented and invested with imaginary social significations, where subjectivity and objectivity are combined into social meaning. This false division between the subject and the object becomes a fundamental antithesis in the frame of traditional ontology and produces secondary divisions between individual and society, time and eternity, phenomenon and essence. However, Castoriadis claims that this primal division is false on a social level, where the real antithesis is located between the psyche and society, since the actual individual himself/herself is already a social institution, informed by language and culture. Even our subjective perception of ourselves is mediated by words, norms, and images that do not belong to ourselves but refer to a public imaginary, already instituted before we were born.

Secondly, the division is also false on an epistemological level, since the very conception of any object (as a signified and evaluated object) can only be constituted by the subject according to the dominant social imaginary significations already invested upon the object. For example, the meaning or value of a tool cannot be restricted to just its practical use, because it connotes also ideas, concepts, and attitudes and symbolizes a broader culture. Archaeological research is based on the inquiry of the symbolic and cultural connotations of tools and relics. Tools can also symbolize world-images or ideologies, as the communist hammer-and-sickle demonstrates. The subjective and the objective dimensions cannot be ultimately divided. Their intrinsic connection remains incomprehensible only if we continue to ignore the social-historical dimension that our collective existence generates, which transfigures, interconnects, and signifies everything that exists within the scope of humanity.

Subjective temporality is the time experienced by a human subject, the temporality that is determined by psychic processes and the flux of the radical imagination of the psyche that corresponds with the active conscious ego. It is clear that we cannot even imagine a completely isolated and firmly closed subjective temporality. Even in cases of extreme autism or comatose conditions, an individual is always exposed, at least corporeally, to both the natural and the social objective temporality. This is the case even in the unconscious mind, as Castoriadis argues while considering the Freudian position that the unconscious does not know time (2007: 376):

> The latter [the unconscious] does not know usual time, diurnal social time. But it is obvious that it unfolds its own time, its proper time. A dream unfurls in a dream time; and it creates, it makes be a dream time. There is a proper temporality of the dream, as, more generally, a proper temporality of the Unconscious. This is not "our" temporality of socialized adults, and noon can be switched to before 9 AM; that matters little, there is a before/after.

The psyche has its own proper temporality, distinctive from social time. Personal, individual time emerges as the superimposition of the temporality of the social imaginary on the temporality of the individual radical imagination. The antithesis between the psyche and society is bridged by the conscious ego, socially informed through education and communication that transforms inner drives to internalized social norms and dominant significations. Language is the carrier of social significations and, in the broader sense of communicative expression that includes oral, corporeal, and visual semantics, language is also the carrier of the dominant social temporality and the social significations of time. The calendar, the days of the week, the months of the year, the seasons and the holidays, all constitute a map of social time that regulates social activities and public behavior. These significations, that regulate personal feelings, drives and conceptions, precede every person, since society is in-itself a plexus of dominant significations, norms, social structures, and behavioral patterns. They are creations of the collective social imaginary, the matrix that generates and eventually validates the social significations that define every society.

The social imaginary is analogous to the radical imagination of the individual, with two crucial differences. The first is the fact that the psyche needs to be educated in order to become a functioning individual capable of surviving. The second is the fact that the psyche exists as actual subjectivity, whereas society exists as the objective magma of individual beings and their relations. Individual and social time are interconnected, although we must accept that in the depths of the unconscious psyche lies the Id, inaccessible to both the conscious mind and society. Subjective temporality is also a multiplicity and subjective time is in-itself magmatic and interconnected with the broader magma of social time which emerges on the surface of the even broader magma of natural time, all of the above forming without ever covering the magma of time in-itself (Castoriadis 1997b: 386). Social time is consubstantial with the plexus of the main and dominant social significations of each society. It has two dimensions, the *identitary* (tautological) dimension, which is calendar time, the standard measurement of time, and the imaginary dimension that assigns meaning to the calendar by appointing significance to temporal instances. *Identitary* social time represents the rhythm by which society measures the natural passing of time and it is the bridge that connects social time with nature. The main attributes of *identitary* social time is repetition and equivalence.

Imaginary social time is determination of the *meaning* of natural temporal instances. Imaginary social time is formulated by the interaction, overlap, and successiveness of socially instituted conceptions, world-images, and socially accepted relations. It is a temporality defined by festivals and sacred days, a mystification of time, the dimension where the *boundaries* and the *periods* of time are imaginarily posited by each society. It also determines what Castoriadis (1987: 210) calls the *quality* of time that defines the social future horizon of expectations. All social representations of time belong to the *time of social representing*, which, despite its tendency to reduce reality to the symbolic, cannot cover up the *time of social doing*. This tendency to reduce temporality to its representation is a tendency of heteronomy. The time of social representing is in a way more independent from natural temporality, since the natural leaning-on of represented social time is more arbitrary than that of the time of social doing, which is more constrained by natural reality. The time of social doing carries within it the practical dimension, which involves the confrontation with external reality, the social co-existence, the moment of transformation. The time of social doing leans on natural temporality and contains contingency; it also carries within it the distinctive ontological category of temporality in-itself, *otherness/alterity*, and the temporal singularity of *kairos*:

> [T]he time of doing would not be a time of doing and would not even be a time at all, if it did not contain the critical moment, the singularity which does not exist "objectively" and which will become so only by means of and for the appropriate doing, its occurrence as such and the point of its realization on the calendar being neither certain nor predictable (whether this concerns primitive hunting or the moment of interpretation in a psychoanalysis). In short, this is what the Hippocratic writings call *kairos*, in terms of which they define time. [...] time is that in which there is *kairos* (propitious instant and critical interval, the opportunity to take a decision) and *kairos* is that in which there is not much time. (Castoriadis 1987: 212)

Eternity and Immortality as Foundations for Heteronomy

Every day, every person, over the course of social life, informs and is informed by social time. Every individual learns the passing of the seasons and the signification of that passing and also learns the imaginary past and future of their society and their appointed place in that history. However, we should remember that social time, being rooted in the outer world, does not have a subjective dimension, besides its imaginary aspects. The conflict between the psyche and society within the individual also manifests as a conflict between subjective temporality, personal time, and social temporality, public time.

The conflict occurs by the different attributes of each, since personal time is limited, finite, and turbulent, while social time claims infinity and stability in order to establish the authority and reproduction of the dominant social norms.

Acknowledgment of our own past birth and our own future death is a socially transmitted knowledge, Castoriadis points out. There is nothing within our individual mind that could make us aware of our own birth and our eventual death, if we did not experience the birth and death of other people. We never witness our own birth or death, only the birth and death of others. The problem of the signification and emotional investment of personal mortality, the inescapability of birth and death as the ontological limits of subjective experience, religious passion and the longing for eternity, all regard the individual. The issues of historical continuity and discontinuity; the foundation, consolidation, and desertion of institutions; the catastrophes of war and extinction, all regard society.

This means that the conceptual horizon of subjective temporality is determined by the social significations of death and mortality. The interrelationship between social temporality and personal mortality is reflected in the political constitution of each society. In that sense, the fact and mystery of death cannot be reduced to a personal existential issue but must be understood as a social issue connected to the institution of political power, social time, and social historicity. Birth and death are the extreme points of reference when human existence touches the primal chaos, the ontological abyss. But no human has been born or raised in the chaos or the abyss, but in a society that encompasses meaning and invests it into the world. The temporality of existence is not restricted to subjective temporality.

The social ceremonies of tradition are focused on preserving and reproducing the dominant social significations by circular repetition. The individual subject must conform to social temporality and moreover, face mortality. Failure to acknowledge mortality is the case of heteronomous societies, which tend to deny mortality by projecting the immortality of the dominant social authority and institution. However, this metaphysical immortality mainly satisfies a social need for coherence and continuity. While the individual subject must accept their mortality, institutions are presented as potentially eternal foundations of social continuity and social eternity that function as a comforting substitute and indirect negation of personal death. The ideology of the eternity of social institutions is one of the sociological foundations of heteronomy, and it is accompanied either by a dissolution of individual subjectivity within the collective, as in the societies of precolonial East Asia, or by a promise of guaranteed personal immortality as long as the person conforms to the dominant norms. Conformity and immortality are essential attributes of any heteronomous society. The trend of conservation and reproduction of the dominant significations manifests in the closure and sanctification of the basic plexus of significations and their institutional forms that is also expressed by the reduction of social creativity to metaphysical factors.

The Creation of Imaginary Social-historical Narratives

Social time is divided into a chronological system of official representations of natural time. This chronological narrative is the primal norm of every social imaginary reconstruction of time and is mainly expressed in two ways. The first is the construction of a *calendar time*, which, protects, reproduces, and imposes social continuity and unity in everyday affairs, unifying every subjective present into a social timetable of circular repetitiousness. The attempts of the leaders of the French Revolution to change the names of the months, to change the official calendar, can be noted as an attempt to rupture incumbent temporality in order to symbolically establish a new era with a new calendar. Those attempts were proven futile, however their echo is still present, since the Ninth of Thermidor, the name given to the month August, is still used as a reference to Robespierre's downfall and as a metaphor for the overthrow of dictatorial authority. The figures of calendar time are the foundations of social coherence that only a common temporality can ensure.

The second way in which social temporality is formally expressed may be called *historiographical*, in the sense of the dominant historical narrative that each society creates as the self-image of its history. Every society presents itself within time as the present of a temporal succession in respect to an imaginary past and an equally imaginary future. This historiographical narrative intersects with calendar time, whose annotations are mostly symbolic reproductions of significant historical events. The imaginary representations of the past contain and justify present ideas and interests and future aspirations. Under the gravity of the present, the past is transformed, regulated, and re-invented toward the future. In modernity, this necessity of past justification has produced, among other things, national legends like that of the Founding Fathers or philosophical allegories like that of the Social Contract, all considered as starting points in history. An imaginary social-historical narrative clothes social-historical reality. In every case, the imaginary institution of society is also the constitution of social temporality, and of the formal history of this temporality. The only restrictions imposed on social chronology is that it has to adjust to natural time, whose instances of daily or monthly circulation serve the standardization of that narrative. Even linear narratives must curve in order to adjust to the circularity of local natural temporality, as the example of Christian holidays indicates.

However, in the case of linear narratives, the arrow of time is ultimately pointed forward and the discourse of time is a discourse of death. The interaction between social and individual time is noted explicitly, since the time-units used to measure temporal rhythm are indivisible points on a linear succession under the axiom of causality. In the case of circular social narratives, the discourse of time becomes a discourse of resurrection, where individual time, essentially linear, is usually absorbed by the community. For example, in Aztec society, time was not an individual matter but a collective subjugation to a preordained fate (Todorov 1987: 69). By their notion of circular temporality, the past prevailed over the present, and events unfolded in repetition so that even the Spanish invasion was interpreted as the fulfillment of a prophecy (Todorov 1987: 84).

Public Time and Space

These imaginary patterns are modes of refuting the mortality of society itself. They are elements of heteronomy, since they attribute societal creativity to metaphysical factors. However, exceptions to the canon of heteronomy have emerged in history, expressing different temporal conceptions. For example, Castoriadis (1997b: 267) locates the emergence of the project of autonomy in ancient Asia Minor and Greece, where and when the dual creation of democracy and philosophy brought into question the traditional religious representations of social time. Direct democracy during the classical period, as outlined in Chapter 2, created a new public space, a space for social deliberation and political decision-making where the functions of government and power could be appointed to every citizen and through every citizen, to all. Social space was subsequently articulated into three, without any *a priori* order, major domains. First, a private space which belonged to the individual and the family, the *oikos* (meaning "house"), a semi-private and semi-public space which was the place of social interaction and transaction. Second, the *agora* (meaning "market" but in a broader sense, beyond the economical function, including public social relations and discourses of every kind) as a free public, thus political, space. And third, the *ecclesia* (meaning "assembly of the citizens"), the place for political deliberation and decision-making. Public time also emerges as free social time, dedicated to the social functions within the new divisions of free public space.

Castoriadis defines public time as the "dimension where the collectivity can inspect its own past as the result of its own actions, and where an indeterminate future opens up as domain for its own activities" (1997: 281). Public time is devoted to democratic self-government and, in that sense, private time is constricted to the time of labor, in direct contrast with modern capitalist society, where private time is considered free and time is public only during the working hours. Free time, time of freedom, must certainly contain a strictly private dimension, but it cannot be contained within the private sphere without losing freedom, since social and individual freedom are interconnected both in space and in time, as the activities of any democratic community show.

An autonomous society, a society that acknowledges itself as the source of all significations and institutions cannot conceal mortality behind fictitious narratives. As Castoriadis points out, an autonomous society depends on the explicit and public acceptance of mortality. In order to open up public time and space to free and equal deliberation, decision, and action, every decision must be open to questioning and every institution, except maybe the primal institution of society as such, should be presented as equally mortal as every private citizen, although of a different duration. A democratic society must recognize mortality as a factum, so that the gravity of every political decision can be fully comprehended. A mortal life is a life of the present, and this present cannot be granted to any authority in the name of eternity. A limited life can find its meaning only in the experience of freedom among other people and that freedom must be socially instituted.

The Time of Our Lives

To connect this philosophical discussion with the fragmented world we live in today, where the dominant social structure is based on heteronomous foundations, we note that these foundations are eroding by the action of social movements and the rise of autonomy. This chapter expanded upon concepts and arguments introduced in Part One of this book and outlined

Castoriadis's radical positions on the philosophy of time and society. It emphasized the creative and indeterminate aspects of human activity and history. This outline laid the ground for further exploration of social time and social space as fundamental dimensions, not only of Castoriadis's ontology but also of the modern project of autonomy. In this context, the global struggle between societies and the elites is the contestation of an actually free public time and an actually free public space. As Jacques Ranciére explains, the contested objectives of this struggle made a prominent appearance in the movement of the Yellow Vests that erupted in France in 2018:

> Occupying also means creating a specific time: a time slowed down in relation to usual activity, and therefore a time removed from the usual order of things; but simultaneously a time accelerated by the dynamics of an activity that forces constant response to challenges for which people are not prepared. This double alteration of time changes the normal speeds of thought and action. At the same time, it transforms the visibility of things and the sense of what is possible. Things that were passively suffered acquire a new visibility as injustice. [. . .] When a collective of equals interrupts the normal course of time and begins to pull on a particular thread—today the tax on diesel, in the recent past university selection, pensions, or reform of employment law—the whole tight web of inequalities structuring the global order of a world governed by the law of profit begins to unravel.[5]

This recent struggle highlights a final important point about time and ontological creation that we want to emphasize. There is an ontological predominance—or primary significance—of the present over the past or the future since the present is the only temporal dimension of actual co-existence, the domain of public time, the moment of praxis, where the instituting is working to overthrow the already instituted. The past and the future have an asymmetrical relationship toward the present, since the past conditions it and the future opens up in a multitude of directions. The present is the ontological field of creation and transformation according to Castoriadis (1987: 201):

> The *present*, the *nun* is here explosion, split, rupture—the rupture of what is as such. This present exists as originating, as immanent transcendence, as source, as the surging forth of ontological genesis. What is contained *in* this present is not contained *there*, for it is burst asunder as a determined "place" in which something determined could simply stand, as the copresence of compatible determinations. Social-historical time—time that *is* the social-historical itself—allows us to apprehend the most pregnant, the most striking form of this time.

This present of praxis, also called *kairos*, is the critical moment, the "singularity" that does not exist "objectively" but comes into being by human action. If there is a place and time to search for personal and social autonomy, this has always been the present, the time of our lives, the era of our times, and now critically in this *decisive moment*.

PART THREE

PRESENT—POLITICS AND CRISIS

6

Crisis and Insignificance

The crisis of social imaginary significations defining our current moment suggests a crisis in mainstream normality. While we have so far discussed this crisis as it relates to capitalism, here we expand our analysis to include the state as a social-historic form. By this we mean the imaginary that posits that there is a single model of "modern society" to which all other societies will evolve toward because of the higher rationality of its institutional arrangements (Wagner 2007). This higher rationality, symbolized by representative democracy and individual rights, is represented by the United States and the United Kingdom, and are, at the time of writing, led by Donald Trump and Boris Johnson, respectively; both are xenophobic, nationalist, and lead political parties that share overlapping networks, objectives, and values with extreme-right and fascist movements. As a social-historical form, the state has normalized these politicians and networks. But, as we argue here, the state also faces a crisis of social imaginary significations as today's social movements provide new sources of meaning. These social movements have their own networks, objectives, values, and temporalities that are distinct from the heteronomous forms of capitalism and representative democracy that the state facilitates.

The Crisis of Western Civilization

The crisis of Western civilization is a concept that appears as early as the second half of the nineteenth century. Karl Marx interprets the crisis as an effect of the fundamental antithesis within the capitalist system, between the static social relations of property and the dynamic forces of production. Others who considered the concept, such as Nietzsche or Oswald Spengler, inspired, whether they foresaw it or not, a philosophical "conservative counter-revolution" and the *kulturkritik* (cultural criticism) movement in Germany, which later produced enthusiastic supporters of the Nazi regime, like Martin Heidegger and Carl Schmitt. Of course, the Second World War was an actual crisis. It was a historical rupture both in human self-consciousness, through the horror of Auschwitz, and in human self-destructiveness, through the horror of Hiroshima. The legacy of this crisis is that Auschwitz is the historical symbol of the brutal immorality of the modern nation state, while Hiroshima is the symbol of the destructive ability that this state holds.[1] These events are milestones of the crisis, which can also be described as the deterioration, de-signification, and decay of the central social imaginary significations of their time, which emerged before and during the revolutions that gave birth to modernity. This decay continued, despite the euphemistic West-European and American "social prosperity" of the Cold War years when Western governments were forced to provide public welfare as a response to the apparently antithetical, but essentially similar, "socialist" bureaucratic paradigm of the Soviets. Nevertheless, this peaceful and prosperous surface was quickly pierced by events such as the radical social movements in the 1960s, the counter-rise of neoliberalism in the late 1970s and 1980s, and the end of the Soviet system soon after in 1991.

For some, like historian (Eric Hobsbawm 1995), the fall of the Soviet system signifies the end of the short, violent twentieth century, whose history has nevertheless spilled into the twenty-first century. The end of the regime certainly signifies the failure of the grand Marxist narrative, which managed to replace religion in some countries while adopting its most essential aspects: prophecy and messianism. However, the collapse of the Marxist Imaginary was a symptom of a wider crisis of significations and deterioration of modern societies, rather than its conclusion, as the following years proved. The scope of this crisis, as it affected contemporary Western societies more broadly, can be more fully grasped, Castoriadis (1997: 262) argued, by observing the collapse of society's capacity for self-representation:

> [T]he fact that societies can no longer posit themselves as "something" (other than in an external and descriptive way)—or that, what they posit themselves as is, is crumbling apart, flattening out, and becoming empty and self-contradictory. This is but another way of saying that there is a crisis of social imaginary significations, that these significations no longer provide individuals with the norms, values, bearings and motivations that would permit them both to make society function and to maintain themselves, somehow or other, in a livable state of "equilibrium."

Identifying the clichéd trend of "empty," "flat," and "self-contradictory" authoritarians ascending to power in the West, like Donald Trump rising from billionaire presenter of *The Apprentice* reality television program to the US presidency or court jester Boris Johnson's rise to kinghood (in the liberal oligarchy sense rather than the literal monarchal sense, but the fact that we must clarify this point because Britain still has a monarchy simply amplifies this absurdity with another) in the UK, Castoriadis (1997: 257) described the depoliticization and privatization emerging:

> [I]n liberal (or soft) bureaucratic Apparatuses, such as Western political parties, we witness a return of a "charismatic" type of authority: charisma is here, simply, the particular talent of a kind of actor who plays the role of "chief," or "statesman."

Writing in Paris, 1982, Castoriadis described this era as the "rising tide of insignificancy." But we now live in a globally interconnected world, surrounded by crises, where the re-appearance of social clashes is occurring everywhere. In our *decisive moment*, it seems that the era of insignificance was both short and insignificant, and that the political and moral void of contemporary elites could engulf them, if not potentially all of us, with a bang, not a whimper.

The decade spanning the collapse of the Soviet world in 1991 to the collapse of the Twin Towers in 2001, for example, symbolizes a kind of historical prologue or epilogue bridging the twentieth century's temporal explosiveness with the twenty-first century's temporal fluidity. In this period, the Zapatista movement in Mexico (which made its initial public appearance on January 1, 1994) emerged as the first popular movement without leaders in the traditional sense (the figure of *Subcomandante* Marcos, now known as *Subcomandante Insurgente* Galeano, originally acted as a publicity symbol, but in recent years has faded into the Zapatista's collective identity). With global communicative and semantic awareness, the Zapatistas used digital mediums to communicate their message to the world in new ways. Their autonomous communities still serve as an inspiration. In this period, the anti-globalization movement, between 1999 and 2003, reacted to the early instances of economic globalization. This movement was global and spatially infinite, not so much due to the international physical expansion of the movement but due to its internal pluralism and complex multiform resistance networks, which posed no territorial demands. The wrath of state force manifested in the cold-blooded assassination of young Carlo Giuliani (1978 to 2001) in Genoa and the use of chemical warfare against demonstrators in Seattle, Prague, and Thessaloniki which, especially as participants in these movements, we will never forget. In the years that followed, a series of riots broke out in the ghetto suburbs of Paris and later in London; riots of the desperate, marginalized immigrant minorities of which the "indigenous" population were terrified.

This outline introduces the problems of crises in state and capital, state violence, and the collapse of mainstream normality that the rest of this chapter expands on. The point is to arrive at an understanding of what the collapse of social validity of state mechanisms (or if you prefer, the "crisis in confidence" that these petrified institutions face), of positive social identification, and of mainstream temporality means in our modern world. We are particularly interested in how these crises open the potential for the creation of free public space and free public time. Surveying recent social-historical uprisings as examples, with special emphasis on those most familiar to us—from the riots in Greece in December 2008 followed by the global Occupy movements of 2011 to the 2019 Yellow Vest movement in France and the revolution in Rojava—we explore these as examples of crises in social imaginary as well as new forms of social-historical creation. To understand the significance of these events, we begin with an analysis of state power as a source of meaning for society, as a fountain for social imaginary signification.

A Specific Form of Power

We use the word "state" in its political sense, which in Greek is translated as *kratos*, meaning simply "raw force." Nevertheless, this concept is not broad enough to include either every form of political power or every form of political institution that has appeared in history. To avoid the fatal mistake of equating the state with political power, a mistake deeply impressed upon modern political philosophy, we should at first provide a general definition of the concept. States exist from the creation of instituted hierarchy, dating at least back to the Chaldean clergy (since there still is doubt about whether the older Sumerians had such a rigid and powerful hierarchy). At the same time, there have been ancient or modern societies without an instituted separate state organization. Some general characteristics may help us distinguish between state authority and political power.

"The state exists," Castoriadis (2000) explained, "where there is a state mechanism, separate from society and effectively uncontrolled, like we see today even in so-called 'democratic countries,' namely countries under a regime of liberal oligarchy." The state mechanism is an exclusive mechanism of authority reproduction, preservation, and distribution that encompasses the political functions of legislature, decision-making and execution, and justice, divesting society of them. The state emerges as the monopoly of legitimate decision-making and violence. As such, it assimilates social temporality and regulates it from above, as the official, dominant social time. It assimilates even the vast, partly independent activities of the economic sphere. Even under the most neoliberal policies, the state provides the only institutional ratification. In another degree, the state itself develops large-scale economic activities in the form of both internal administrative and external business enterprises. Even before the rise of capitalism, the state tried to regulate and control commerce and economy in favor of the ruling elites.

For example, the state of Castille during the Middle Ages managed to control and regulate the livestock traffic of the herds, providing privileges and issuing prohibitions, so that the wealth from pastoral activities was channeled from the mountains to a small landowner elite. The state of Venice, at the peak of its glory, had imposed confinements on trade for outsiders, allowing German merchants to trade only inside the walls of Fontano di Tedeschi. On the other side, foreign merchant communities in Constantinople, with privileges earned by political diplomacy and military force, managed to impose their will on weak imperial governments of Byzantium in the thirteenth century. During the fourteenth century, the example set by the bourgeois Italian merchant-bankers was shaping northern European expanding cities, where banks were established along with strong bonds of allegiance between the wealthy bourgeois and the new states.

The drive toward unlimited expansion of commerce and economy stretched across the Atlantic to, as Charles C. Mann (2011) describes it, establish the "permanent European occupation in the Americas" in 1492. By founding *La Isabela*, in what is today the Dominican Republic, Cristóbal Colón "began the era of globalization—the single, turbulent exchange of goods and services that today engulfs the entire habitable world." This globalization has historically been described in primarily economic terms, but it included a biological dimension as well (Mann 2011). The Columbian Exchange, and the "ecological imperialism" that followed, marked the twilight of traditional indigenous civilizations (by genocide, ecological transformation, and cultural assimilation) and the beginning of the violent expansion of Western European domination that established the Western European political and economic paradigm as the predominant model of social organization. Mercantilism enforced the concentration of political power to the state and created the conditions for the development of an internal, national market, dictated by merchants. When the Industrial Revolution brought about the industrial organization and the complex machine apparatus, the commercialization of land, labor, and means of production created, for the first time in history, a "free" market where everything could be priced and sold according to a price system. As Karl Polanyi (1944) has shown, this new institution that became the dominant value system subjugated society to a semi-independent economic sphere where the state had the role of legal patron.

This model of organization evolved to include the marginal independence and predominance of the economic sphere over all aspects of modern society. It originated from the conjunction of private capital and state mechanisms that replaced the withering feudal patronage relations. The Enlightenment revolutions instituted ostensible jurisdictional distinctions. And modern political philosophy proposed the "division of authorities" and the placement of constitutional restrictions. Yet, we cannot see any actual division between the legislative, juridical, and executive authorities (not to mention the so-called fourth estate, that is, the press) in practice. The convergence and interweaving of state authority and private capital continues relentlessly.

The monopolization of political power and legitimate violence by the state is a result of the problematic division that has been imposed between instituting society and instituted authority, a division that, as Castoriadis (1991: 157) illuminates, underlies the very concept of state organization:

> Explicit power is not identical to the state. We have to restrict the term and the notion of state to a specific *eidos* [form], the historical creation of which can almost be dated and localized. The state is an instance separated from the collectivity and it is instituted in a way that it continuously ensures this separation. The state is, typically, what I call an institution of the second

order, belonging to a specific class of societies. I would insist, moreover, that the term "state" be restricted to the cases where there is an institution of a state apparatus, which entails a separate civilian, military or priestly "bureaucracy," even if it be rudimentary, that is, a hierarchal organization with a delimitation of regions of competence.

The construction of state institutions is founded on a sanctification of authority and the restriction of the political community within the boundaries of a small, oligarchical elite or even a dynastic family. Even in the quasi-autonomous city of classical Athens, where the political community was limited to indigenous men, something unacceptable in any era, this community was by far more inclusive than any state organization, since any free citizen could and should equally participate in the institutions of government, without anyone retaining an authoritarian status that would elevate him above the community. The Greek democratic *polis*, Castoriadis (1991: 157) explained, was not a "state" since explicit power for positing laws (*nomos*), acting in common (*dike*), and with purpose (*telos*) "belongs to the whole body of citizens." In our project of autonomy, the imaginary political community of free and equal individuals obviously includes, virtually and ideally, the whole of humanity.

Modern nation states were founded not on divine providence but on the authority of an arbitrary national "will." As mechanisms of hierarchical bureaucracy, they are supposed to, according to the dominant Western founding myth, represent the nation, namely society mutilated into a nation. Two specific nation state institutions and social functions that incorporated the techniques of authority were national mandatory education and national mandatory military service, propped up by national taxation. Today, both are being abandoned by most Western states (not Greece), gradually handed over to private capital. Nevertheless, during the formation of nation states in the nineteenth century,[2] both institutions played a vital role in the ethnic and linguistic homogenization of the subjugated populations. Mandatory education and military service constituted a broader oppressive educational mechanism with the responsibility to safeguard and reproduce the basic national myths. In this way, the nation state absorbed crucial aspects of the socialization process which typically belonged to the broader family or clan. The nation state, appearing as the "representative" of the "unified will" of the people and founded on a paternalist political theory, managed to substitute family on a broader social scale, diminishing it to mere parental and fraternal relations.

The nation state, however, is a complex social-historical political formation where the twin currents of political republicanism and economic industrial capitalism converge. Those currents, which belong to the wider magma of the Euro-Western civilization, have deep roots in late medieval years. They exploded to conquer social reality through the successive revolutions of the late seventeenth and eighteenth centuries. Old social significations of feudalist and monarchical theology crumbled (in the periphery of the Western world, for example, in the Balkans traditional significations and practices of patronage and family connections still survive, if not in formal law, certainly in behavior and custom) and new imaginary ideals like monetary circulation, unlimited economic expansion and growth, rationalistic sovereignty, individual profit, capital independence, and the marginal independence and predominance of the economic sphere over society, shaped the world according to their image.

The equation of power and state was enriched by the rise of the nation state with the *metaphysics of nationality*, which consumed and dominated the world, being unquestionably adopted even by multinational societies (like the United States, that manifold, multilingual, and multicultural social mosaic). Nationalism seeks to destroy the evidence of historical facts which are heterogeneous and discontinuous in favor of a fictional homogenous and continuous narrative. The reduction of historical time to the substantive conception of the nation eliminates historical temporality, creating a pseudo-historical national myth. A myth so far removed from lived experience and social sentiment that it has to be violently impressed upon the social imaginary, with rigorous programs of national education, national army recruitment, national holidays, and the nationalization of religious and political propaganda. Castoriadis observes that the nation fulfills a function of social identification "by means of the threefold imaginary reference to a 'common history'—threefold, because this history is sheer past, because it is not really common, and, finally, because what is known of it and what serves as the basis for this collectivizing identification in people's consciousnesses is largely mythical" (Castoriadis 1987: 149).

Immanuel Wallerstein highlights the relation of the national imaginary to social temporality, contemplating on *pastness*, the foundation of social and collective identities that correspond to individual self-perception, since "pastness is a central element in the socialization of individuals, in the maintenance of group solidarity, in the establishment of or challenge to social legitimation" (1988: 78).

We could argue, therefore, that the temporal mode of the national imaginary is pastness and, in particular, fictitious pastness. Wallerstein points out that the "concept of 'nation' is related to the political superstructure of this historical system [capitalist world-economy], the sovereign states that form and derive from the interstate system" (1988: 79). Similar to Wallerstein, Ernest Renan, in his 1882 essay "What is a nation?" admits that forgetfulness and, explicitly, historical error, "are essential in the creation of a nation."

More than the traditional, medieval, or archaic states, the modern nation state, whether of the "Western" or of the "socialist" varieties, cannot be historically separated from the economic mechanisms of global capitalism and all its transformations, even though in theory it is supposed to be independent from the "free market."

Techniques of Control

The historic experience of the twentieth century was a bloody verification of the synergy between the nation state and international private capital, regardless who the owner of the social means of production was—private companies or "the workers'" state. Castoriadis demonstrated that a new oppressive social formation, bureaucratic capitalism, emerged within the state mechanism and obtained authority while claiming no ownership over property or wealth. The twentieth century was also the period when the conversion of nineteenth-century disciplinary Western societies—defined by the organizational paradigm and timetable that applied to all social institutions of public education and production emblematized by the industrial factory—concluded and moved to twenty-first-century globalized societies of bio-political control, where mass media, advertisement, state propaganda, digital images, and market values invade private life. In this period, the techniques of control have transformed from discipline to manipulation. We can see the strategy. It moves in tandem with the rise of consumerism, the end of the predominantly male-oriented market as women and young people appeared in the sphere of production and consumption, the invention of television and direct access into the sanctum of the private house, the global spread of organized mass sports and entertainment, popular music and life style trends, and finally the use of mobile devices and algorithms for data-driven exploitation and surveillance.

The successful application of these techniques concluded the colonization of free, personal time, namely non-labor time, by state and capitalist structures, transforming it into private time, namely non-public time. Public social temporality always reflects the dominant social relations and serves, both as calendar and historiographic time, their reproduction and consolidation. However, the further development of bio-politics by means of cultural homogenization and material abundance was a radically new social-historical phenomenon with a radically new psycho-political impact. The colonization of personal free time by market services and entertainment products resulted in the multiplication of private spaces within individual life, as well as to the fragmentation and privatization of public space. Lewis Mumford asserted that the essential symbol of industrial capitalism is not the steam engine but the alarm clock (1934), the mechanism that divides the day into countable working hours, equivalent to arbitrary value points. The daily TV program—the symbol of post-war bureaucratic capitalism before the internet—divided into broadcast zones that match the divisions of the social time of production, morning shows for housewives, noon cartoons for children, and Sunday sports for working people. It remains an anthropological and sociological relic from the era of Western consumerism.

Against this mainstream culture, the rebellious 1960s gave rise to forms of cultural resistance and examples of a radically different temporality. The social movements of the situationists, the hippies, the leftists and the anarchists throughout the Euro-Western world experimented with communal ways of life, private and collective psychedelic experiences, psycho-geographical projects. They explicitly sought to break the boundaries, first of mainstream social time, secondly of subjective and natural time itself, through the radical negation, inversion or perversion of the dominant calendar, historical patterns, and personal experiences. Yet, those controversial and multifocal active denials of social normality and normative temporality that momentarily ruptured the enclosure of social imaginary were quickly assimilated. Their symbols and images involuntarily expanded the cultural range of the mainstream social time they had put under question. The new counterculture that appeared in the social-historical magma was used as a bridge for the colonization of private life by instituted authority. Images like the symbol of peace or later the symbol of anarchy were assimilated by the advertising and cultural industry after the removal of their initial revolutionary content.

The expansion of the cultural range of mainstream social time produced a risk for authorities, even as this radical culture became de-personalized. At the same time the techniques and mechanisms of public control became more personalized and applied on an industrial scale. This bubble began to burst in the mid-1980s, the glamour and kitsch decade which now seems like the swan song of an idiotic feast. The imposition of neoliberal greed to the highest ranks of power led to social clashes across multiple levels and a dispersion of social coherence alongside the unification of international capital. The assimilation of former Soviet states by the dominant capitalist paradigm spurred the globalization of transactions and information, incorporating this new jurisdiction into global, market-driven exploitation, increased poverty, and inequality. We already mentioned the anti-globalization movement that first promoted a symbolically influential interconnection of the oppressed in an imaginary community of global solidarity. And we have mentioned the brutal execution of Carlo Giuliani at the 2001 G8 summit in Genoa by the state, as part of that movement. So now we look at another technique of manipulation.

The Retreat to Force

When the nation state's validity collapses it retreats to force and then violence becomes a technique of suppression complementing the methods of manipulation outlined earlier. For example, during this century's uprisings, riots, and social rebellions in Greece, state repression was reinforced by these means:

(a) Technically with antipyretic uniforms, plastic bullets, and armored vehicles.

(b) Strategically with crowd control techniques that segmented the urban fabric into delimited and surveilled zones in collaboration between international police agencies.

(c) Legally with draconian penal legislation that restricted civil rights and upgraded minor crimes to felonies while anti-terrorist laws were also applied, inhibiting constitutional liberties.

(d) Ideologically, as fascist and absolutist ideals were spread. Collaboration between the Nazi Golden Dawn Party and mass media produced propaganda to undermine the deeper social significance of the rebellions.

But these means are not limited to Greece, as Palestinians, Egyptians, Chileans, Sudanese, those in Hong Kong, and black and indigenous communities in North America can testify. They are enabled by interstate treaties and agreements that strengthen trans-governmental collaboration and interdependence through a plexus of the international military-industrial complex (led by the United States, Britain, China, and Russia). This plexus drives the synergy between private interests and political lobbies with enough force to dictate the conduct of warfare, foreign and domestic. It includes semi-independent networks of state and private capital shaping the fields of justice (privatization of prisons) and public services (privatization of health care, education, garbage collection, and water) worldwide. These techniques include deployment of private mercenary services alongside national armies (the infamous Blackwater (now Academi) responsible for the 2007 Nisour Square massacre in Iraq, for example), along with the surreptitious use of drones and "autonomous" weapons. The Greek state's resort to violence can be understood in this context of larger trends.

Globally, state violence is inseparable from state politics. The political personnel that climb the authoritarian hierarchy are carriers of the dominant significations that inform state institutions and at the same time are subject to the pressures that these institutions exercise by their function. They, at one and the same time, uphold the dominant function of the state while the state affirms those who aspire to advance its power. Violence and war are not an antithesis to politics but an available option with variable costs and, as an extension of state politics, an instrument. As heads of state like to say, "All options are on the table." To carry out its violence the political establishment often resorts to para-state organizations. This, combined with the relapse of nation state official rhetoric to obscurantist schemata of the past, is another indication of the signification crisis. In these instances, official rhetoric turns to the extreme right, to religion, to nationalism, to conservatism and pre-Enlightenment political theology. The Nazi Golden Dawn Party's rise to the upper echelons of official Greek politics, participating in parliament from 2012 to 2019, exemplifies this.

The Collapse of Dominant Significations

The current crisis is not just a financial crisis, as we have argued, but a crisis of significations. Across various forms of capitalism we see the weakening of the dominance of economic significations over the other spheres of social life, the arrival of social movement–led temporalities, and the emergence of new forms of consumption that are consistent with the perpetuation of the autonomous project through self-education and collective work. The signs were visible from the beginning of the century, when the old, mummified significations of obscurantism resurfaced on a global scale, when new social movements emerged to redefine and reclaim public time and space. The situation is intensified by the steady growth of megacities, global hubs that overshadow the states that carry them. Since 2011, we live, for the first time, on a planet where more people live in urban centers than in rural areas. While humans become more urban animals, they also become less political, since the inhuman architecture of megacities leaves no room for public space, nor time for collective deliberation, public communication, and democratic decision-making. Before the housing bubble burst in the United States, there were the suburban riots in the capitals of Europe. Then came the riots of December 2008 in the cities of Greece, which had a deep and widespread social character. That December, the impulsive and massive demonstrations in every city of the country were led not by "professional" revolutionaries, but by high school students. Crowds of students besieged every police station in the country, full of rage at the cold-blooded assassination of sixteen-year-old Alexandros Grigoropoulos by policeman Epaminondas Korkoneas in Exarcheia, in the center of Athens. People from across society, across generations, joined the students and their parents.

This rebellion against state and police brutality was explosive. The government withdrew the police from the streets. The revolt revealed the gap between the state and society, not only as a social disassociation with state power but also as an *antithesis of interests*. In Greece, as Chapter 3 demonstrated, modern history is a story of collaboration between Western-oriented state mechanisms and international capital at the expense of the people. Trust in state institutions has always been weak. Greek society experiences state violence as a traumatic reliving of its recent history. It remains a common sentiment; the feeling that state bureaucracy serves its own interests, which depends on private capital rather than social approval.

A New Social Temporality

That December shattered the traditional *metaphysics of rebellion*, both of the hegemonic version which argues for an enlightened avant-garde to lead the riot and of the teleological version which sees rebellion in an apocalyptic manner as the event to mark the end of history. Of course, nothing like that ever happens. Rebellion metaphysics includes a *metaphysics of violence* which may lead to the withdrawal of society from the political sphere. It adopts the Christian (shared by the Enlightenment deists of the eighteenth century) perception of time, as a temporality of prophetic promise and messianic fulfillment. It conceals time under the schema of cause and effect, as a linear transition from an absolute, pretemporal *prime cause* to a foreseen, post-temporal *final effect*. This schema places rebellion at the extreme point, end or beginning, of history, like Christian theology places the Second Coming at the end of days. This metaphysics has a genealogical relation, ever since the medieval Christian revolutionary messianic tradition (Cohn 1957) was inherited by Marx and passed on to the movements of modernity. This messianic element allowed, in the former Soviet bloc and elsewhere, the fusion of Marxism with traditional ethnic prejudices and religious idolatry. This strengthened the authority of Marxist-inspired regimes over a variety of populations.

This *metaphysics of rebellion* withered after the December 2008 riot in the atmosphere of general puzzlement that followed. The riot unearthed the spirit of solidarity and defiance which would continue to grow during the crisis that followed. December left us with the taste of free public temporality experienced in the streets, which were flooded with those who gathered, organized, demonstrated, protested, and fought against oppressive mechanisms and would meet again in larger crowds in the years to come to demand direct democracy and political emancipation. Social time was liberated from the monotonous rhythms of production or mass entertainment and regained its creative depth, as each moment felt like a nexus of possibilities in the openness of public space and free passionate human communication.

December 2008 was a historical event which differed from other uprisings in Europe, like that of the Parisian suburbs in 2005, because it was not only the socially excluded that led the riot but also the politically excluded, the middle and lower strata of Greek society. Those who made their appearance at the central stage were the school students who besieged police stations with oranges and demonstrated against state brutality. It was also an event that spread throughout the country, since riots and demonstrations erupted in forty-two Greek cities with an impressive temporal depth, an evolution in time that spread beyond the beginning of 2009. The prevalent images of fire and destruction that have since then been impressed on social imagination don't tell the whole truth. Public building occupations, popular assemblies, self-organized cultural events were the actual essential manifestations of the rebellion. An event is singular in its particularity and cannot be predicted according to other events. The links and connections between events can only become visible a posteriori, since an event inspires further events. Further events that share a common thread of significations, that share a common future horizon of expectations, change the significance of the initial event, since they transform important original elements in their own social-historical context, instituting a new originality. That moment of December echoed a long history of tension and frustration between the people and the state in Greece. It also echoed global contemporary tensions between society and authority institutions, being the first among successive popular uprisings. As an event, it was singular but was also connected to similar singular events that form the discontinuous history of the struggle for individual and social autonomy.

The Occupy movement followed in 2011, occupying main squares in Greek cities, notably Syntagma Square in Athens, for nearly three months of social deliberation and clashes with the police forces, starting from a demonstration against the first Memorandum of Understanding signed between the bankrupt Greek state and the IMF, and in resonance with similar Occupy movements in Spain and the United States. It had the temporal structure of a limited duration of social co-existence and experimentation with direct democracy. This included a multiplicity of parallel events, festivals, demonstrations, but mainly, by self-organizing the occupied square on the basis of direct democracy. Open popular assemblies were held daily where thousands of civilians had the chance to participate, as proto-institutions of public deliberation that issued resolutions against the economic, social, and ecological crisis, along with open committees drawn by lot, cultural events, and self-organized services for food and accommodation. This created a free public space and time in the political center of Athens, opposite the seat of parliamentary oligarchy, where direct democracy could be practiced in public through self-experimentation and collective innovation.

The Occupy movement also created a free public time in the heart of the dominant social temporality, disrupting it, a public time of deliberation, self-organization, decision-making but also of social interaction, play, and artistic expression. Thousands of people participated daily, sharing particular projects, getting to know each other, forming personal and social relationships, creating a collective present projected onto a common future horizon. Come 2012, social temporality was bound once again, but not settled, along with politics, within the walls of parliament. After years of police violence, state terrorism, and political upheaval came a series of elections that diminished the hold of traditional establishment parties (the Pan Hellenic Socialist Party and conservative New Democracy (ND)) that ruled the country since 1975. Two elections, in six months, brought to power two successive unstable governments comprised of the alliance between formerly left SYRIZA (Coalition of the Radical Left) and the always far-right Independent Greeks (ANEL). This coalition seemed to be the establishment's last bet, since they "stabilized" the status quo before splitting up in 2019 in view of new elections. SYRIZA lost to ND, first in the Euro-elections of May 2019, then in the Greek elections of

July, bringing ND back to power. During this period, social rage dispersed into individual agony, but it also inspired collective efforts outside the state and capitalist economy: local struggles against authorities, hubs of a different, restricted economy within an egalitarian and democratic communal self-organization. Social networks continue to grow, local resistance communities continue to fight, and history remains turbulent, global waves smashing hard against the walls of authority.

In the years following the 2008 revolt in Greece, local communities rebelled against state decisions to sell or exploit natural resources. At Lefkimmi, on the island Corfu and at Keratea, near Athens, communities violently resisted the construction of garbage dumps in their regions. At Skouries, Halkidiki, near Mount Athos, a broad social movement emerged against the exploitation of the mountains and forests for gold mining against the interests of both the Greek state and the transnational El Dorado Gold Corporation. In Epirus and Western Greece local resistance movements have been organizing from below, against oil extractions, manifesting in forms of horizontal democratic networks that create common events, like the demonstrations in Ioannina in 2018 and Athens in 2019 where thousands gathered in protest. In all cases, social movements organized in terms of direct democracy, with communal assemblies, prompting wide social solidarity far beyond the boundaries that the forceful response of state oppression generated.

The Invasion of History in Mainstream Temporality

While the temporality we described in preceding sections refers to the Greek experience, similar social-historical phenomena made their appearance worldwide as spatio-temporal instances, moments of global transformation of societies. Occupy, for instance, created globally synchronized temporalities, with common demonstration dates, with instant information exchange, and with intercommunication between focal points around the world. Global multiplicity manifests through the idiosyncrasy of contemporary communication and information, especially via the internet. It creates a newfound sense of *globality*, expressed politically as the networking of social movements. But it also appears as a sense of a *global social temporality*, a planetary *synchronicity* that contains local social temporalities. This creates a universal chronology and history, which supports a sense of *diachronicity* worldwide.

In recent years heteronomous social time shook on several occasions. Neoliberalism's austerity policies and the financial crisis violently disrupted the rhythms of labor and production. The strategy of the "shock doctrine," described by Naomi Klein (2007), brought the depreciation of labor and the liquidation of labor time. Unemployment, part-time employment, precarious gig economy work, zero hour contracts, and variable timetables amplify these problems, as does the rapid reduction of purchasing power among the majority, which upholds the significations of time and money in the imaginary core of the system. On the other side, however, social movements also disrupted established social time, with combustive gatherings in public squares organized anonymously via the internet, social media, and huge demonstrations. Variations of these disruptions occurred in the Middle East and North Africa during the Arab Spring uprisings against dictatorships and destitution. And similarly, in Western city centers during Occupy. But, prior to that, the disturbance of mainstream temporality was symbolized in December 2008 in Greece by the image of riot police encircling the plastic Christmas tree of Syntagma Square, to protect it. It was brand new, since rioters set fire to the one before during the first week of the uprising. This image—the oppressive forces of the state guarding the lifeless symbol of the "festive" normality of Christmas, brutal force defending the official temporality—was a symbolic admission of the importance of established social temporality for authorities that had to maintain not only the dominant societal hierarchy but also its temporal skeleton. But this was symbolic in another sense too. Modern rebellions express the rejection of core capitalist imaginary significations, like the primacy of profit, unconditional industrial growth, the mass production and consumption of cultural products, and the objectification of people and planet. The values of solidarity, social freedom, equality, and decency re-emerged at the core of social-political action.

One of the explicit messages of the December 2008 riots was that free public space and time belongs to society and is created by self-organized social, political, and cultural activities outside and against the capitalist mindset. This radical conception of free public space stands at the core of the contemporary project of autonomy. Free public time became a shared experience during those days, penetrating social normality. The riot was described as "a riot that came from the future." It was a social-historical moment that shook the waters, uncovering isles of free human interaction based on solidarity and equality. This is why we didn't see the "working class" or any organized, impersonal political party; instead we saw society unbound, the social individual, the democratic subjectivity. These temporal isles already existed in the margins of modern Western societies, in the form of social centers, occupied buildings, and local movements. However, restricted to that margin, they developed into semi-closed spheres of an imaginary openness. This theoretical openness suddenly became social-political action, praxis, by the invasion of history in the channeled waters of mainstream temporality.

The project of autonomy re-emerged on a global scale amid the crisis, after a period of apathy and insignificance. The reaction of the state was violent and multifaceted. However, it is important to look beyond the authoritarian reaction against recent social movements in order to evaluate the imaginary significations of autonomy that rise from the temporal turbulence. In doing so, we see that the public demand of social movements worldwide is direct democracy. Every self-organized public space, open community, and network of social solidarity that has emerged is self-governed in terms of direct democracy. This explicit democratic demand brought forth the issue of social transformation, the rejection of dominant instituted authority, the possibility of an autonomous reinstitution of society. This demand has a long history as Castoriadis (1997: 276) traces:

> Direct democracy has been rediscovered or reinvented in modern history every time a political collectivity has entered a process of radical self-constitution and self-activity: town meetings during the American Revolution, *sections* during the French Revolution, the Paris Commune, the workers' councils, or the Soviets in their original form. Hannah Arendt has repeatedly stressed the importance of these forms. In all these cases, the sovereign body is the totality of those concerned; whenever delegation is inevitable, delegates are not just elected but subject to permanent recall. One should remember that for classical political philosophy, the notion of "representation" is unknown.

What could be the meaning of the word "revolution" after the collapse of the *metaphysics of rebellion* in the twenty-first century? Answers may be found in recent emancipatory struggles for free public space, free public time, and direct democracy. Of course, the Occupy movement did not result in revolution anywhere, or in any process of radical self-transformation of society, since it did not have the space or the time. But the claim for a radical, democratic reinstitution was explicitly posed. On a local level, in several parts of the world, networks of limited self-institution emerged where there had previously been an extended political desert. There are many, on a variety of scales, in a variety of cultures, with a variety of functions toward the common goal of social liberation. Here, to close this chapter, we draw insights from just an inspiring few.

In 2016, the French *Nuit Debout* movement created a new sort of temporality which, as Jacques Ranciére (2017) emphasizes, transcended simply being against government measures and decisions by reframing the space and time of being-in-common:

> It started from labor conflicts, conflicts concerning workers and it became a kind of, what I call, an opposition of worlds. No more an opposition

of forces, but a conflict of words. And of course, what symbolized *Nuit Debout*, meaning that we don't sleep at nights, like the proletarians of the 19th nineteenth century, also was this idea, which I found quite exciting, of changing the calendar, saying that the movement was a movement of March and that after March 31st, there would not come April 1st, but March 32nd, 33rd etc., etc. Well, I think there is something important, which is part of all those movements of the squares, the idea precisely of a kind of displacement. Normally, protesters march in the streets. And there was the idea now that the point is not to march in the streets against the government, the point is to create some kind of specific forms of spatialization and temporalization of the movement.

The temporality that spans beyond insurrectional events to characterize the formation of a common way of life and overcome identity politics is known as the *duration*. This can lead to a political semi-secession as exemplified by the ZAD (Zone to Defend) movement at Notre-Dame-des-Landes. The movement began as a demonstration against a military airport in the 1960s and grew to be a movement of defense of a self-governed community and land, which continues after the government abandoned the airport plans in 2018. Over this period ZAD experienced a deep transformation, as Dr. Kristin Ross (2018) explains, in the relationship between time and a common way of being as the *duration* unfolded:

[I]n the case of the ZAD, the unity was provided by opposition to the airport. So it was a clear project and that brought people together. As time went by, that changed. And here is the importance of *duration*. It is that, as time went by, they discovered not just what they were opposed to, but also what they were for. And what they were for was the defending of what they had become. In other words, of the kind of community, of the kind of collective that they had become, in very real terms. The years of shared experience, the different people that had come in, the memories and again, the physical relationship to the land, which they are constantly working on and also the battles with the police. So there is a change in what [Gaston] Bachelard calls the muscular consciousness of the land which has become part of the value that you are defending. And still, you have eclecticism within the group, nothing of that has solidified as homogenous.

These movements posit a new temporality between the ephemeral and the enduring, the local and the global. They put into question the borders of established identities, established temporality, and order. As Ranciére (2017) explains, there is an inner correlation between these movements and a correlation of temporalities, in the sense that they are efforts to overcome established social divisions that reproduce inequality:

> [W]hat has been important in the recent movements is precisely the ... idea that the question of the universal is really at play in the very form of the movement. So, it is not the specific object of the power that is either particular or universal. The point is whether you deal with it in a particular or universal way. Particular, meaning that I am interested in this or that kind of fight and universal, meaning that I think that in this particular thing there is a question dealing with the way in which it has to be dealt with, not from the point of view of this or that identity but by trying to make it universal and dealing with it in a way that it possesses a capacity of everyone.

That people could be participants in social movements based on their own involvement and commitment, while social movements can approach problems from situations of conflict that concerned everybody, is a tremendous advance for modern social movements. Additionally, however, what is evident in these movements is the desire of the people to create a political public time based on their refusal to be represented. As Castoriadis (1997: 313) said, the revolution begins when "the population forms its own autonomous organs—when it enters into activity in order to give to itself its own organizational forms and its own norms."

Finally, an inspiring example of this revolutionary activity has been the Kurdish revolution for autonomy and direct democracy in Rojava after 2011, inspired by Murray Bookchin's project of democratic federalism. This revolution has managed, in the throes of war no less, to defend their communities with people's militias against the onslaught of the Turkish state as well as the Islamic State, and through numerous betrayals by the United States, *and* to politically reinstitute their community as autonomous communes, in terms of equality, freedom, and direct democracy leaning on the physical nature of their surroundings with minimal mediation. This highly unlikely revolution in the Kurdish regions of Syria demonstrates the power of human freedom. Their militias and public assemblies comprised of free and equal men and women are consciously designed not to reproduce authoritarian hierarchy but, instead, to create a new, practical education in the horizontal institutions of direct democracy, self-government and autonomy.

This chapter has sought to demonstrate how social movements have created new social-historical forms within the crises of social imaginary significations of state, capital, and mainstream temporality. We pick up this thread in the following chapter by exploring the question of who the revolutionary subjects of the autonomous project are by distinguishing important differences between the concepts of constituent and instituting power.

7

The Invisible Subject

The twenty-first-century experience in forms of direct democracy that we outlined in the previous chapter, albeit on a limited or local level, brought forth the important question of who could be the *political or revolutionary subject* of a radical social transformation. This question is critical for the emergence of actions, ways of being, organizing, building, and understanding that proximate autonomy in our *decisive moment*. Unfortunately, the answer to this question, which is connected to issues of political decision-making and power, is sought by some in an anachronistic return to revolutionary dogmatisms of the past. If Marxism seemed, and is, bankrupt at the end of the twentieth century, it is still haunting Western political thought in the twenty-first century. No matter how distant a theory is from reality, reality cannot be enclosed in the walls of a theory. Discourses among radical theorists, looking to locate elements of their own ideological identity within social movements, reveals that the quest to identify an ideal "system"—a transcendent structure of power—and the search for the ideal "subject" of that system—despite all honorable intentions—are operating on a new *metaphysics of authority*. This chapter interrogates concepts of the revolutionary subject in relation to the project of autonomy and direct democracy. Drawing from the example of Greek social unrest since 2008 and the global Occupy movement, we explore who the subjects are that practice direct democracy in moments of radical social transformation. We juxtapose understandings of the revolutionary subject that Castoriadis held against Marxist concepts such as Michael Hardt's and Antonio Negri's "multitude" as well as nihilist visions. This is important in order to distinguish the difference between constituent and instituting power. We look beyond recent history to explore subjects of social-historical transformations and evidence of human self-awareness. Finally, we return to consider subjects as agents of self-institution, social movements and their correlation with the individual, and social transformation for the objective of self-governance.

Direct Democracy and Jurisdiction

In our experience, direct democracy is the only political form that allows free public deliberation and action that includes everyone, as an equal, free, and responsible person. First, lack of indirect representation, respect for individual opinion, free speech, outspokenness, rejection of hierarchy, discussion, and open voting on public issues and not voting for representatives, and free public time and space are the essential features of any democratic political procedure. Secondly, the experience of the global Occupy movement and specifically of the huge public gatherings in Syntagma Square show that every directly democratic assembly has a corresponding jurisdiction. The Syntagma public assembly of summer 2011 had complete jurisdiction over the occupied square, the public common ground. There, the movement self-organized rapidly, with a variety of interconnected political and practical functions, beside the daily general public assembly. Solidarity kitchens provided food, not just for communication teams and information networks, but for all. Free radio, such as the self-organized radio-station of the people, *Radio Entasi*, broadcast from the first week of the occupation, through all of Greece, with coverage including live reporting during violent oppression. Medical teams provided free medical care to everybody, which became especially important during police aggression. Artistic and musical teams, discussion groups on various issues, free lessons, a kindergarten, and a free community emerged under the tents and banners of the protesters.

Anybody could voluntarily participate and help in any of these activities; in this new social environment trust and solidarity toward everyone seemed natural and obvious. Everybody gathered every evening near the center of the square for the general public meeting. Everybody could speak on their turn and every issue and proposition was discussed, voted on, and decided by all. Practical decisions were made quickly, theoretical discussions could last for hours. Nobody complained, since public temporality was filled with new meaning and every moment impressed a memory of actual public freedom. Accordingly, local directly democratic assemblies formed afterward in different neighborhoods of Athens and had jurisdiction over their neighborhood areas. But a single assembly cannot have jurisdiction over the whole country or exercise political influence over the geopolitical space of a nation state if it is to be consistent with direct democracy. Only a vast network of nested assemblies and local communities self-governed by direct democracy, interconnected but autonomous, could provide a scalable answer to this problem. There is no ideal formulation, but rather a set of formulated ideals—democracy, equality, freedom, and responsibility. We see assemblies created among the Yellow Vests, but their function and responsibilities are different from those created in Rojava—the former are efforts to organize the struggle, the latter are the institutions of a society.

But, why should such a network be restricted or defined by national borders? It could expand to a certain region or potentially to the whole world, since it would not be an expansion of a univocal authority, but an expansion of equal communication and free interaction between autonomous communities. Direct democracy itself is the only place and time when we can seriously contemplate direct democracy. This claim may seem redundant, but its important implications can be seen by considering another limited communal form that has been created in Greece, the form of the *public social space*. Examples such as *Nosotros* in Athens, *Micropolis* in Thessaloniki, *Alimoura* in Ioannina, among others, are free social spaces where direct democracy is experienced as not only a form of decision-making but also a form of collective creativity. Ranciére (2017) defines a free social space that corroborates our own experience:

> A free social space is a space where the very separation of spheres of activity—material production, economic exchange, social care, intellectual production and exchange, artistic performance, political action, etc.—is thrown into question. It is a space where assemblies can practice forms of direct democracy intended not simply to give an equal right of speech to everybody but to make collective decisions on concrete matters. In such a way a form of political action tends to be at the same time the cell of another form of life. It is no more a tool for preparing a future emancipation but a process of invention of forms of life and modes of thinking in which equality furthers equality.

Besides serving as forms of political praxis, these free social spaces give form to the activities of constant reinstitution and political education. And this re-creative circulation of praxis and reflective critique generate social reinstitution and autonomy. As we stressed in Chapter 2, any theoretical model that aspires to be a complete and ideal simulation of direct democracy will fail. And, as we argue next, if we think of direct democracy in terms of the system of state politics, which denies the subject of radical social-historical transformation and is restricted within national borders, we will hit a dead end.

Piercing the Traditional *Metaphysics of Rebellion*

Every political philosophy that refers to metaphysical regularities that supposedly govern history needs a transcendental subject to incarnate the imagined "natural laws" of society, at least if there is no god. This metaphysical subject can be "the ancestors," "the faithful," "the Greeks," "the Germans," "the proletariat," or any other term general and obscure enough to describe a transcendental collective will that overcomes and encompasses individualities.

Every heteronomous imaginary institution finds its justification there. To despoil the power of the individual person, authority replaces it with a generic "subject" or a legal entity. So the quest for a carrier-subject of the collective is the theoretical reef where radical political philosophy crashes. It is the metaphysics favored by the left. Who is the privileged revolutionary subject? Is it the workers? Is it the farmers? Is it the students? Is it the unemployed? Are they self-conscious actors determining their own history or actors in a predetermined play? Who will revolt, and in the name of whom? Yet, in these new directly democratic assemblies described earlier, there was no univocal, super-physical distinct subject or a historically privileged social group—just free individuals self-organizing their common activities in terms of autonomy. Everybody, from every social layer, was there, except the mechanisms of the state or private capital and the persons that incarnate them. Even more, in enduring directly democratic struggles, the actual subjects found themselves changed. Politics is not a field of essences but a field of relations. The process, described as people abandoning their social functions, can be found in many directly democratic uprisings across place and time. Experience showed that the only actual political subject of direct democracy is the physical, individual subjectivity. Maria, George, Nick, Tonia, and so on, every one of the real individuals were there, as free political persons and autonomous individuals with personal responsibility of thought and action and an equal right to public social power.

Castoriadis defines *human subjectivity* as an autonomous individual with reflective contemplation and deliberated activity—contemplating on action and acting consciously. But this action and this contemplation cannot be restricted to the private sphere. It presupposes free public space, free public time. Even the ability of free thinking can be eliminated by authority if access to public discussion, public opinion, and public criticism is denied, as Immanuel Kant has demonstrated. And a general public assembly, at the time of decision and the time of execution, is the public space where autonomous subjectivities meet and interact in the political manner of collective praxis.

Whereas the free market, *agora*, (in the ancient sense, not its modern capitalist meaning which is about who holds the most bargaining power or brute force), is the public space where autonomous subjectivities meet and intercourse in a social manner of leisure and recreation. Autonomous subjectivities, self-governed individuals—the range of their political activities supersedes the sum of their private activities, since it refers directly to a wider horizon, the social-historical horizon. Social relations themselves constitute yet another organic layer of implicit power where there is no absolute or relative authority granted to anyone over everyone, such as in the petrification of power in state institutions. Within directly democratic social relations, political power is potentially exercised by everyone, since anyone participates publicly in the democratic institutions, by lottery or in turns (elections, being an aristocratic institution, are reserved for technical positions and functions).

Limitations and Horizons of Social Movements

If we commit the mistake of appointing a general term like "the nation" or "the party" as the foundation of political authority instead of the real individual citizen, then we reinvent a transcendent, invisible subject, widening the gap between society's real political activity and a supposedly metaphysical subject will. Even the term "multitude," proposed by Marxist political philosophers Toni Negri and Michael Hardt, a term found in Spinozean political theory, is a poor substitute for real people and raises more aporias. Is every multitude political? Is every gathering of people a multitude? Does it depend on number? On activity? Can it be defined *a priori* or *a posteriori*? And so on. If the subject that redistributes and exercises political power is not every actual citizen but some invisible collective subject, there rises again the problem of representation. And there emerges an additional problem, the problem of the social majority over the minority, which are presented as constants, whereas in a direct democracy this problem is not so difficult, since the majority and minority are variables that shift according to the specific issue under discussion. People voting for a specific action can easily find themselves on the same side as their previous opponents when discussing another action. Similarly problematic is the other concept coined by Negri (1999), the "constituent power of the movements," which proposes the implicit substitution of the subject by the movement. Like other efforts of the meta-Marxist thinkers, this conception bears the hallmarks of a latent Marxism, the quest for a privileged revolutionary subject, the division of society into ontologically and existentially contradictory classes, the quest for a sociological foundation of authority and the subsequent erection of an "absolute" justice.

Of course, we should also consider social movements as very important carriers and manifestations of the project of autonomy, as long as they really express the ideals of freedom, equality, and solidarity. Not every social movement is an autonomous movement or a movement for autonomy, although self-organized democratic movements are primary political means toward this cause. Therefore, to concede some constituent power to any movement, without further definition, opens the door to totalitarianism. For example, every actual social movement is, by definition, both partial and specified such as the movement against state terrorism, the student movement, the workers' movement, the ecological movement, and so on. Every radical social movement is actively juxtaposed to established authority and eventually confronts it within a limited fragment of time, at a specific social-historical moment. This confrontation happens in a limited fragment of space, on specific demands, which remain partial, regardless of their future ramifications. Hence, an individual can participate in many different social movements, at different times and places. Together, this is the power of every social movement: the ability to directly address the present within a future horizon. Access to an open future is established when the movement realizes the values and functions of an alternate social organization on practical, tangible issues, opening fields of social freedom in contemporary reality. But when a specific movement wins or loses its respective goal, it dissolves in social reality, since actual participation in a movement is itself partial and temporally finite, in the sense that it lasts for whatever time the issue exists.

Social movements, as streams within the social-historical magma, can become matrices of significations and institutions that continue to resist and restrict established authorities. However, experience shows us that even if the ideas of autonomy can be manifested and realized by social movements, these are not the only form of action. For example, two of the first and most influential social centers in Greece, *Nosotros* in Athens and *Micropolis* in Thessaloniki, were not created by social movements but by the initiative of people who actively participated in social movements. And this makes sense because the direct political purpose of a specific movement is confrontation and liberation of public space, not institution. It makes sense that the people who form the movement should proceed to self-organizing their social reality, expanding the free public space and time liberated by the movement, to retrieve it not for the movement, but for society, as free autonomous individuals. This fine distinction may seem obscure, but it is an important distinction between the limited temporality of a social movement on a partial issue and the indefinite temporality of an actual autonomous social institution. For example, if a student social movement managed to create the public space for radical democratic institutions of education, then the initial movement would have won and dispensed within broader directly democratic formations that would potentially include everyone. A social movement can answer the main political question, namely "who makes the political decisions?" only negatively by responding that state and/or economic authorities do not have the authority to monopolize political decisions, for example. But a social movement cannot respond positively, claiming that the movement should retain political decision-making exclusively for itself without falling toward totalitarianism. The only positive answer could be that only society has the authority to make political decisions. A response that must be realized through institutions that allow potentially every adult person to participate freely and equally in political power.

Of course, the whole of society cannot actually participate in a singular social movement. Only afterward can we ascribe the term "the movement," in the general sense, to the magmatic streams of limited social movements and public activities that eventually correlate with broader parts of society to perform a major social transformation. For instance, consider the question of whether the resultant of a variety of movements can also be called a movement. This question not only invokes Russell's paradox about the impossibility of the Set of Sets but is empty and descriptive. "The movement" of 1960s radical America is an *a posteriori* description, and not a sociological analysis. Despite their common grounds and shared meanings, the anti-war movement and the civil rights movement obviously had different apparent demands, different scope, different means, and different impacts, and these differences scaled down to even more distinct movements under their broader and respective civil rights and hippie "umbrellas." Every movement is not only partial but, in a way, also exclusive since only the presently active can claim participation in a movement. However, their ultimate values and goals should refer to those beyond the movement, even the inactive, sometimes even the dead, and definitely future generations. For example, the ultimate values and goals set by the protesters of the 1960s for civil rights and social justice still remain relevant in our times, but also could be identified in earlier revolutionary movements, thus justifying their legacy. How are the presently active defined as people of the movement? By their presence in the activities of the movement. If only the insurgents deserved a claim on political power after their victory, then this self-reference would undo the ultimate purposes and initial cause of the movement. Remember the communist movement, how its power became petrified in party and state bureaucracies and how it was transformed into iron tyranny.

An autonomous social movement of direct democracy should vindicate public spaces of freedom not for itself but for society. Like the creation of free public space and free public time regards not only those that have fought to create it but all the people. Similarly, we should create public institutions of political deliberation, decision-making, and action that are not separate from society, nor rule above it, but are within the active layer of social relations. Should these constitute an authority of "the movement"? Of course not. On the contrary, free institutions are required, open also to those that did not actively participate in the movement. (We will make an inquiry into the concept of authority later on.) Every directly democratic political formation must determine the limits of its jurisdiction, if these are not determined by external conditions. Neither a singular movement nor a singular assembly can become the central political institution. When the Occupy movement took over Syntagma Square in Athens, 2011, the movement began dispersing when it exceeded the limits of its jurisdiction, and the few people remaining who tried to transform the square into a centralized institution of self-governance failed. This failure demonstrated that free social institutions should resume responsibility for their respective communities, actual and/or imaginary and multiply into broader networks of free social interaction, so as to combine locality and globality in a complementary network of autonomous communes. Our societies are divided by internal borders, while nation states are being molded into international organizations. The project of autonomy involves the transgression of those borderlines, exposing the deep divisions between society and established authorities.

Every democratic public institution is complementary to others and requires constant revisal by the instituting society. For this to happen, political issues must be publicly debated in a manner that involves everyone personally so that all can deliberately partake in the solutions. What must be explicit is that the relation between dynamic social movements and institutions of direct democracy is not contradictory, nor antithetical, but complementary and interactive, a harmony produced by different temporal tonalities. Negri's conception of the constituent power of social movements fails to define which social phenomenon can be considered as a movement. Is it any collective motion of any part of society? And what about reactionary, extreme-right or racist movements? Is it any collective motion of any part of society against established authorities? And what about the syndicalist movement? Is it any collective motion with a popular demand? And what about the Islamic movements? We cannot avoid the issue of the ideological context of each movement, which is its most essential determination. What are the imaginary significations that inspire a movement and the set of values that are at the core of its actions? The issue of which political ideals and values shape the movement is also part of the main issue of which political ideals and values shape every primary institution of society. But this is a problem that can only be practically resolved in the process of *institution* itself. For that, a singular movement or social motion is not enough, it requires the active and deliberate participation of the people, or their majority.

We understand that, good intentions aside, a movement exercising authority singularly would be very dangerous. Isn't that what the Bolshevik movement was? Can the workers' movement alone set the law in the name of society as a whole? Can the workers' movement singularly manage production without the help of an ecological movement to test the products? Should there be a super-movement, an umbrella of partial movements? Or should every movement, by definition partial, resume absolute authority over its area of interest? There were the movements of the Parisian people behind the barricades in 1871, but the institutional form of social freedom was the commune that addressed the whole of humanity. There was a movement of the Russian people, but the autonomous institutions that emerged after the February revolution of 1917 were the Soviet councils who addressed workers' internationally. The first politician to grasp political power, "in the name" of a movement was Vladimir Lenin (1918), who wrote that it was necessary to learn how to harmonize the democracy of the working masses "with *iron* discipline while at work," and with "*unquestioning obedience* to the will of a single person, the Soviet leader."

Transgressing Bipolarity

It is no coincidence that the concept of the constituent power of the movements seems to be founded on a Manichean division of society, which echoes the

Friend/Enemy division that Carl Schmitt, the Nazi legislator, proposed as the anthropological principle of political society. Of course, any internalization and universalization of the Enemy category has authoritarian ramifications, depending on who decides who falls under that category. And who determines that? The sovereign. However, the project of social and individual autonomy cannot be a mere reversal of polarities. It must transgress and destroy that bipolarity, oriented toward a new social coherence, a new ontology, in terms of equality, solidarity, and freedom. A counterbalancing theoretical attitude at work in our contemporary historical vertigo is the rejection of humanism and the rejection of human rights. Here, the polarization of the metaphysics of authority is reversed, with primacy given to the proprietary aspects of social relations, rather than to the subject, physical or transcendent, of social activity.

Of course, we cannot deny that in our naked reality, where every signification and evaluation stems from the abyss of the social imaginary and manifests in the social-historical field, every value is ultimately relative and, seemingly, essentially an arbitrary human creation. But this basic assumption loses its meaning if we ignore the concrete social phenomena that rise from these arbitrary imaginary significations, which provide the worldview and self-image of a society.

We should be the last to forget the totalitarian ramifications of Western rationalism but neither should we underestimate the social and political achievements of the Enlightenment in the battle against political theology and God. Could we imagine, by invoking the post-modern relativity that all values rule, a project of individual and social autonomy without an essential frame of universal values, like freedom and equality? Are not the concepts of freedom and equality, if not truer, more desirable social imaginary significations than oppression and exploitation? Of course, if the question is posed in a theoretical vacuum, we can give any answer we like. If we talk about abstract social units instead of living, actual, physical, and passionate human beings, then we can support any claim, as the ancient sophist rhetoric has already proven. Ancient skepticism, Pyrrhonism, like post-modernism, ended in an empty negation of any moral evaluation that resulted in an indifferent affirmation of all practical reality. But, like Aristotle said, when criticizing Plato's *Republic*, let us look into factual reality. Every institution of society is ultimately arbitrary as a creation of the social imaginary and this is the ontological and anthropological precondition for the possibility of any discourse on human freedom. If there were any biological or metaphysical predetermination of social values and predestination of society, then there would be no actual political questions, only technical ones. Something similar was proposed by Marxist regimes in their effort to prove their superiority, supposedly secured by solid historical "laws." Every society is instituted arbitrarily, but in a specific time and natural environment with material and historical limitations. There is, however, an objective criterion to distinguish between heteronomous and autonomous societies. That is the explicit public acknowledgment of self-institution and the creation of a free public space and time for equal deliberation and political action upon this self-institution. Problems generated by the ultimately arbitrary mode of institution can be discussed and resolved in a reflective and public manner. The only firm ground in such a fluid social reality has to be a set of fundamental, moral, and political axioms that refer directly to personal freedom, political liberty, and social equality as necessary and self-explanatory significations of direct democracy.

The huge social-historical transformation known as the Enlightenment instituted universal human rights. It is a set of significations raised against the metaphysical concept of absolutism by Divine grace. As such, they demand the accountability of authority to the people and acquire a sphere of personal immunity against state violence. As such, human rights are efforts toward a delicate balance between individual privacy and the social pluralism of multiple interest groups. They also imply a perception of the distance between society and state authority mechanisms that rule from above and may turn against society; mechanisms that must be restrained because they monopolize legitimate violence. The interpretation of human rights can be positive or negative depending on the meanings we attach to the words "equal," "free," and "the pursuit of happiness." If we give the name of freedom to mean national security, the name of equality to mean homogenization, and the name of happiness to mean private material pleasure, then we have a document laying out the concession of public power to the state or any other paternal disassociated authority. If we give the name of freedom to mean, rather, self-governance; the name of equality to mean, instead, social solidarity; and the name of happiness to mean public creative activity, then the words regain their true force and we have a declaration of human liberty against tyranny.

As long as a global network of direct democracy seems like a distant future horizon, human rights are a significant weapon of society against totalitarianism (Paul 2014: 83). As such, and despite its historical distortions and transformations, universal human rights remains a document of human self-awareness. It stems from the acknowledgment that only humans create justice and set laws, and justice and laws are set by humans as humans, beings born and raised into a self-justified or self-justifiable social reality. The mode of being human is not just biological, but essentially social-historical. Human rights are considered universal, as being primary to all religions or cultural ideologies. However, if we want to be logically consistent, there is nothing outside humanity, physical or metaphysical, to safeguard these *self-evident* and *unalienable* rights. In reality, as we know, these rights have been proven easily alienable from oppressive authorities, and political or economic tyrannies, as has been historically demonstrated by slavery, among other examples. Our own philosophical stand, considering temporality in terms of ontological creativity and society in terms of imaginary self-institution, does not give space for axioms about human nature. The declarations of human rights, many as they are, are also socially historically defined and we should defend them as steps achieved toward human liberation in the larger struggle against heteronomy, and as political affirmation of autonomy, not as God-given attributes, which they are not. The issue of human rights is not a matter of typical logic or speculation. It is a matter of politics and social reality. The objective for social movements should be to expand human rights as elements of an autonomous social reinstitution. We should not deny the political aspect of the individual, but rather transform and open the political sphere directly to society, so that people can become equal not in oppression, but in freedom.

Instituting Subjects

If the subject of radical social-historical transformation is not rooted in the *traditional metaphysics of rebellion*, and becoming equals in freedom requires opening the political sphere directly to society as we have just argued here, then the new communal institutions of direct democracy that emerge locally set a paradigm of political activity and self-organization beyond borders and without leaders, and this political activity is already a praxis of autonomy and the free creative synthesis of a social instituting imaginary. Against the globalized network of authorities and corporations that materializes and gestates the new, depersonalized, and decentralized version of global capitalism, we can develop our own networks of social solidarity, political freedom, and direct democracy, and create a free public spatiality and temporality. By breaking down ideological dogmas and barriers that dominated and subjugated the revolutionary movements of the past, we can reinvent our vivid, playful contact with the isles of social struggle, with the demands of local and global communities that carry the meanings of autonomy on a practical level, with collectivities based on the creative power of free individualities. And this, of course, has radical implications for the social imaginary of modern democracy. Social movements today, for instance, reject the principle of political representation, reject the conceptual core of representative oligarchy. For instance, the Yellow Vests' call from the popular assembly of Commercy in 2019 is explicit on this point:

> If we appoint "representatives" and "spokespersons," it will eventually make us passive. Worse: we will quickly reproduce the system and act from top

down like the scoundrels who rule us. These so-called "representatives of the people" who are filling their pockets, who make laws that rot our lives and serve the interests of the ultra-rich! Let's not put our finger in the gear of representation and hijacking. This is not the time to hand over our voice to a handful of people, even if they seem honest. They must listen to all of us or to no one!

From Commercy, we therefore call for the creation throughout France of popular committees, which function in regular general assemblies. Places where speech is liberated, where one dares to express oneself, to train oneself, to help one another. If there must be delegates, it is at the level of each local yellow vests people's committee, closer to the voice of the people. With imperative, revocable, and rotating mandates. With transparency. With trust.[1]

This correlation of individual, collective, and social that transforms and is transformed by reality rescinds traditional norms of enclosed political organizations in favor of a plural, multi-conceptual, and multicultural interaction in terms of public self-governance. A democratic network of autonomous individuals within autonomous collectivities means much more than a simple counterpoint to the mainstream.

8

Power, Authority, and Freedom

As we argued in Chapter 7, the democratic network of autonomous individuals within autonomous collectivities is more than a simple counterpoint to the mainstream. This is because the issues of power, authority, and freedom that they aspire to resolve present a rupture with traditional ontology. As we argued in Chapter 1, this includes a rupture with traditional left approaches to power and authority, such as those found in the Marxist Imaginary, regardless of revisionist attempts. That is not only because of the primacy of economy that Marxism proposes over social life, or its supposed "natural laws" and pursuit of economic growth, but also because it is necessary to resolve the distinction between *political power* and *state authority* in directly democratic and self-reflective ways that traverse the passage from old to new ways of being. Both trends of contemporary radical thought, the attribution of political power to the will of a collective subject and the counterbalancing elimination of any subjectivity in favor of a transcendent structure of power, as we argued in the previous chapter, are founded in a common, implicit equation of political power and state authority. This view perceives all political power as an authority separate and above society. Unquestioned acceptance of this equivalence, which forms the core of the social imaginary of heteronomy, obscures the attitude of liberation movements on the problem of authority. This obscurity was located by activist and thinker Murray Bookchin in his book *The Communalist Project*

(2002) where he uses the anarchist experience of the Spanish Revolution (1936 to 1939), to denounce anarchist delusions on the problem of power, namely the illusion that political power can be completely abolished. It is an illusion which he finds "as absurd as the idea that gravity could be abolished." The basic—however, not the only—questions that Bookchin asks are: Can there be a society without political power? Are contemporary forms of political power the only alternatives? Is our only option before the problem of political power a radical denial or rejection? Is it, finally, possible to realize an abolition of all political power? The issue under question is the issue of political power, not as a particular instituted regime but as an immanent foundation of every society.

To address these important questions it is necessary to reflect here on the imaginary institution of society. To do this, we use this chapter to expand on the concepts of *legein* and *teukhein* applied in the creation of the social imaginary. This leads us to understand significant threats to the stability of heteronomous societies. As we saw in earlier chapters, democratic politics is not restrained to the domain of explicit powers. We argue that this implies a public dispute and transformation of instituted significations on the social-political level. To demonstrate this, we consider the formation of self-instituting societies in late medieval Europe and how the positive project of social-historical creation continues today.

Legein and *Teukhein*

As we saw briefly in Chapter 5, Castoriadis argues that every society is self-instituted as *legein* (language and imagery) and *teukhein* (technique and practical reason) and, with these, creates its own myths and establishes its own arithmetic. Social imaginary significations, impulsive creations of the social imaginary, manifest in two interwoven dimensions. To recap, the *ensemblistic-identitary* dimension is determined by the categories of identity and functionality that correspond to the functional aspects of *teukhein*, for example, an object as a tool, and the *identitary* elements of *legein*, for example, language as a code, or a hierarchy of codes. In this dimension, social imaginary significations are formulated in terms of identity, non-contradiction and the excluded middle (or third), by the rules of formal and mathematical logic. The imaginary/poietic dimension is the dimension of symbolization, evaluation, and signification beyond functionality. It is the imaginative and creative aspects of *teukhein*, for example, the sanctification of an object as holy or symbolic, and *legein*, for example, language as a play of meaning, or *phatis (langue)*, in the terminology of Castoriadis. In this dimension, social imaginary significations are correlated by relations of indetermination and cross-reference, which are neither coincidental nor necessary but associative and open.

Every social institution must inject a meaningless world with a coherent meaning to satisfy the human imaginary urge. Power exists in every society as an implicit substratum of social imaginary, namely as the implicit, instituting power expressed through language, custom, and behavior in a manifold way. It is manifested publicly and realized in the secondary institutions of explicit power, which Castoriadis defines as the instituted powers that are "capable of formulating sanctionable injunctions." Explicit powers formulate the *political sphere*, which is the political dimension of public spatiality, the space of political deliberation, decision, and the political dimension of public temporality which is the time of decision-making and political action.

In the case of heteronomous societies, the meaning of social existence refers outwardly to an entity or domain that regulates and sanctifies social reality from beyond. In this way, social institutions and imaginary significations are presented as petrified, eternal, and unchangeable. Explicit power and public space and time merge within the enclosure of significations as an enclosed sphere separate from society. This finds the antithesis between private and public as an unbridgeable gap. Sanctified explicit power becomes established state authority, in the service of social stability, hierarchical order, and the consolidation of ruling elites. Heteronomous social institutions strive to remain unaltered within their imaginary enclosure.

Threats to Heteronomy

What threatens the stability of a heteronomous society? Castoriadis mentions four threats. First, society, as a being-for-itself, institutes its imaginary on and within its natural environment, the prime physical ontological stratum. However, natural phenomena of this physical environment are in themselves chaotic, undeterminable, and coincidental. There are natural phenomena that can and have destroyed societies. Apart from violent phenomena like volcanoes or earthquakes, there are delicate ecological processes which, when disrupted, lead to the exhaustion of natural resources and to consequent social collapses, as occurred on Easter Island (Diamond 2012). Moreover, the natural world has no meaning in itself, society invests it with a nexus of significations that can never completely cover all natural phenomena, including those of human physiology. By its very presence, the natural world tests the limits of any imaginary signification that wants to explain it.

In our times, this interrelation between society and the prime physical stratum is under dramatic pressure due to the overexploitation of natural resources, aggressive neoliberal policies against the environment, and techno-urban expansion. We are members of the first human society in history with the ability to completely destroy its broader ecosystem. Every prior human society that exhausted their respective ecosystem collapsed and only speechless ruins remain of their civilizations, like the headstones of the Moai in Easter Island, Mayan pyramids in the jungles of Mesoamerica, and cities of Anasazi in the southwestern United States. Contemporary global Westernized societies are beginning to understand that the dominant social significations of capitalist growth and profit maximization are incapable of explaining and justifying planetary destruction.

Secondly, social imaginary significations can never fully tame the psychic core of the individual, nor stop the constant flow of representations, emotions, and desires that is the human radical imagination. Despite the impressive power of education, every human being is themself a source of representations and significations, and a nexus of possibilities.

Thirdly, society is never completely isolated; there are always different societies around that represent different magmas of social significations, and their presence threatens the sanctity and authority of established institutions just by comparison or contradiction. Heteronomous societies downgrade "foreigners" to consolidate the status of their own institution. This is the root of racism. Ancient Sparta forbade its citizens to travel to other cities in order to avoid indulgence in foreign "temptations." In our times, however, means of communication and interaction have covered the globe, transgressing state borders and transforming the very concept of locality, which is now projected globally. Autocratic and dictatorial regimes try to block access to these global networks and control information and communication because they are threatened by the very presence of an outside world. Nevertheless, our contemporary, ostensible openness of inter-social relations is only skin-deep and unilateral since communication and interaction are restricted to functionality, namely with regard to technique and financial transactions. Therefore, globalized capitalism rules over a variety of essentially different social institutions around the world, enforcing a homogenization of political and economic functions that leaves other social divisions, prejudices, and traditional hierarchies vivid in the lower layers of societies under exploitation.

An official and local temporality are both formulated that are contradictory in many aspects. The state official tries to follow global capital circulation and temporality and regulate social functions accordingly. The local dominates the calendar and historicity of social relations, following ancestral timelines of eternity and repetition. As time moves on, global temporality corrupts traditional temporal rhythms, sometimes dispersing local communities into misery and dragging individuals into psychological devastation, as has happened with the native populations in the Western hemisphere and Australia. However, not even this communicative globality could be historically possible without the cognitive openness that occurred with the emergence of the project of autonomy. This openness that created a new perception of the Self and the Other, attached a new sense of positive curiosity to old social transactions and began the new adventure of the quest for knowledge and meaning. Today, another sense of social globality seems to emerge through the worldwide interconnection of social movements and autonomous communities against the globalization of state and capital.

Fourthly, society itself exists within time-in-itself and is always subjected to alteration, temporal change, and its own history. No society, no matter how rigidly enclosed in its own proper time, can ignore that there is a future. Every society formulates expectations, aspirations, and fears toward this future, forming a social imaginary representation of it and itself within it. Even more, under every social institution, no matter how heteronomous, there is always a subterranean instituting social imaginary at work that gradually transforms the significations of the social instituted imaginary.

In the face of these four threats, heteronomous societies constitute a closed system of imaginary significations that conceals the fact of their own self-institution from themselves, attributing their existence to a more stable, metaphysical eternity. Laws are invested with absolute authority, beyond any discussion, while the issue of truth is never raised, since truth is supposedly written and safeguarded in Holy Scriptures. Institutions of explicit power are raised above social control and a layer of ruling authorities rises and monopolizes governmental structures, diminishing the political sphere and subjugating public space and time.

Political Power and State Authority

Returning to those questions that Bookchin raised, it is useful here to distinguish between *political power* and *state authority*. Power derives from the Latin verb *posse*, which describes an ability or capability in the broader sense. Authority comes from the Latin word *auctoritas*, which describes dominion in a legal-institutional sense. A society without institutions is obviously unthinkable and the existence of a variety of institutions is an indication of social imaginary creativity. The variety of societies in any given historical period is unquestionable and even today, ethnologists discover tribes in remote areas that maintain a Neolithic way of life that is no less complex than our own in its beliefs and customs. As a manifestation of this creative instituting ability, implicit power is social power in the sense of the ability of a being to produce a change in its external environment and transform its internal condition.

As instituting power, this capability is manifested in every domain of the social-historical sphere in the form of *legitimate* social imaginary significations. Explicit, instituted authority crystallizes on the surface of social relations as the primary function of preservation and materialization of these significations. Heteronomous societies attribute this ability, this collective creative power, to metaphysical entities, generating the alienation of human social relations within authoritarian institutions, the latter that are considered as manifestations of a higher, atemporal, authority. The subsequent (logically, not chronologically) separation of power from society is expressed as an *antithesis of principle* between the private and public sphere, which absolutizes the distinction between the two domains that are always different but not necessarily antithetical. This antithesis between private and public manifests within social temporality as an antithesis between private time of "freedom" and public time of labor. This radical separation of private and public, implies another separation between individual and social since both are the conceptual foundations of the equation of political power and state authority. The state in this case is being represented as the "guardian" of the individual from society, while actually operating as the guard of private capital from individuals and communities.

Political time, which is the time explicitly set for political decisions and governmental action, seems to rise above social temporality according to the degree of independence of authoritarian mechanisms from social relations and is delimited, along with a diminishment of political space, within the walls of the ruling elites. These strict divisions of social temporality become focal points of the tension between instituting social imaginary and instituted social significations, between public time colonized by authorities and private time of the isolated individual. These temporal antitheses that divide both personal and social life reproduce the antithesis between private and public that originates in the equation of public with state, after the vaporization of political powers from the people.

The distinction between the public and private domain is a necessary element of any society. Even in tribal societies with no private property, there is still a personal private inner space of the individual consciousness, at the very least. In every society every individual is given a personal name that indicates a fragment of privacy, even if privacy does not exist as an independent social signification or sphere. This distinction is also impressed in social chronological systems, as a distinction between personal and public time, which intersect within calendar time. Imaginary significations attached with specific temporal moments or significant days of calendar time connect personal history with social historiography in a way that the life of each individual is inscribed on the structures of social temporal annotations and is assimilated within the actual and conceptual societal proper time.

Utopia without Political Power?

As we introduced in Chapter 6, the conceptual equation of power and state that corresponds to the antithesis between private and public has held down radical political philosophy for centuries. Early Marxists and anarchists adopted and reproduced this equivalence and formulated the utopia of a society without institutions of political power. Marxists considered the use of state authority necessary for the destruction of the state by inflation of the apparatus itself, a paradox that, as history has proven, leads to totalitarianism. Anarchists, on the other hand, tried to rescue the concept of freedom not by rejecting the primary equation, but by rejecting political power along with the state. A direct consequence was the identification of any politics as *state politics*, which resulted in the conceptual entrapment of a political denial of politics as such. Within that entrapment, a variety of anarcho-individualistic attitudes flourished along with ambivalence before the issue of social institution and communal organization. This was expressed by anarcho-syndicalists as a series of contradictory political choices during the Spanish revolution, like refusing to fully support the collectives and the directly democratic communes of self-organized people, while at the same time participating, with three appointed ministers, in the official social-democratic government. A political philosophy that accepts the equation of power and state and perceives the political power of society as a privilege of instituted authorities can only result in an absolute affirmation of authority or a rejection of power. The latter, besides generating a plethora of contradictions, is an essentially defensive attitude. Any movement that proposes nothing more than radical denial is condemned to blind resistance and circular self-reference. Freedom, if not realized through democratic, open social institutions of political power, if it fails to become the essential criterion of politics, is rendered to an existential and individualistic concept and is exiled from the political domain to the netherworlds of utopia.

Democratic Creation

The core of the political activity of autonomy, consistent with a radical political philosophy, should be the rejection of the equation of power and state, denial of state and hierarchical imaginary significations, the attribution of power back to society, with emphasis on individual subjectivity, the formulation of a really directly democratic power of the people, and the abolition of state authority. The attribution of public space and time, and the political powers it includes, back to society, transgresses the false antithesis between the political and social domain. Consequently, the project of autonomy presupposes an openness of meaning, which cannot be carried individually, but must be realized socially in order to create the social preconditions for the emergence of autonomous human subjectivities through education and praxis:

> Democratic creation breaks the closure of signification and thus restores to living society its *vis formandi* and its *libido formandi*. In reality, it does the same thing in private life, since it claims to give to each person the possibility of creating the meaning of her own life. (Castoriadis 1997: 343)

However, this openness cannot withstand the restrictions placed by heteronomous societies against time, it cannot be associated to any eternity of the beyond, and it has to recognize time as the inevitable change and alteration of all that exists, as being-toward-becoming rather than simply being as a permanent state. An autonomous institution assumes the social-historical and political risk to open itself voluntarily to the wilderness of a fluid and unknown future, while heteronomous societies move backward with eyes fixed on the past. Moreover, social autonomy corresponds to a different social proper time, a public temporality where laws and institutions are disputed and transformed. Instead of the eternal authoritarian legitimacy of heteronomy, the questions of legitimacy and responsibility remain constantly open to time and public opinion, since direct democracy explicitly acknowledges mortality and offers ways of coming to terms with it on both a social and a personal level. Instituted laws appeal to everyone but anyone can appeal against an unjust law since these are explicitly acknowledged as social creations, and therefore are relative, imperfect products of humans within time.

An autonomous society, by acknowledging the mortality of its institutions, acknowledges that all laws and social conditions will eventually change, intentionally through politics or unintentionally through external factors—temporal, natural, or social—and chooses explicitly to determine this change by public deliberation and political action. Without this acknowledgment of personal and societal mortality, without this rupture, the individual is entrapped in a circle of a meaningless imaginary eternity, under the domination of petrified, sanctified, authoritarian significations. If this acknowledgment of mortality remains personal, without social reference, it cannot suffice to inspire the liberation of public time but rather private fantasies of escape.

To summarize our argument so far, our contemporary reality, our present, and our past are formed by the historical struggle between the powers of social creativity and state authority. The contradictory co-existence of these currents within the social-historical magma generates social tensions and collisions that vitiate dominant imaginary significations, condensing political time to free moments of rebellious public temporality and miserable periods of brutal state oppression. While a world of dominant imaginary significations wears out, a new world defined by solidarity, globality, and freedom rises. Among them, a variety of revolutionary phenomena appear on the surface of a turbulent reality, changing it irreversibly. What we have not fully considered yet in this reality is how important features of our contemporary world, such as the internet, are shaping our ontologies. This is the subject that we turn to next.

9

The Ontological Revolution of the Internet

The market and the state are not alone in shaping present societies. The internet has fundamentally transformed our ways of being in the early twenty-first century. On the one hand, the unbound character of its time and space has come to define a whole new dimension of our social-historical reality, thus providing opportunities for freedom. On the other hand, as we have argued, it is also a site of ideological contestation that has had profound effects on liberal democracy. This digital dimension of life is simultaneously a new platform enabling the institution of a multiplicity of social and individual subjectivities while at the same time amplifying the state and capitalism, which aspire to leverage this dimension for the enhanced pursuit of unlimited growth and rational mastery. Because of the significant role that this digital dimension plays in our lives, it is useful to examine the problems and prospects that it presents for the project of autonomy.

An Anti-humanist Nightmare?

When Martin Heidegger predicted the end of philosophy during his infamous last interview[1] in 1966, the *Der Spiegel* journalist correctly asked, "Who or what will take its place?" Heidegger responded, "Cybernetics," thus directing his descendants' attention toward the cybernetics movement, which was introduced earlier by Norbert Wiener as the scientific study of control and communication systems of human beings and animals. Cybernetics combined the theory of information with the theories of control, that sprung up during the Second World War, to describe thought as calculation using the algorithmic paradigm of Turing machines. More recently, neurologists have made claims in the traditional epistemological field of philosophy, proceeding from this ontological basis, equating human cognition to cybernetic systems (Dominey et al. 2003). However, the emergence of the internet refutes any such claims since this technology's content and utility can only be described by means of a social epistemology based on the understanding of social significations as continuous creations of an anonymous collective. Regardless of whether cybernetics represent the completion of Cartesian humanism, as Heidegger declared, or its destruction, as cognitive scientist Jean-Pierre Dupuy claims (Dupuy 2000), most post-structuralists, deconstructionists, and network sociologists, like Bruno Latour for example, used cybernetic systems as examples of the dehumanization of social and ideological formations and as justifications for a profound anti-humanism. Underlying these theories and the recent claims of neurologists and neuroscientists in the fields of consciousness and thought is a simplistic ontological axiom that seeks to replace the active subjectivity of the individual with an impersonal, dynamic plexus of information, discourses, ideologies, and neuronal synapses. Maurice Merleau-Ponty (2007: 352), a close acquaintance of Castoriadis, warned of these dangers and their corresponding implications, such as the "post-truth" and "fake news" era which are defining features of the ideological war that characterizes our *decisive moment*:

> Thinking "operationally" becomes a sort of absolute artificialism, such as we see in the ideology of cybernetics, where human creations are derived from a natural information process, but which is itself conceived on the model of human machines. If this kind of thinking takes over humanity and

history, and if, pretending to be ignorant of what we know about humanity and history through contact and through location, it sets out to construct them on the basis of a few abstract indices as a decadent psychoanalysis and culturalism have done in the US, since man truly becomes the manipulandum he thinks he is, then we enter into a cultural regimen in which there is neither truth nor falsehood concerning humanity and history, then we enter into a sleep or nightmare from which nothing would be able to awaken us.

The cybernetic anti-humanist nightmare is a reduction of human theoretical activity. This activity, as Castoriadis (1984: 219) reminds us, is more than simply the discovery and exploration of new regions, its progress confers "new significations upon the already available 'categories' and, even more importantly, posits/invents new 'categories.'" Thought as a creative action, beyond algorithmic calculations, being itself a *vis formandi* of the world of social significations, presupposes human subjectivity and the conscious activity of the actual individual. However, this individual cannot be radically separated from his or her social-historical environment; that is, his or her ontological horizon within which any concept is formulated, evaluated, and justified. The anti-human aspect of the internet presents a serious problem for the project of autonomy. This chapter explores this problem by considering the relationship between digital subjectivity, the actual individual, and the social-historical environment. It examines the issues that arise when these relationships become unbound, and how the promise of digitally unbound space and time give rise to movements such as the transhumanist movement, the emergence of e-sports, blockchain technology, new means of communication, and the creation of a whole new domain of digital reality within the social-historical. Despite many problems, the internet also offers many positive possibilities, such as a new sense of globality and interconnectivity. Thus, the internet can be used both as means of liberation by social movements and as a weapon of control that can subvert those movements.

Beyond the Digital *Ensemblistic-identitary*

The emergence of the World Wide Web in the 1990s and the global expansion of the internet during the first decades of the twenty-first century indicate the fallacies in the cybernetic program to mechanize the mind. We stand witnesses to a semantic colonization of the cybernetic system, a social imaginary creation and expansion within the digital *ensemblistic-identitary* organization that cannot be described by mechanical or cybernetic terms. Paradoxically, cyberspace, as a new being, a form of alterity, seems to both exacerbate and capsize the polarization between the operational and the symbolic. The creation of the internet might be more than an epistemological revolution, to use the terminology of Thomas Kuhn (1962). It might be an ontological revolution. We selected the word "ontological" to describe the emergence of more than just a new social-historical being (such as the elementary information unit, which appears as a particle or wave charged with significance), the emergence of a completely new plane of reality, within the social-historical field, that has the ability to become independent of the basic physical plane on which it is, ultimately, founded.

Cyberspace creates, from the point of view of human subjectivity, *sub specie humanitatis*, a completely new objective surface, a *novus locus* for reflection and self-determination. The World Wide Web constitutes a form of objectivity, whose manifestation, appearance, and significance has nothing in common with its material substructure or physical foundation. Namely, what we see and transfer via the internet, the semantic information, is something completely different than its material bearer, the electronic wave or particle. It is so very different that we could not describe it as the surface of a material structure, like, for example, a building that is perched on the joints of its skeleton and refers to them directly or indirectly. Neither can we describe it as the semantic codification of a fixed system, since the code on which it is matriculated remains strictly operational while the significations that are transmitted construct and refer to autonomous semantic or imaginary inner universes.

What appears on the screen is a visualized meaning, clearly autonomous as regard to its content and its significance. It constitutes the element of a digital universe, which is formed as spectral hologram of multiple private worlds, a new level of social reality with distinct properties and attributes. The epistemological attributes of the digital world are the predominance of the visual, due to the complete absence of tangibility, where the objects exist exclusively as phenomena and immaterial representations, and the de-corporealization of the subject, in a quite platonic plane of social existence, where the social-historical actualities are virtually multiplied. As such, cyberspace indicates an implicit metaphysics of space since within its boundaries, as a superset, time becomes insignificant and is rendered to a simple logistical calculation, no more a rhythm of distortion or a rate of entropy. Only outside of the digital boundaries, on the physical plane of the actual technical structures—the servers, hardware, the time it takes to run processes—does time exist as time. Only on the outer surface of its ontological sphere, on its foundation of reality, is the digital universe exposed to temporal becoming.

An Avatar for Human Subjectivity

This is only one aspect of the internet, however. Another aspect is the social-historical dimension, as a human creation and the problematic relationships which it erects with its social environment from the point of view of individual subjectivity. The emergence of the digital world within the social magma results in the emergence of a new avatar for human subjectivity, a bodyless being, fabricated by the actual individual, which constitutes both an ideal shadow and a selected reflection of the latter. The digital identity of each user is already a multitude, a conscious re-composition of the individual, based principally on their own self-image, on the self that the individual herself or himself chooses to fabricate from the fragments of her or his personal existence. The user creates a digital shadow, an "ego" free from corporality and its restrictions. This avatar is suited to become a field for the imaginary, for free self-recreation, and, as such, it reflects and encompasses the elements that the individual recognizes or invents as the prominent elements of his social and private self-image, in constant reference to the Other without the endangerment that the corporal presence of the Other brings forward. The digital being is thus constructed as an infinite reflection of the individual within the digital objectivity, no longer as a subject, but as an imaginary representation. Here, any terms of Truth are constantly variable. Here, from this variability, is where movements such as the transhumanist and cyborg movements draw from, rebelling against an imperfect human existence, aspiring to liberate themselves from biology to control human evolution through rational mastery, to eradicate aging as a cause of death, uploading their minds into the digital ocean, merging with machines to reinvent themselves in an image of their "higher" ideals (O'Connell 2017: 3).

While the variability of Truth of an unbound domain, such as in the digital, may give rise to such movements aspiring to transgress the physical boundaries of the material world, the digital communities within cyberspace, however, are imaginary communities devoid of any actual territoriality—communities instituted on the basis of choice and free recognition. The borders of these communities are not external, like actual territorial borders or mortality, nor are they imposed by any social-historical "necessity." They are specifications of taste, which overcome any spatial division, beyond the divisions that the individual herself places upon herself. This does not result in chaos but, on the contrary, in an unconscious self-institution of the rules of every digital sub-space. The absence of external necessities in this space renders those rules arbitrary and, at the same time, highly venerable. Consequently, what constitutes a delinquency *within* the internet is any attempt to restrict the freedom of informative and semantic circulation and re-construction. The outlaw is not a hacker who tears down firewalls, but rather is any formal authority which tries to impose censorship. Any effort to tear down obstacles blocking the flow of information, censorship, is not a denial, but, on the contrary, an affirmation of the nature of the medium, the uninterrupted, free flow of information and re-creation of social imaginary forms. That is why efforts to control the flow may backfire, as in the case of the "Streisand effect,"[2] because censorship and concealment are methods that radically oppose the nature of the internet and its constantly re-creative topology.

Invasion into the Social-historical

The foregoing observations could be misunderstood as a description of the isolation of the actual individual from their social-historical environment or as a description of a novel solipsism. However, the digital world is neither in social-historical isolation nor in cognitive encapsulation. On the one hand, it is obvious that every digital reference reflects manners and trends that are also active in social reality. This is one side of the coin, the reflection of real social-historical life on the screen. The simultaneous worldwide spread of information in real time actually creates a universal social temporality with attributes like un-territorial circulation, global communal networking, and the ability to re-present contemporaneous events of potential synchronicity. It also creates a universal social historicity with attributes like the ability to preserve, accumulate, and perpetually represent cultural events of a potential diachronicity. Thus, the immanent historicity of society not only emerges but also expands as an aspect of the social imaginary through this phenomenological timelessness of the internet that manifests as the conjunction of a synchronic present with a diachronic past toward the future. Although the internet formulates a global composition of distinct social temporalities in a universal social time, within cyberspace the experience of subjective temporality crumbles before the infinity of every possible enclosed proper time of each web page, every digital game, and each enclosed cyber-world.

Digital space and time invade social-historical reality. This can be seen in the black economies of online gaming and the respective e-sports, where players compete for huge amounts of money as in real-life Olympics, in digital stadiums with multiples of fans. This trend is prominent in East Asia, where some players enjoy celebrity status. But these black economies are more important, with digital game artifacts being exchanged "underground" for real money. Of course, every game-world is but a codex written by the programmers of each company and one would expect that the companies would easily control the pseudo-economies of each game. Yet, in the most popular online game-worlds, like the *World of Warcraft*, black markets have emerged beyond administrative control. These black markets, just like in real-life economics, have created respective economic bubbles where the prices of digital artifacts soon skyrocketed, and millions of actual US dollars were exchanged, invested, won, or lost. Regardless of any administrative efforts, these black markets cannot be confined by anything less than the complete withdrawal of the game itself, since infinite digital space is available to erect their own "underground" hubs. This "invasion" of digital economics in the actual social-historical field has resulted in concentration camps in China, where prisoners are forced to play online games beyond exhaustion, in order to collect valuable artifacts for the prison bosses to sell in the digital black markets.[3] Meanwhile, private companies emerge in other parts of South Asia, which hire professional players to supply to the same growing demand.

The invasion of digital economics is especially visible in the world of cryptocurrency as well, where the global market capitalization of the top one hundred digital coins is steadily worth hundreds of billions of US dollars. Digital currency's dark sides, based on blockchain technology, cast shadows over its benefits in the social-historical field. Bitcoin mining alone may consume more energy than Argentina, with devastating ecological consequences.[4] As a store of value, blockchains place billions of dollars at risk during bear market "corrections" and hacks, the ups and downs of daily market volatility in capitalization are like tsunamis crashing on the shores of digital value. Some segments of the community promote extreme ideological commitment to hyper-capitalism—elevating market mechanisms and auctions above the guarantees of human rights. And yet, blockchain technology does not currently live up to its own value proposition of decentralization, as the top two cryptocurrencies, Ethereum and Bitcoin, experience the centralization of mining, with the top four miners in Bitcoin and the top three miners in Ethereum controlling more than 50 percent of the hash rate.[5] There are alternatives, such as FairCoop,[6] working to build a self-managed and autonomous socioeconomic ecosystem based on justice and equity. They operate on an ecologically friendly Proof-of-Cooperation algorithm combined with open public assemblies. But states around the world are also working to control these technologies, through the creation of new laws and financial regulations, in ways that aim to perpetuate the dominant heteronomy of capitalism.

Freedom *versus* Censorship

The digital impact on the social-historical landscape is not merely negative. As we have alluded to before, from the perspective of social movements and freedom there are many positive aspects. From the Zapatistas, to WikiLeaks' innovative publishing techniques, to the "Arab Spring," to the Yellow Vests, we experienced an "invasion" of the internet into history, in the manner that movements which appear firstly online are reproduced, introduced, and transferred in the actual social reality. Indeed, in an emphatic way, when freedom of communication and interaction collide with a regime of censorship and obscurantism, as happened in the Middle East, it was not by accident that social media, like Facebook, assumed a liberating aspect in the Arab world, in ways freedom struggles and those who had been organizing for decades could take advantage of. It was because their function suggested ways of free communication to a society of closed, critique-proof imaginary significations. The digital subjectivity, without the burden of corporality, found the significance of freedom in its individuality. The most surprising thing was that the actual individual came down onto the streets to protest and thus placed her or his actual corporeal body in direct danger in order to defend this significance, which illustrates an important point: politics requires actual, corporeal participation, not just digital communication. The new ontological attributes of constant communication and non-material objectivity have the potential to liberate the individual from the necessities of material identities. Thus, the constitutive material foundations of belonging were shattered, and new, completely imaginary instituting forms have emerged.

The global Occupy movement, as well as the recent Yellow Vests movement, first started through digital messaging and then quickly overcame digitality without much effort, thus creating another form of free interaction, bringing forth the project of direct democracy into the actual, face-to-face dimension of social reality. The individuals that occupied public space first met in the cyberspace of the internet without the need of a rigid ideological pact to ensure everyone's presence in an ideologically confined space. On the contrary, what occurred was a free and conscious reclamation and opening of actual public space. Public space enabled social place outside state authority. The faceless multitude or the masses are not the appropriate concepts for the foundation of a free community of individuals. Contrariwise, we saw an infinite networking of collective personalities. "Portals" of communication and "interfaces" of action were freely created, where each individual could participate where she or he chose, exactly because the concepts of desire and reflective choice replaced duty and metaphysical necessity.

Autonomous individuality, reflective thought, free public space and time, the collective individual, all were concepts that emerged from the depths of a society ruled by the imaginary of heteronomy, outside and against it, in a most practical manner. The fact that this spirit of freedom spread like fire throughout Western societies proves that direct democracy appears as an almost natural way of social institution when in the free collective individuality, the actual individual becomes the subject of political decision-making. It also suggests that the manner of free networking in the digital world reflects ways of networking in the real world, which have remained regionally isolated until now.

This virtual space of the internet expands with a plethora of websites, portals, and other forms that are constantly created, communicated, and recreated. Cyberspace, without a tangible outer limit, equals the sum of the cyber-localities that exist at any given moment, but expands chaotically, and can be presented as a potentially infinite superset that is also available as a locus for the transmission and transmutation of social significations on the scale of global, yet personal, human interaction and communication. A form of communication that is simultaneous, free, and essentially incorporeal, also allows minor or suppressed ideas to be presented worldwide, on a level platform so that local confrontations or resistance can address a global audience. Where there may be absence of any censorship authority inside the means itself, such as surveillance or marketing algorithms, the success or rejection of any transmitted information/significance depends on the broader socio-historical environment of the recipient. Where there is such authority—which is very nearly everywhere, in every Google search, Amazon product listing, and social media interaction—we must question the information we consume and the deep internet forces that govern the distribution of what we digitally input into it. These conflicting characteristics make the internet both dangerous for authorities, who are vulnerable to the internet, and a useful political tool and platform for authorities to exploit—such as the Cambridge Analytica scandal discussed in Chapter 1, but also Edward Snowden's NSA leaks—which is dangerous for everyone else.

Whereas the establishment clashes with society over public space in social reality, in digital reality there is also a clash between state and corporate organizations and the society of individual users. There is a clash between narratives that flourish in the absence of independent truth values. Donald Trump famously asserted that he would not have been elected without Twitter, whereas the far right has been using troll techniques and internet tools to spread messages of hate. During the Coronavirus pandemic, conspiracy theorists peddling falsities, such as China deliberately spreading the virus and anti-vaccination misinformation, were getting millions of views on

YouTube.[7] The extreme right-wing, aided by Trump's anti-China claims and suggestions that people could inject bleach to combat the virus, used these conspiracies as scapegoating tactics to recruit and build their movements. This is characteristic of the ideological conflicts defining our *decisive moment*, as this conflict extends between the digital and social-historical fields. The movement for digital freedom meets the social movements in the internet, thus transferring social conflicts to channels of digital communication and hubs. The struggle between state services and hacker communities intensifies and escalates proportionally to the social conflicts of actual reality. Efforts to control the internet have resulted in, among other things, the emergence of distributed consensus platforms such as blockchains and distributed filesharing systems, next generation "Web3" technologies that advance properties such as immutability and censorship resistance, decentralization, and disaggregation. New digital tools, platforms, languages, and ethics are created, but the question about whether or not these could be conventionalized—as in making public key cryptography easily accessible for common use—is posed by necessity due to the dangers that authoritarian control of the internet presents.

The Digital Magma of Consciousness

The imaginary multiplication of the digital person is nevertheless accompanied by a semantic leveling of the actual person to the specular dimension. Cyberspace is the surface of visible representations that addresses the sense of vision and the semantic field that is defined, first, by the visible dimension of reality and, secondly, by the sense of hearing as a sensationalistic addendum to the visible world. Not only is the reception of digital information primarily visual, but the navigation and use of the internet is also based and constructed around the sense of vision. The visual dimension is just a surface layer of the representative magma of consciousness to which all senses participate equally, but also a dimension to which the blind members of humanity have limited access. So, although cyberspace claims universality, this universality is not accessible to all and so is, for many practical purposes, fictitious. Therefore, beyond the *ensemblistic-identitary* dimension of the internet as a functional network for the direct transfer and spreading of information, its imaginary-semantic dimension as a cyber-world for representation and reconstruction of symbolic significations and meanings presents a horizon of limited amplitude but of a potentially infinite semantic depth. The fetishized images that reflected the iconic significations of modern society become encoded points of diversity in a digitally indifferent space, able to include any possible meaning of the global social imaginary.

To summarize the arguments that we have made in this chapter, the relationship between digital subjectivity and the actual individual and their social-historical environment is deeply problematic. It is a relationship of pure reference without external restrictions where the individual imagination can roam unbounded. Besides the obvious psychological perils for the individual, which have resulted in the founding of gaming rehab clinics and the danger of an acquired digital autism, the internet opens new areas of endangerment as regards public discourse and public deliberation, since the internet public space is an indirect public space and not subjected to the social variations, natural alterations, and political restrictions of actual public space and time. It lacks the accountability of actual public life and the temporal and objective directness of corporeal presence. However, the reciprocal relationship between the digital and the actual has unraveled established political rules of conduct, Donald Trump's presidency among the most striking examples. In contrast to the use of the internet by social movements, the dominant majority leans toward a manner of "public" privatization such that the de-corporealization of consciousness within the internet most often results in a de-corporealization of the sentiment that produces a fictional digital public discourse, which, however public, is projected from the actually private space of the home.

Respectively, the direct and constant flow of information corresponds equally to a semantic downgrading similar to the dialectics of quantity and quality raised to the superlative. The contraction of the temporal duration of the dissemination of information to near zero causes a proportional contraction of the information's impact on the corresponding significations. The potentially infinite repeatability of information weakens its temporal gravity on the social imaginary. The object, having been signified as the social representation of the object itself, now becomes a representation of the representation and so on, while the gap between actual and mental experience widens.

The problem grows with the accumulation of information in a digitally unbound space and time where such vast quantities of information emerge from the depths of this realm to overwhelm the temporal bounds and rhythms of social-historic society. This is particularly important as regards the social imaginary and social-historic creation, specifically as it pertains to education and politics to empower the public to participate in and shape society. For how can a public that lacks the time and space to deliberate on relevant information reflect to make decisions on the important matters that affect them? As Castoriadis (1997: 55) pointed out, the problem is not simply that access to information impacts the public's experience of direct democracy:

> The problem is not to equip everybody with a portable version of the Bibliotheque Nationale or the Library of Congress. On the contrary, the maximum of information depends first and foremost on a reduction of data to their essentials so that they can readily be handled by everyone. [. . .] Democracy is not the right to vote on secondary issues. It is not the right to appoint rulers who will then decide, without control from below, on all the essential questions. Nor does democracy lie in calling upon people to voice their opinions upon incomprehensible questions or upon questions that have no meaning for them. [. . .] "In full knowledge of the relevant facts": in these few words lies the whole problem of democracy.

Today, each of us has the equivalent of portable versions of all encyclopedias on their smartphones, but the reduction of data to their essentials is still necessary. Algorithms and filters may help this, but the answer is not the reduction of human activity to the digital *ensemblistic-identitary*. The answer is free public space and time for deliberation and processing of information to move closer toward true knowledge, to avoid what Merleau-Ponty described previously as a deep sleep, a cultural regimen in which there is neither truth nor falsehood concerning humanity and history. This requires a form of digital autonomy, complementary to actual democratic institutions of social autonomy. The next and final section of this book considers the erosion of the global significations of economic growth and the future of autonomy and direct democracy as they relate to the kind of public space and time that is required to process and deliberate on this information.

PART FOUR

FUTURE—AUTONOMY, DIRECT DEMOCRACY, AND LIMITED ECONOMY

10

The Collapse of the Old and the Emergence of New Significations

We have argued that the heteronomous significations of capitalism promote the dominance of the economic sphere in the modern world, such that it has supplanted all other modes of being. This supports the assumption that capitalism is eternal, and the religious belief that markets know more than people. With the methodological objective of rational mastery comes the determination that societies can be managed with calculation and economic precision. This is done in order to reinstitute itself as the dominant institution of society. Part One of the book analyzed the ambiguities and uncertainties of these dynamics in the first two decades of this century, such that in Chapter 1 we observed the social imaginary significations of capitalism faltering, but in Chapter 3 we reviewed the process of how capitalism sought to reproduce itself in modern Greece, in ways that support the Western Imaginary and impose on Greece the society of the individual, where the individual is "seen as an atom linked to other human beings only through instrumental rationality" (Wagner 2007). In this chapter, we continue to analyze this human transformation. Then we look at forces that are currently contributing to the erosion of the global significations of economic growth, including the bureaucratic capitalist mode of production in China. We argue that these forces contribute to an uncertain future for people that capitalism categorizes as workers and consumers. This uncertainty is important because it weakens the signification of capitalism's dominance over society.

Homo Computans

When somebody has a lot of money, they feel like they own the world. Common people have known that for a long time. It is not certain if it is a capitalist or precapitalist trait. However, very early, in antiquity, Athenians instituted restrictions on private wealth. We may have to deal with a primal aggressiveness associated with accumulation of wealth that runs through human history. Regardless of where the trait comes from, capitalism certainly universalized the belief that the economic motive is fundamentally what puts human life into motion. "By hook or by crook," Castoriadis (2005: 96) said, "economic motivation tended to supplant all other motives. The human being became *homo oeconomicus*, that is to say, *homo computans*. Duration was reabsorbed into a measurable time imposed upon all." This sense, that everything belongs to economy, is not just the fake byproduct of some central planning. As we have argued, it is preceded by the emergence of contextual significations: capital growth, profit as the primary objective and unquestionable human purpose, and money as a distinctly traded product. These imaginary significations have been universalized and dominate the world. As a result, not only do capitalists feel that way, but also those who aspire to be capitalists and even those who are desperate, who have no capital or hope. Economic domination of social life has enabled the emergence of the individual as a new type of product.

Before Neoliberalism

Some years ago, a representative of the fishermen of the Gulf of Amvrakikos in West Greece was complaining on a local radio show about the flocks of cormorants that naturally consumed large quantities of fish every day. With quick calculations he counted the cost of the cormorants' dinners at around 50,000 Euros per month. A man, already drunk, who overheard, cried out, "Wow, 50,000 Euros! That's 25,000 ouzo shots! Double!" Many would agree that such quantifications are stupid. But we can find them in numerous examples of everyday life, in social and financial relations of any scale. And with these examples we can ascertain that there is a universalization of stupidity. A stupidity that today is the dominant way of human life. But let's take those anthropological types, the fishermen's representative and the drunk, and try to imagine a journey to their past lives. They were born in the currently drowned villages of the banks of the Achelous River of western Greece. Drowned in the artificial lakes created by the erection of hydroelectric dams, they spent the first years of their lives in the dispersed temporal duration, the dispersed social time of a mountainous community culture. But, rapidly, with similar velocity to that of the space shuttle traveling at that very same time to the moon, "capital growth" came. Now, one of them counts his own life and the life of the cormorants in Euros and the other in drinks.

Achelous, from the dams downward, is caged. The river is unable to enrich the land with its natural fertile earth, which it had deposited for more than half a century. During this time, extensive use of agricultural chemicals has destroyed whatever ecosystem had survived the construction of the dams. The broader sea region around the river delta was impoverished. Littoral land has become degraded. The first dam was raised in order to provide cheap electricity to PESINE, an aluminum extraction company, that, wherever it operated, left desert in its wake. The description of this vicious "capital growth" cycle could go on forever. But there is no real interest in calculating the financial cost of this extended ecological catastrophe. Examples of similar ecological catastrophes are in the thousands, but profit and growth drive them all. A growth that the capitalist system needs in order to exist. A growth that demands that everyone learn to quantify in whatever units, even if seemingly stupid, that express the pain that social-historical alienation produces.

A New Product: The Individual

Since the late 1970s, with the emergence of predatory neoliberal economics which the Mont Pelerin Society campaigned for and Margaret Thatcher and Ronald Reagan officially adopted, capital circulation was liberated in a seemingly inevitable globalization of the market. It was the first shock for the old industrialized countries of the West which resulted in the destruction of their productive sectors. During the 1990s, neoliberalism began the large-scale destruction of private property when a variety of small and medium enterprises of every sector in Europe and the United States closed or went out of business, while many large-scale companies transferred their production and manufacturing units to "emerging" Asia, Latin America, and Eastern Europe. The assertion made by economists that capital growth would cause money to flow to the rest of society is reality turned upside-down, since the flow of money is almost exclusively directed upwards. Hourly wages in US industries and manufactories are reduced. Thousands of workers across Europe are fired daily.

"There are only individuals, there is no society," Margaret Thatcher infamously claimed in 1980, having witnessed the withdrawal of syndicalism and the welfare state and as the anthropological type of the product-person—the individual-being-as-product—then emerged; a product that can only be perceived as isolated and individualized, in order to be countable for capitalist consumption. "To everyone separately, from everyone separately," former Greek prime minister Kostas Simitis would repeat, twenty years later, as a member of European social democrats who eagerly sought the realization of neoliberal financial policies. In the past, private media corporations like magazines, newspapers, and news networks sold their readers to their patrons. In modern energy markets, consumers are sold along with the stocks of energy corporations. These types of transactions have expanded globally with profound ramifications. When Nestle buys a water spring in Greece (not any water spring, but the most emblematic) what it actually obtains are the Greek consumers of mineral water. When, in 2014, the Greek government planned an education-employment offer based on vouchers, what it really sold were Greek students to private education systems. Phone and communication companies do nothing less than buy and sell those who communicate. They buy and sell the communication time of the people. In great malls, corporations buy and sell public space and those who use it. By this formula IKEA constructs big malls that contain a little public space, an open lounge, or a small square with indoor trees, fountains, and benches.[1] This synthetic public space in a private mall is centered on the temporal rhythm and goals of profit maximization and growth.

De-signification

In the global market, labor has been experiencing the process of de-signification since the early years of capitalism under the economic dogma of production cost reduction and profit increase. Despite everything else, and in order to perpetuate itself, this dogma also inspired mass production of millions of useless objects and the human needs and jobs for them. As such labor-rental is today expanding to take an increasingly central place in the global market. Newly industrialized countries in Asia, for example, sell their work force— not because of trends toward urbanization, but because of the destruction of local societies—in the global labor market. This vast labor market, which provides the lowest labor costs possible, creates and supports a social layer of Westernized consumers that represent 5 to 10 percent of their societies' overall population. This 5 to 10 percent amounts to several million people, if we count just China and India alone. An inflated global market formed around wealthy individuals in the Western minority world who rule over millions of people in the majority world struggling in inhuman conditions to ensure the conspicuous consumption of the few.

The increasing number of platform workers doing microwork in the gig economy symbolizes this tendency. These workers are located primarily in low-income and middle-income countries in Southeast Asia and sub-Saharan Africa and sell themselves as "on-demand" and "online freelance" workers for temporary data entry, transcription, and translation services for clients based in the rich countries. As more of the world connects to the internet, more of this cheap and precarious labor will drive down wages and disembowel security in the global labor market. As the CEO of one platform put it:

> There are 7.1 billion people on the planet, there are 2.4 billion people on the internet . . . They're what I call "PHDs," poor, hungry, driven. . . . They're willing to work on any sort of job, right, a lot harder than maybe you or I are, for less money . . . it's highly competitive and it changes dramatically as the internet gets turned on in various countries. . . . And those [unskilled] rates are going down because the more [workers there are], when you're talking about unskilled jobs there's almost no floor as to where those actual prices go.[2]

All this is widely understood, and it is hard to find anybody who will deny it. However, economists claim that, despite the dire consequences of capital growth, there is no other system capable of mobilizing the whole of humanity. They claim that the expansion of economy over all domains of life, transforming everything to merchandise, ensures the demand for these products. Therefore, capitalism is inevitable and the best possible system.

Capitalism as a Total Social Fact

Neoliberal economists claimed two decades ago that the initial shock caused by the globalization of markets would eventually balance out with the globalization of production. The exact opposite has happened. Small-scale economy, in the form of small agriculture, manufacturing, and construction are all being dislodged from the global market. Nothing similar can survive the environment of a super-sized global economy. No bank or financial organization will provide money to the millions of small-scale producers in order to ignite competitive growth. It has been decided that markets nowadays dance a different tune. Many professions are lost because they cannot survive in this reality. Positions of skilled labor in production and construction are nowadays few and scattered around the globe. Billions of unskilled hands in Asia, Africa, and Latin America are, aside from entry into the gig economy, available for any productive plan of any corporation that can afford them. No matter how low wages in the West are dropping, they can by no means compete with the inhumanly low wages of the newly industrializing countries. In countries of applied financial crisis, like Greece, a selective deflation is being imposed, leading to large profits for large-scale corporations and brutal impoverishment for small-scale businesses and middle-class professionals.

There is no reason why the existing regime of aggressive global capitalism, with its calamitous impact on societies and nature, should be "inevitable," especially, when we know the efforts that state and corporate officials make to achieve these conditions, by oppression and manipulation. The neoliberal dogma of *sancta realitas* is not only theoretically shortsighted and morally blind but also de facto condemned by the devastated social reality it has created. Moreover, borders and enclosures have never managed to contain human communication for long. Even before Western civilization forced itself upon the world, global interactions between societies had already corroded boundaries that nation states imposed. The modern drive toward a global market instilled a sense of urgency into those that supported this drive, and who were already plagued by a feeling of anxiety, that something would catch up with them. We don't know what could have happened, for example, if, after the 1989 Tiananmen Square massacre, the Chinese state didn't so thoroughly and hastily co-operate with the institutions advancing global capital (Klein 2007). We could say the same thing about East European countries, where a post–Cold War democratization in traditional Western terms was averted, since it would be a drawback for the champions of global "free-market" economics.

In general, we have to admit that without the transformation of the nation state, the deregulation of governments' financial policies, and the complete liberation of international capital flows, this globalization of capitalism could not have been achieved. The disorganization of the nation state in the financial field took place through a unique process of absorption and neutralization. While initially the state set the paradigm for capitalist corporate formations, subsequently they exceeded it through the dominance of the central signification of capitalism, economic primacy, and the profit motive. Public, state, or semi-state services were transformed into public or state companies, evaluated in terms of financial output and put on the stock market. Every country, every nation state functions like a big corporation. Consequently, public space, supposedly managed by the state in the name of society is now subjected to the "laws" of market antagonisms. Therefore, when corporations demand the annexation of public space for commercial exploitation, arguing that, this way, public space will become more useful, they really mean useful in terms of private profit. For us, public space is not only the common space itself but also the people gathering there, their culture, and interactions. These people are gradually transformed into customers, consuming the commons like industrial products. The domain of public power is gradually transferred from the nation state to financial organizations and private capital. With this in mind, we can see how international organizations composed of bank and investor lobbies are becoming a new formal center of decision-making over the economy, and since everything is absorbed by economy, a new formal center of absolute power. The state is restricted to the role of police enforcer.

To comprehend the transformation of humans into consumers/products, it is informative to consider the past attitudes from those countries which were slow to embrace capitalist growth. During the 1950s and 1960s, when cinema dominated Greek social life, some people stayed in the theatre to watch the movie for a second time with the same ticket, not because they enjoyed it, but because they felt that this way it was cheaper. When we heard these stories in the 1970s, we laughed. However, later, one way or another, we all learned to understand that this attitude toward life based on the quest for profit would eventually expand to encompass most activities in the public sphere. So, during the 1980s and 1990s, Greeks consumed the newly instituted public health system. They consumed so much publicly subsidized medicine that Greece acquired some of the most resistant viruses.[3]

Public service policies promoting consumerism and the citizen response to consume more penetrated every management sector of the public commons: energy, education, health, communications, water, food, and so forth. It is an imperial privilege for capital investors to have already ensured the consumers of their product, as is the case with public space. At first sight, this situation resembles the relationship between the dealer, the drug, and the addict described by William Burroughs in the prologue of *Naked Lunch*. The difference is, of course, that public space and the commons are not drugs. But this obvious difference is not enough to push aside the initial simile. It only highlights the collapse of significations that define global capitalism, the transformation of social values into market values. Global capitalism gains ground, abolishing any limit to growth that the state or nation present, while simultaneously imposing new limits and divisions of an economic nature on the conquered lands. China is buying lands in Africa while European capital seeks expansion in Eastern Europe, as is Israeli capital in Greece and in the East Mediterranean, as is US capital in Latin America and the Pacific, and so on.

The forced opening of the densely populated Asian and smaller East European, African, and Latin American countries to neoliberalism has caused tremendous social changes with tumultuous political consequences. The states of these newly developing countries were transformed into state corporations that enable, protect, and impose the most relentless form of capitalism. Globally oriented financial lobbies search out these spaces to advance capital growth, where state borders can be used as an instrument to control immigration and population flows. In this globalized social reality, capitalism

1. crushes national sentiment and addresses labor and consumer populations on a global scale, by exploiting the masses of poor for cheap production on one hand, while intensifying the spread of advertising and consumer exploitation globally on the other;
2. occupies ground without any delimitation or commitment, considering land as earth's gift to capital;
3. separates from the nation state political formation, which it initially co-existed with, reducing it to a throughput and policing role.

If we take into consideration that even in Europe capitalism was never the sole social structure but co-existed with political models of liberal oligarchy (along with their imaginary signification plexus that includes the welfare state and basic constitutional rights, which are irrelevant in a purely capitalist framework), we can detect, behind this economic neoliberalism, the absorption of social life under economy, and a tendency toward a homogenizing capitalization—viewing everything as an asset to be converted into capital—of every dimension of life, private and public. This is capitalism appearing and operating as a "total social fact" (Mauss 2002: 100-102).

China, Bureaucratic Capitalism Par Excellence

In the global economy of production, the paradigm is set by the dominant productive countries. The scepter in this case is held by China. Castoriadis describes capitalist bureaucracy as a hierarchical scale of internal apportionment between directors and executants, without any limits on exploitation; an advanced stage of monopoly capitalism. This mechanism is imposed on the working masses that theoretically form its "base," but in reality, are placed outside and opposite it. In China, we witness the unfolding of this totalitarian capitalism: an autocratic administration ruling over a large pool of slave labor stripped of any basic human right with the help of a brutal state as partner. We also see this model, this orientation, replicated in Europe, in Halkidiki for example, where the Eldorado Gold corporation with the help of Greek police forces, the national government, and state courts violently confront local communities who dare to resist. Moreover, throughout Europe, the new model of food production and standardization, on both medium and large scales, and other sectors such as construction are based on a type of slave labor which subsumes isolated workers, in many cases immigrants.

But China, as a symbol of this new productivity model, signifies much more. It managed to combine an already instituted rigid bureaucratic state mechanism and a vast subjugated population into a nation-factory of producing for global scale. This "achievement" of a totalitarian capitalism raised China to the first place among productive countries in the world. China produces whatever global capitalist centers want it to produce. Most importantly, it produces a new paradigm of space-time arrangement of human social activities that imitates Western patterns in a most denuded and cruel manner. China dominates world production without creating much that is socially meaningful. It has adopted Western forms of life to reproduce them erratically, void of substance. Chinese super-growth and super-production leads the models of capitalist growth worldwide. This Asian capitalism reaches new heights of fetishization and alienation by disconnecting the product, from Western fashion to electric guitars, from its social history and reputation. In the past, every product was accompanied by its "myth," even if it was nonsense. Our present globalized culture of production and consumption is not really reproduced, but re-printed, like a new version of an original movie that has been lost. Contemporary culture is re-printed in the global factory of China, which produces not only industrial products but also whatever is worth producing, without thinking about quality or functionality. A large variety of traditional craft products of the "developed" European Mediterranean countries are no longer manufactured by local societies and communities there but are massively and industrially produced in China and other "developing" slave labor countries.

The dominance of China and the newly "developing" productive countries—developing in quotes because this word is a euphemism for countries building the pad from which they can launch capitalist growth from—is accompanied by the dominance of production for the sake of production. The globalized productive economy requires a constant and standard consumer base. This situation applies not only to the common, but also to a variety of technical and industrial, products (with a ready-made consumer market, formulated in the past) that were till recently—from the theft of indigenous land in the Americas to the theft of user data in digital platforms—the flagships and "myths" of North American and European industries. The bulk of these products are now manufactured in China in such a vast quantity and such a poor quality that the myth that accompanied the label collapses. Even if a consumer obtains the "original" product, there is no satisfaction since the mass production of "knock-offs" have depreciated the brand value of their "status symbol."

The Global Signification of Growth Weakens

This semantic retreat of capitalism, which at first seems like a self-entrapment, since it spreads according to the spreading of mass production, penetrates every consumption sector, until it meets the anti-consumerism movements that emerged in the 1960s and 1970s. Does it really meet with them? Certainly, it does not meet with them in the sense of a vast political movement or a common political aspiration. Along with the retreat of consumerist myths, people create anti-consumerist myths, forming an anti-consumerist lifestyle, a lifestyle popular in the old industrial societies of the West. This in itself is not by definition bad. It may prove to be a favorable condition for the rebirth of political deliberation and social interaction without, however, being itself a sufficient condition. In any case, the point is that the dominant imaginary of capital growth is weakened due to these two factors: the exclusion of the vast majority of people from the sphere of consumption and the dethroning of "label-myths" that forces consumerism to retreat.

The fact that neoliberal policies have produced nothing positive may be due to the weakening of the social imaginary signification of growth and not, as Jeffrey Sachs has claimed, due to the reluctance of neoliberal masterminds to put themselves to work, as the masterminds of the Marshall Plan did during European "reconstruction" in the 1950s. During the post-war period the social signification of capital growth reached its climax, both in the Western (as private capital growth) and in the Eastern (as state capital growth) spheres of influence. However, in the late twentieth and early twenty-first centuries, we experience the collapse of this signification as the absurdity of its content becomes obvious. We disagree with Naomi Klein's assumption that the loss of Western capital's adversary, the Soviet Union, politically liberated rampant capitalism because we know that on a political level this fact had little influence on the political directives set by European governments and the social movements that were developing in Europe. It is a frequent mistake made by thinkers in North America since they experienced the Cold War and anti-communist hysteria from within the core of the Western "camp." People there, even great thinkers such as Noam Chomsky and Howard Zinn, often perceived the Soviets as the adversary of the West, while political movements in Europe had already experienced firsthand the "betrayal" of the communist regime.

At that time, from the late 1980s to 1991, nobody could predict the time and the manner that the so-called "communist" states would implode. But today, looking back at history, we understand that their systems were paper towers, with foundations already eroded by the dominant capitalist significations of economic growth, financial motivation, and consumption. Other dominant significations of Western societies also found their equivalent in the social reality of communist states, except the idea of democracy and political freedom. Similarly, the excluded element, political democracy, is also considered needless by the designers, managers, and international corporations of globalized capitalism. On the contrary, democratic movements and institutions are considered a grave threat. "In order to have a democracy in society there must be a dictatorship in power,"[4] Anatoly Chubais, Boris Yeltsin's minister of privatization, who Jeffrey Sachs has called "a fighter of liberty," once declared (Klein 2007).

A Personal Mission to Advance the State

"Free people and free markets are parts of a common plan," Milton Friedman used to boast. However, a glance at China is enough to disprove this claim, since the attachment of democracy to free trade was put aside in favor of the brutal imposition of neoliberal politics during his visits there. One could claim that Friedman was the abettor of the Tiananmen massacre. But China also offers another example illustrating how the separation of state authority from society is nothing more than individuals who at any given time govern in favor of their own private interests and their elites. The Chinese Communist Party and the Chinese state in total had, in a way, deposited its future, already from 1980 onward, to the advice and guidance of Friedman and his pupils. Privatizations, price liberation upwards, slave labor conditions, starvation wages, and the creation of a new global regime of Chinese capital were not to be stopped before some thousands of bodies in Tiananmen Square. Similarly, the millions of victims of collapsed traditional societies are not enough to stop the subsequent marching forward of Chinese industrial growth, nor the transformation of Chinese peoples' lives into living hell. Advancing Chinese capital globally is now the private mission of all the lower and higher officers of the Chinese Communist Party and the Chinese state.

A Disfigured Future

The transition of the Chinese mega-nation state to a symbol of economic growth projects the elements of capitalist self-destruction to new heights.

Globalized Chinese capitalism may prove to be the Trojan horse for the collapse of the central significations of the system, but these situations do not invite peace or prosperity. Capital growth on this level invites the possibility of analogous environmental and social catastrophes of unknown ramifications. Along with the inflation of the banking and stock-market sectors, unchecked industrial growth and financial deregulation create an unprecedented historical economic turbulence that is not preconditioned by any particular planning. It is the mindset presented in Martin Scorsese's film *The Wolf of Wall Street*. Financial planning in China, Russia, or Brazil doesn't require any sophisticated mathematics or science. The plans are exclusively based on elite political decisions. These are arbitrary ratiocinations like the aforementioned ideas expressed by Chubais, the Yeltsin-era privatization tsar. Everyone knows that corporations, banks, and financial organizations use "investments" as an alibi, while their actual directive and aim is nothing less than guaranteed and direct private profit regardless of the long- or even mid-term consequences.

A very important phenomenon that follows the collapse of local societies, which Western authorities actually try to utilize with some planning, is the massive immigration of populations, on a scale never seen before. In the new markets that open up there is no place for people who not only experience absolute poverty but also asphyxiation in an environment of fear and brutal oppression supported by the alliance between governments and corporations, state, and capital. Selective assimilation of refugee populations is some sort of plan, but the Mediterranean is already full of victims of authoritarian regimes in North Africa, Middle East, and Central Asia. Who cannot see that European officials try to take advantage of this immigrant flux in order to secure a cheap and fresh work force for a more competitive production? Fiscal adjustment plans and austerity memoranda imposed on southern European countries are accompanied by the adaptation of a new labor market where the product under negotiation is not actual labor but the workers themselves. Assessment programs imposed by governments on civil servants and teachers are actually programs of ideological classification in the sense that what is primarily evaluated is the employee's faith and compliance to the program itself and the policy it supports. What is actually evaluated is not work performance, but the workers themselves and their relation to the political administrator.

The objective is to introduce a global "labor market" attached to a global economy with a globalized production. There is an attempt to degrade labor as much as it takes in order to deprive it from any significance. Future generations will face a situation where labor is devoid of meaning. In such a situation it will be difficult to imagine or defend workers' rights. This planning by financial authorities and organizations has essentially two aims which use mass immigrations as an instrument for political control and private profit. These migrations—forced by civil wars, imperialist expansion, climate change, and the rise of religious fundamentalism—offer weak alibis to states for dividing society into inter-social zones of legal exception. The state of legal exception is not actually absolute, since those zones are not external but internal societal zones. It is a condition of modular classification, imposed on society in the form of laws and edicts with the application of state violence. For example, the classification imposed on immigrants is double, both at the border, where entry is permitted on terms of nationality, and in the interior, where they become denizens without national identity. National identity is a classification label, stripped of political power that does not ensure any rights, since it is the state's prerogative to recognize, verify, or remove it. Thus, firstly, it is the state's prerogative to exploit immigration flows in a way that would not threaten social stability toward a regression capable of undermining the rise of a new political and economic landscape further oriented toward rational mastery and growth. Not that any regression, toward more isolated forms of nation states, for example Britain's vote to "Brexit" from the European Union, could derail or control capitalism, but it might unleash hidden or suppressed social forces. The second is to utilize these immigrations to increase European and Western productivity on a global scale, without the limitations of previous welfare and syndicalist policies, and to promote the depreciation of labor and the degradation of its place in production. Establishment of a vast, cheap, and dehumanized labor market, where the worker is rendered an expendable non-person, is meant to safeguard the expansion of global economy and the correlative globalized mass production.

To achieve these goals, EU officials are enforcing an austerity fiscal program on European societies, starting from the southern European countries. It is an effort to modify social human behavior in accordance with the directives of a globalized capitalist market. A program that is guided by force and a demand for the total compliance of those who execute it and those who suffer it. When the Greek prime minister George Papandreou announced the first Memorandum of Understanding to the Greek public on April 23, 2010, he spoke about the loss of national independence. This same phrase was repeated by the following prime ministers Antonis Samaras and Alexis Tsipras who signed the next Memoranda on 2012 and 2015, respectively. National independence may have been lost, but it is uncertain whether EU programs and regulations will ultimately manage to save the countries that gave birth to capitalism or transform them to something entirely different.

It is sad to see the demonstrations of worker syndicates amounting to nothing and the French people voting for Marine Le Pen of the far-right National Front party. It is sad seeing the German middle class consuming itself, and enjoying it, while drinking cheap beer and wine. Or to see Londoners trying to live an imperial myth that has long since collapsed. But the most inhuman cultural type of the human-product that causes sorrow along with disgust is to be found in cities where elites gather, along with lobbyists and financial officials—the Jeffrey Epstein's of the world. Human trafficking, prostitution, and especially child prostitution is flourishing around financial centers in places like Frankfurt, Hong Kong, and Moscow, where expensive and forced sex workers gather around the "wolves" of the global economy. Two decades after Castoriadis described *homo computans*, we see this anthropological type re-evaluating everything, including humans, in market values. This, of course, began long before we could acknowledge it. Labor wages could never be accurately estimated within the general policy of capitalist market evaluation.

> Labor power has no exchange value determined by "objective" factors, for wage levels are determined essentially by formal and informal working-class struggles. Labor power has no predefined use value, for productivity levels are the stake in an incessant struggle at the point of production and the worker is an active as much as a passive subject in this struggle. (Castoriadis 1997: 111)

Syndicalism appeared as the possibility of regulating this uncertainty under the focal point of workers' consumption power. The struggle between labor and capital resulted in broadening capitalism, mainly through the expansion of consumerism after the Second World War. This lasted till the 1970s. Now, near the end of this decade as we have described, we enter a new phase of capitalism, which addresses the individual rather than society. It is also an era of emancipatory movements as the individual aspires to become itself.

Dead End or New Beginning?

The introduction of these changes to the position of individuals within society occurred in a social-historical framework when finance influenced the temporality and spatiality of human activities to an almost absolute degree. Anti-conformism for example, which during the same time manifested socially as a "movement," would remain marginal, while privatization of existence would quickly be identified with commercialization of existence, somewhere far away from any version of personal autonomy that inspired emancipation movements. This way "emancipated" individuals would be utilized by economy as the new product either in the sphere of consumption or in the sphere of capital production. Any capital investment now needs individuals-workers that actually care and put their personal efforts in service of the plans of "their" corporation. An ideological faith in corporate strategies is required, something expressed explicitly in China with hymns and anthems collectively sung by workers at the beginning of every working day.

After years of downward spiral, this perception of syndicalism has lost any representative capability it once had. It is nearly impossible for any syndicalist bureaucracy, which is part of the broader political system shaken by the same impossibility, to represent societies so atomized and fragmented. The individual no longer feels the urge to take advantage of syndicalist achievements or actively participate in them, because every person can perceive themselves as unique through private consumption of public space. So, social public space transformed into private space for public consumption requires, in order to exist, this type of individual-as-consumer. Moreover, the range and capability of individual consumption has increased to a great degree due to technological evolution and the over-production of useless commercial products that have now occupied an important place among "necessary" goods. Syndicalism, where it wasn't already complicit, had little more to give, let alone that the new status of labor would be determined by the immigrant or the refugee, willing to pay their fortunes to work in the fields of Greece, Italy, or Spain and the sweatshops of Holland, Belgium, France, or Germany. With that granted, resistance to the reduction of workers' rights seemed insufficient before the magnitude of this new global reality. The inability to fight causes defeatism.

The seemingly triumphant individual became, in the late twentieth century, a dead end in itself. But actually, in human history there are no dead ends, in the sense that every dominant social model is always opposed to marginal or latent social powers. Capitalism has proven its ability to assimilate differential forms of social institution and various imaginary significations, as long as they don't threaten the hegemony of the dominant financial significations. But even this prominence of financial significations and profit motivation is not unopposed, since new significations emerge against it during our times. We could argue, for example, that the place of the individual within society, however upgraded, affects the whole spectrum of human activity, especially economy in the time of its total universalization. The dominance of individualism creates an environment suitable for a new financial dimension based on the individual replacing the product. This is the point of the saying, "If you're not paying for the product, you are the product" on which companies like Google and Facebook have built their business models and which characterizes so much of our digital age.

This individual becoming the product has crucial political ramifications in a time when the political system is put under question amid the general collapse of central social imaginary authorities of any kind. Loss of the political system's representative capability did not destroy it but downgraded it to the point where the basest and lowest tendencies of the elector masses rose to the surface, as we see in the case of extreme-right and neo-Nazi parties. This has been widely observed in many European countries, but significantly has occurred in the United States with the election of billionaire businessman Donald Trump to the presidency in November 2016. Today, there is no actual social-political party. People are no longer flowing toward political parties in any country and official politicians no longer express even the slightest aspiration for real change. Almost half of the voters no longer vote, and the excuses given are trivial, like "I fell asleep," "I had no time," "I went on vacation." These are expressed not only by those who could be classified as apolitical but also by those who are politically concerned. This transformation of the position of the individual shakes social bonds, reversing the polarity of their relationship to the collectivity. The political system, political organizations, parties, and syndicates are incapable of representing something that is beyond representation. Human individuality has escaped the normativity determined by the community, the syndicate, the party, or the organization. On the one hand, the individual transcends the collective organization in the realization of their aspirations, while on the other hand dominant social imaginary significations of political representation collapse.

Today, personal expression is mostly located in the private consumption of capitalized "public" space. However, new significations are being created and meet with this dominant individualized person outside of the sphere of globalized capitalist economy. The next and final chapter focuses on these developments and argues that new types of collective organization are appearing, which not only place limits on growth-oriented economics but also challenge the dominance of economy over the rest of social life. These developments are important for advancing the project of autonomy.

11

New Forms of Social Networking and Local Autonomy

In previous chapters we have argued that we live in a *decisive moment* characterized by multifold planetary crises that threaten nature and society and the rise of new ideological conflicts which include new social movements, but also the weaponization of technology, state violence, and the rise of reactionary movements. We weighed differences between ancient and modern forms of democracy and, by using the example of modern Greece, looked at how the West has abstracted away notions of direct democracy in order to impose liberal oligarchy driven by the pursuit of rational-mastery, unlimited growth, and expansion. This included the privatization of public space and the transformation of space and time into sources of individual consumption rather than locations of social and public deliberation. We reviewed key concepts in Castoriadis's philosophy including ontological creativity, social-historical time, and the foundations of heteronomy. This led to an in-depth exposition of the crises in social imaginary significations followed by social movements enacting social-historical creation and the important differences between instituting and constituent power for the revolutionary subject. We considered the differences between political power and state authority for social movements before turning to examine the ontological effects of the internet, as a new platform defining our lives and which is unbound by the social-historical field from which new forms of individual and collective digital identity rise. The forces contributing to the destabilization of the significations of economic growth, as de facto motivation for all human activity, are many. And we argued that despite the dehumanizing impact of the internet on individual and social behavior, these developments create the potential for advancing the project of autonomy. We then turned to account for the de-signification of global capitalism and the rise of new significations. In this final chapter, we explore how autonomous individuals and communities find meaning in global culture which includes, importantly, the rise of new types of collective organization imposing limits on growth-oriented economics. We highlight aspects of recent social-historical creations that amplify the new significations and meanings and are alternatives to those perpetuating the domination of unlimited growth and expansion, suggesting a forward movement for the project of autonomy. These creations include different forms of free social spaces—from occupied factories to free solidarity networks and collectives—which illustrate the importance and significance of the project of direct democracy today.

Homo Anti-economicus

Contemporary political collectivity is nothing more than a network of autonomous individuals and now is the time that we experience its birth. The sovereign individual wants to be able to choose the mode of their life, the mode of their work, and the mode of their creativity while at the same time seeking the reason for the way they live and the reason for which they work, in other words, the meaning of their labor, why and for whom they will produce, and most importantly, what they will produce, transforming their work into a proposition toward society. A multitude of independent small producers, individually or collectively, create around their activities small independent markets, temporary, or stable. The most progressive among them create networks of social transaction and solidarity, oriented to move out of the official framework of a capitalist economy. It is a movement toward a self-limited economy that opens a new public space based on the contemporary sovereign individual and the networked collectivity that they create with their equals. New significations are posed concerning the manner and the organization of social life. Even if these significations are miniscule relative to those of global capitalism, they are enough to showcase their critical and dynamic potential.

But to understand the importance of these new significations, we must look back. Forty years ago, the question that circulated among intellectuals was if an alternative model of financial growth—different than the one adopted by the West, with its known catastrophic consequences—existed. Was there, for example, a socialist model of growth? Today, the question is modified: Is there an efficient model of green growth? Recent debates around a Green New Deal, discussed in Chapter 1, are the most obvious example. Of course, contemporary financial growth seeks an epithet as a euphemism, to justify itself. But back then it was searching for ways to achieve globalization, while, growth itself was already a common dogma of states worldwide. Castoriadis rejects financial growth. He conceives it as a signification integrated into the hegemonic reasoning of the dominant system, a supposedly self-evident hegemony. Even so, Castoriadis does not speak of an "other" economy, but of the limitation of economy. He suggests a political proposition that is nothing less than a total political transformation:

> Today, all the movements we are talking about aim in one way or another, to one degree or another, at surmounting and abolishing this division between directors and executants—between direction and execution. To the extent that they are not simply movements of explosion and expression but also movements of creation, of social institution, they express and embody people's aspirations to autonomy. They thereby herald and prepare the sole possible radical transformation of society: the advent of an autonomous

society, a society that, for the first time, assumes responsibility for its self-governance and that itself lays down its laws. The unifying logic of these movements, and their connection with the project of society's radical transformation, are to be found in this, that they already embody, be it in a partial, fragmentary, and fledgling way, the following central political significations: self-management, self-organization, self-government, self-institution. (Castoriadis 2010: 164)

Castoriadis described a direct democracy that would overcome present national forms of social life. He understood that a non-banal dimension of reality is offered as an alternative to quantification and calculation, where capitalism transforms everything quantifiable, wherever it rises and whenever it rises, into a quantity for consumption. But he also traced new significations that were being created and emerging. In 1981, he spoke of the revolutionary changes taking place in Western society through the implicit and explicit struggle for gender equality as an example of social transformation or quiet revolution:

What did, and what still do, all these movements express, whether we are talking about the workers' movement, the movement of women, of the young, or of ecologists? In my opinion, they can be grouped together under the same signification: movements toward and for autonomy. We're dealing here with attempts by different categories of people who aim at no longer being subjected to the institution of society as it is imposed upon them but, instead, at modifying it. Through the combined effect of the women's movement and the youth movement (which are closely connected, moreover, in a nonconscious and subterranean way), the institution of the family has already been modified in its very reality. (Castoriadis 2010: 91)

Children of the late 1970s are middle-aged now, in the first decades of the twenty-first century. If Castoriadis was right back then, we should be experiencing the results of the dissolution of old significations and the beginning of new social imaginary creations. As we have argued, our present supports those observations. Growth, and quantification, the dominant social significations of capitalism for over a century, now recede for reasons unforeseen by economists. Despite their retreat on the semantic, symbolic, psychical, and practical level, financial and capital growth have now been globalized, something predicted by most during the 1970s; less predicted has been its disastrous and irreversible consequences.

In such an environment autonomous individuals define their activities as structural resistances that, as such, bring along new significations of radical and universal change. These are almost ignored by mainstream hegemonic discourse since they occur in a different temporality of semi-illegality. Similarly, a segment of the left still under the spell of growth's tautological justification and the objectives of modernity are unable to see the problem of social-historical alienation and the wider and deeper project of autonomy as a struggle against heteronomy spanning a period from the ancient world through to today's global struggle. In today's struggle, sperms of a new public space in the context of social freedom appear worldwide. A new anthropological type is being outlined, let's say a *homo anti-economicus*. This human type emerges within a new public temporality that, compared to the vertiginous acceleration of the capitalist juggernaut, seems to move in slow motion. However, every particle of reality they conquer becomes, in a way, part of their movement, since they reinstitute it according to their own public temporality. By determining their own private and public time, autonomous individuals gradually undermine social imaginary foundations that has for more than two centuries seemed indestructible.

New Significations

The significations behind nation state structures also retreat and, in their place, a global human being rises, who is not restricted to a single definition. This person is the global financial human, whose activities transgress national borders, not because of international supply chains or product transportation but because of the global range and reference of producers and their merchandise. Every producer addresses a customer with global characteristics, within a rather homogenous global consumerism. But this person is also the global cultural human, since whatever new art is created now has a global range and reference. When we mention, for example, New Greek or New Turkish cinema, we actually refer to subcategories of a global cinema. The same applies even to contemporary Iranian cinema and to Japanese cinema, which, even in moments when it describes the most ancient and particular Japanese traditions, uses the Western or rather global cinematographic idiolect. The same is apparent in the domain of music, hence the labels "ethnic" or "world music." "Imagine" by John Lennon is so simple that it resembles rhythms from all over the world. The songs of Janis Joplin or the solo of Jimmy Hendrix did not address a limited internal market but people everywhere. But now the same, mutatis mutandis, can happen with a small band from Athens, Istanbul, or Moscow; a cultural globalization that occurred before the financial one and mostly due to the people rather than the planning of the music industry, which was eventually against this people-driven progression as it transgressed the "holy" regime of copyright. A recent example of how this people's cultural globalization spread can be found in the myth of "Sugar Man," that raised generations of rebellious youth in Johannesburg.

Every art and, moreover, every technique, is deeply affected by the globalization of production that came after the globalization of mainstream culture. For example, the invasion of the Japanese saw to cut timber in Europe displaced traditional European saws and with them a whole culture of saw-manufacturing and usage techniques. It seems reasonable that a tool of limited use replaces one with long duration in an age characterized by acceleration and ephemeral relationships. However, loss of a culture means loss of a particular reading of reality in whichever domain this occurs. Conclusively, we should note that the financial version of this global human type obstructs and hinders the cultural version. The devastating capitalist onslaught eliminated local cultures, the seed of an actual global civilization. Castoriadis, in 1997, described the dismal period of triumphant capitalism, without however betting on its future survival. He had already pointed out the self-destructive tendencies of the capitalist system. And the words he wrote, just months before his death, are particularly prescient:

> In such a situation, there is no point in discussing any "rationality" of capitalism whatsoever. The regime has shunted aside on its own the few means of control one hundred and fifty years of political, social, and ideological struggles had succeeded in imposing upon it. The lawless [anomique] domination of the predatory "barons" of industry and finance in the US at the end of the nineteenth century offers us but a pale precedent. Transnational firms, financial speculation, and even mafias in the strict sense of the term are now roving the planet, and they are guided solely by the short-term view of their profits. The repeated failure of every attempt to protect the environment against the effects of industrialization, both civilized and savage, is only the most spectacular sign of their myopia. The foreseeable and terrifying effects of "modernizing" the other four-fifths of the world play no role in guiding present-day policies.
>
> The ensuing outlook is not that of a general "economic crisis" of capitalism in the traditional sense. In the abstract, capitalism (global companies) might do better and better until the day the sky falls on our heads. That would suppose, among other things, that the ruination of the old industrialized countries, particularly in Europe, and the exit of billions of persons from their age-old world in order to enter into technicized, wage-earning, urban societies in the as yet unindustrialized countries might be able to pass off without major social and political hitches. That is one possible perspective. It is not certain that it is the most probable one.
>
> Analysis can go as far as to pose these kinds of questions. The rest depends upon the reactions and actions of the populations of the countries concerned. (Castoriadis 2005: 121–2)

As Castoriadis suggests, social insurrections, social explosions and riots—pulsating social movements—are not events that drop from the sky but manifestations of a continuous turbulence within social-historical time. His prediction that the system is incapable of handling the "exit of billions of persons from their age-old world" cannot be ignored.

Beyond State and Capital

During the 1960s and the 1970s anthropologists noted that, despite the brutalities of colonization and the violent shredding of "undeveloped, prehistoric" Africa, the traditional anthropological "African mentality" still survived. Communities in India still maintained ancient methods of manufacture and agriculture. Traditional cultures had not yet vanished. Castoriadis during that time suggested that those cultural forms may still contain the possibility of an original and positive contribution to the necessary transformation of society. But what is the situation now? Today many traditional cultures and communities across Africa, Asia, and Latin America have been sacrificed on the altar of global capitalism. But at the same time, against this desolate reality, another social reality emerges, initially manifested as the people's resistance before global capitalism. In India, as well as in Latin America, given the cultural differences between these regions, a reconnection with traditional communitarian cultural traits appears, either through an invasion of these significations into instituted social function or by the recreation of autonomous communities wherever possible, with the Zapatista movement being a prominent example among many. In Rojava, communitarian traditions blend with the modern project of democratic federalism. In Western countries, where very little tradition has survived, a new form of networked collectivity appears at the junction between accumulated knowledge and new significations of social liberation, which may be a predecessor of future communitarian forms of autonomous living.

So, we observe across the global horizon the almost simultaneous appearance of new, egalitarian, and democratic manners of social organization, where economy is subdued in the service of the other domains of private and public living. In every case, despite the "measurability" of the phenomenon that proves its global extent, we cannot presume that such radical change is near to reaching the majority of humanity. However, the fact that millions of people aspire to self-government and experiment daily with forms of free interaction, political autonomy, direct democracy, and social solidarity indicates that we are probably in the beginning of a historical period that will set new social determinations and transform relations between people, capital, and the state. Resistance to the capitalist juggernaut is not solely produced and reproduced by social movements in the traditional sense, but rather by the self-institutions of new social functions in communitarian form. These communities manage to operate almost self-efficiently through the network of open relations, without maintaining any form of distributive bureaucracy (like traditional collectives), by the self-regulation of individual relationships between producers and consumers, for example, on terms of equality, freedom, and solidarity and with a sense of common good based on these principles. This new global trend toward a limited economy, where financial functions are restricted in the service of other human social activities, direct democracy, and personal freedom is detected not only in the seeds of a new, social, and free public space and time or within the new networked collectivities. It also penetrates all the levels of the instituted social structures more or less, and its advance is combined with the retreat of consumerist myths in a way that causes great distress to the servants of free market economy, who complain about the "reduction of demand." This reduction of demand is another symptom of the recession of the social imaginary significations of financial growth and consumption.

Across "undeveloped" and "developing" capitalist countries the capitalist storm macerates the social fabric and destroys whatever is left from traditional communal cultures, while in some countries communitarian values and forms of living are recreated, utilizing both their communal traditions and anything useful provided by contemporary technological global civilization. A part of the general population of these countries tries to shield itself against financial expansion, misery, and poverty by choosing, not a wealthier, but probably a frugal alternative way of life, which nevertheless offers a more free and meaningful public space and time for social and personal activities. The social imaginary significations that inspire these communities have global as well as local references since they contain universal meanings and values, like respect for nature, quality of life, social solidarity, and democracy.

Democracy is not perceived by these communal populations as the need for a "democratic" capitalist state, but as a democratic and open form of living and interacting with the earth, air, and water.[1] This conception of democracy is not far from the direct democracy proposed by modern Western social movements. Meanwhile in the "developed" Euro-Western countries, the majority of the population, the "99 percent," suffer the consequences of austerity policies and financial recession. Increased inequality in productive relations occurs globally and the globalization of production casts aside the independent small producers who try to defend themselves; some create their own limited markets, as we have mentioned, around their specialized products that are also alternative manufacturing propositions to possible consumers and, eventually, to society. Gradually, new social relationships of trust are formed between small producers and their customers, who besides the product itself, exchange knowledge and opinions about the construction and quality of the product. The most common questions asked are not how much, but how, why, from whom and for whom.

The relationship between the ability of "offering" and the ability of "having" is, in these cases, determined by self-efficiency, equality, and solidarity, whereas in the capitalist system it is determined by the right of the powerful. When small, limited markets interconnect to form broader networks, they acquire the capacity to create hubs. They manifest the ability to create public space and time in the context of individual projects, ideas, collective decisions, and actions. In any case, no one could point to this trend as a way out of the mainstream financial crisis. Nobody enters these procedures with a profit motive, or with aspirations to make a fortune. What essentially drives people to such alternatives is a representation of themselves within a community of people. What is of main interest is their existence within the community not in terms of capitalist competitiveness but in terms of social trust and free co-existence. When we claim that these experiments are not a way out of the mainstream financial system, we just mean that they do not yet produce outcomes of scale necessary to reverse growth or displace those central social significations experiencing collapse, nor do they create the necessary preconditions for displacing the existing heavy capitalist machine.

These new communities or independent markets erect an obstruction to growth expansion while at the same time conquering space for the seeds of new communitarian forms of autonomy to take root. This new type of collectivity appears in many different social sectors and domains, like food production and distribution, communications, education, manufacturing, and so on. But hubs that collect all these different functions thus providing a relative autarky suitable for an independent communitarian form of living are rare. Perhaps if the creation of hubs was rushed, it might result in the formation of a new bureaucracy and to a subsequent collapse; perhaps the reinstitution of a public and free space and time extending to the whole of society, against state and capital mechanisms cannot be constructed with the building materials of the past, but with new materials not yet fully created. Future institutions inspired by the project of individual and collective autonomy are not in need of some historically privileged "subject" to exist, as we have argued, but in need of a free public space and time to rise, and the self-conscious desire to do so. It is not a procedure addressing where or how the "subject" would dissolve within a new bureaucratic mechanism, it is a procedure that bears nothing in common to the birth of syndicalist organizations or political parties or co-operative associations under state custody. The social imaginary significations and social-historical conditions that birthed these formations of the past are now absent. Today work, production, and the welfare state are dissolved and deregulated, and the state withdraws from the management of social functions, except those having to do with the representation of power and the legitimization of violence. Most importantly, the conception of collectivity on which these formations were based has altered. But what are the preconditions for the new networked collectives to exist and expand beyond the jurisdiction of state and capital?

Common Ground, Common Time

The space of the new collectivity is the public space created by the interaction, communication, and networking of free individuals. The hubs and joints of these networks formulate the broader public space, their *agora,* the space where ideas, opinions, inspirations, and suggestions regarding the commons freely interact, circulate, and become issues of public debate. The necessary precondition for these individuals and these networks to exist is the *common ground*, which can be actual or virtual, as a common reference. Regarding the ground upon which all human activities of the private and public domain take place, we are specifically interested, here, in the ground upon which small-scale production operates and within which free public space develops. In terms of the mainstream capitalist system, the common ground is perceived as the place of initial capital accumulation, as extended capital, something radically against the values of human solidarity, social equality, and human interaction that require a limited market. So, a major political demand rises, the demand to reclaim common ground, to reclaim public space, whether we refer to rural or urban space and land. This reclaiming of public space plays a major role in contemporary social movements and social clashes. There are vast agricultural lands in the countryside and thousands of buildings and spaces in the cities chained and sealed as corporate or state property without being ever used for anything meaningful. Moreover, during the aforementioned process of nation state degradation, the most important lands were given over to capital through privatization, lands on which a social public space could flourish.

In Athens, there are huge free spaces or urban forests, like in the cases of Elliniko or Nea Philadelphia. The bestowal of urban land to private capital is an indication of the political authorities' vulgar cynicism. Public ground is given to private capital with the obligation to manage it. It is as if someone occupied the delta of a river under the promise that they would ensure that the river flowed to the sea. In Greece, coastlines, forests, water springs, mountains, and rivers—anything that could be exploited to turn in a profit—are pillaged by private corporations under this catastrophic logic. Certainly, today there are no instituted social functions to reclaim this stolen ground in the name of public freedom. Yet such instituted social functions, not as initial capital accumulation and property, but as common ground are a necessary foundation for new demands. The major political demand we describe takes the form of a *public reclamation of common ground*. This political demand accompanies new autonomous formations from their birth onwards.

Common Ground *versus* the Regime of Taxation

As already mentioned, new networked collectivities of a limited economy, which create around them a public space-market, must detach themselves from the determinations set by the social temporality of the capitalist clock. But beyond this, there are established institutions that hinder the emergence of new communitarian social functions, namely the legal and judicial mechanisms of taxation. The social temporality imposed by the tax system, which is adjusted to the terms of capital growth and a corporation-state, can only be evaded through illegal means. Moreover, the economic aggregate of a limited economy, a non-expansive economy that does not infiltrate every domain of human life but is limited to a small collective, is a non-taxable aggregate for these reasons; the "surplus value" of such an economy is not financial, but social. It lies outside of the vicious circle of finance, outside of the banking system, outside of state loans and subsidies, with limited input and a network of mutually complementary self-sufficiency. When such efforts meet mainstream markets or the state, they nevertheless pay indirect taxes. Let us recall the neoliberal argument that, by the liberation of capital flows and the new type of stock-market growth a "trickle down" phenomenon would occur, which would send money downward. This argument was used for the scandalous reductions in the taxation of private wealth and the destruction of state welfare policies, with horrendous ramifications for society. Trickle down proved to actually mean trickle up, moving money faster to fewer and even richer pockets. If we reverse the argument, it seems more just to demand the exclusion of the whole spectrum of social networks of limited economy and public spaces from state taxation. After all, these efforts are created and self-managed without any intervention by the state and, in terms of advancing social-historical creation, are against it.

As we have noted, the main issues of individual or collective enterprises that propose an alternative organization of public affairs and a new way of life to society are the common ground upon which these networks form, and the taxation of their activities by state authorities. Some might argue that these are the same problems faced by a multitude of small independent entrepreneurs and startups who thrived for a brief period but are now cast into poverty and annihilation. They equate their sudden success to the brief period of capital growth or a successful round of venture ("angel") capital injection, and conclude that a new clever innovation to capture profits will restore their prosperity. But how is this possible at a time when ideas and techniques of limited economy infiltrate the social layer of small producers, a time when the contraction of demand seems to be a manifestation not only of the loss of consumption power but mainly also of the collapse of consumerist myths and eventually of the signification of financial growth itself?

Common sense also reverses this argument, allowing us to broaden the reference to the political demand for free public space and time. The propositions for the common ground, a free public space-market and a limited or restricted economy are formulated not in the manner of hegemonic reasoning but in a practical manner, in the form of social functions with the ability to spread without being hindered by typological limitations of familiarity. They are propositions articulated as a reinstitution of social functions and not as the program of any political party. It is an institution of new social functionalities that will possibly replace lost significations of the old world; not just replace them but give birth to a new world that today looks fragile in this ferocious transitional period.

As regards the common ground, we have mentioned that it lies at the center of social collisions worldwide either on the small scale of networked collectivities of individuals or on the large scale of independent communities, as those in India or Latin America. Taxation, on the other hand, is a very difficult battleground, since taxation systems have been technicalized to a degree that any effort to avoid them is considered an act of delinquency. As the Panama Paper's investigation revealed,[2] the global elite have concealed their own private wealth—at the expense of public well-being—amounting to billions of dollars in tax havens. This has everything to do with individual greed and nothing to do with the daily battles for personal and collective survival, particularly those examples aspiring to develop a common framework of social and political legitimacy that we are concerned with. These two issues are preconditions for the existence of a limited economy where an independent market and a free public space facilitating free and open human interaction and political deliberation could nurture the seeds of an actual direct democracy. These are also issues that rise before every effort to articulate a specific political proposition for societal liberation in the sociohistorical environment of a new globalized reality, "beginning with work and production."

Ancient Communitarian Significations Invade the Modern West

We are more or less aware of the constituting terms of recreated communities in India or Latin America that draw from their own communitarian traditions, some of which are ancient in origin. Their efforts to detach themselves from international agricultural corporations are crucial, since most of their productive activities are agricultural. Productive plans imposed by Monsanto and other companies have pushed thousands of small producers to suicide in India. Today, the trend toward communal independence and a return to traditional ways of production and communitarian forms of living is on the rise. Communal self-efficiency is influenced by external factors, like fluctuations in the global cereal stock market for example, in a ferociously industrialized neoliberal state like India. International pharmaceutical corporations drag countries to international courts when they dare to challenge their corporate monopoly on medicine by breaking patents, which make otherwise cheap medicine expensive and so thus not affordable by the population. The question for self-governed communities in India and Latin America is whether they will manage to survive the onslaught of global capitalism.

To answer this question, we should look again to the global references of these communities. Vandana Shiva (2005) has expressed them in the Western idiolect, as the "democracy of water," "democracy of land," and "democracy of sustenance." The resistance of these semi-traditional communities against global capitalism also has a global reference since it is simultaneously a defense of life itself and a proposition for an alternate way of living. These global references will become meaningful when introduced to the relevant self-governed communitarian networks emerging in the old industrialized countries of the West as nothing can be perceived on a global dimension nowadays without conjoining what "the West can contribute." The possibility of new communitarian forms of living emerging in this part of the world can dynamically nurture the seeds of a global transformation of society toward autonomy, precisely because it implies the displacement of the social imaginary significations dominating the world for the past two and a half centuries.

Beyond Social Economy

We will attempt to point out some characteristics that appear within Western societies that strengthen this possibility. But before that, an explanation is necessary to be clear what we mean. We do not refer to any form of "social economy." Social economy was born almost concurrently with industrial capitalism, without ever overcoming it. Social enterprises, in their efforts to adjust to an economy of profit growth, were either reduced to oblivion or assimilated by the free market system. By "assimilation" we mean their transformation to purely capital corporations regardless of the survival of any characteristics of self-management that may remain. Their version of organization was the exception that supported the norm of private and corporate capital enterprises. Social economy never managed to root out the profit motive from its financial function, considering it as the inevitable and unique reasonable motivation. This is also the case today, when, in the time of global financial crisis, forms of social economy are used as the pillow that protects the system from its abrupt fall. In reality, the redesigning and promotion of social economy is planned to create an unemployment buffer around municipalities and local governments to ensure a limited flow of capital into societies that have fallen victim to financial growth, and toward the restoration of public trust for the financialized economy.

This is illustrated by the fundamental difference between the contemporary financial and growth crisis and the crisis of the 1930s. Today, behind the crisis is the recession of the imaginary of capital growth, whereas back then exactly the opposite happened, despite the stock-market crisis of 1929. In 1929, whole towns in the United States rebelled, while today millions of poverty-stricken citizens did not even participate in the global Occupy movement that expressed society's anger and resolution. Back then, Western populations still aspired to progress. Now no one expects anything from the future promised by the establishment. For instance, nobody speaks of the "American Dream" anymore and even Donald Trump recognizes it as an aspiration that is no longer alive as he campaigns to "Make America Great Again." The distance between these two slogans is the distance to the promised land, which has lost all meaning. The victims of the contemporary crisis find themselves in a void of significations haunted by ghosts of aspiration where social economy seems more like a derelict nursing home of the future than an actual financial alternative.

The Movements for Limited Economy

Social movements for a limited economy integrated into a free public space and time, and inseparable from it, have made an appearance long before the financial crisis of 2008. What characterizes these movements is the creation of new meanings and significations, where we see the ancient communitarian significations at play, rather than their purely financial functions. Let us mention some examples from our own experience. The *Peliti network* in Greece[3] for the collection and preservation of seeds under extinction is a community of more than two thousand individuals, groups, and families spread across the country. The reasons behind the formation of this social network was not profit or finance, but literally an alternative way of life as regards production, sustenance, work, and ecology. Around this community a new public space and a limited market are created where economic functions are almost invisible. These new conceptions of agriculture, from the time that they are practiced, have influenced the choices of numerous people, regardless of their personal interest in getting involved in a different kind of agriculture. There is now a wide and free public space for the exchange of seeds, knowledge, goods, and experiences beyond state and capital mechanisms. Hundreds of suburban small-scale farmers around big cities interconnect with consumer networks. Small-scale producers are driven to them by the possibility of greater independence from the asphyxiating vicious cycle of loan and profit or from the pressure of middlemen and the need to constantly increase productive capacity; small-scale producers and farmers feel more free and calm in an environment of limited level transactions. Consumers are driven by the quest for a better quality of life, a personal relationship with the producers, a fresh social trust. Within this framework prices are publicly regulated. Here economy is limited, and the profit motive is replaced by a different set of values that refer to a non-financial motive and aim to reproduce the social relations of egalitarian public temporality.

The reasons behind these phenomena are not restricted to a reaction against capital and the growth economy. Besides, the idea of production and consumption outside financial growth developed in Japan during the 1960s because of the great scandals in the sector of food production (Latouche 1993). Later on, these ideas spread across the countries of the industrialized West. So, the reasons that gave birth to this trend are not economic or financial. The fact that it penetrated essential domains of human activity like sustenance farming and agriculture, creating new forms of public spatiality and temporality, is an indication of the spread of this phenomenon. We can detect similar efforts in every sector of manufacture, from daily products to construction. In reality, new conceptions, ideas, and meanings create new needs that cannot be satisfied by the globalized industry. Enterprises in remaking and repair multiply, aided by the poverty created by the crisis and the march of neoliberalism over societies.

Between 2010 and 2011, in the free social center *Nosotros*, located in Exarcheia, Athens, free carpentry lessons on repair and renovation were given with great success. The people who participated did not do so just to increase their market value and working skills. The main reason was to invest their work, and consequently their lives, with new meaning. If they simply desired a place in the official employment market they may as well have joined the schools for skilled labor offered by the state of Germany across the southern

European countries. But what they actually sought was ways to express the new significations of personal and collective freedom. These lessons led to the founding of Athens Wood School[4] in 2017, a collective carpentry school that also teaches a different approach to our relation to nature. The same applies to students of free self-education lectures, to people joining free courses given by collectives, to people who educate themselves by participating in the free activities of social movements. Serge Latouche (2009: 47) describes this new social trend in its broadened form within the societies of the European South, where

> [T]he local is not a closed microcosm, but a knot in a network of virtuous and interdependent transversal relations, with a view to experimental practices that can strengthen democracy (including participatory budgets) and make it possible to resist the dominance of neoliberalism.

These people fight to invent and create a life of decency with strategies based on the development of a network of social relations inspired by solidarity and mutuality, while pointing out that this "alternative" requires self-organization, wit, and a form of black-market economy. This is the situation of the networked collectivities and the new limited economy markets. Individuals participating in the new social movement toward a limited economy and social liberation seek and try to create a new normality, to create a new temporality and a liberated public time. They seek an escape from the capitalist clock. An escape from the idea that time is money. They try, in short, to create a new social normality beyond economy. This supersedes both those who criticize growth for purely ecological reasons and also Latouche's project of de-growth, since in reality, no society can find its justification outside itself, beyond self-reflection and deliberation with others. The new significations and meanings that comprise these new multilevel and multifaceted societal movements of our times herald the beginning of a radical transformation of society by positioning the elements that will re-determine itself. These elements are neither economic nor financial in manner.

We are able, schematically, to outline some of them:

1. The emergence of a new type of collectivity as a network of individuals, where the individual can present their project within a rudimentary free public space and time.
2. The creation of a broader free public space, not necessarily geographically determined.
3. Emancipated individuals can choose between transforming themselves into products or into autonomous persons. The second choice does not mean creating a political party or movement but putting in motion direct democratic functions that refer to daily human activities.
4. The networked collectivity, comprised of autonomous individuals, attempts to create its proper temporality by controlling the temporality of its activities.
5. A common feature of this movement is limited economy and the effort to restrict the financial function so that it is in service of human activities. It is a feature that can be detected horizontally and vertically across the social spectrum.
6. This limited economy within a free public space-market also influences small businesses that operate within the mainstream market economy.
7. Self-education and mutual training and research become integrated functions within this free public space and time.
8. The investment of work and production with new significations. People attempt to integrate themselves into the rest of social activities. People seek free space and free time.
9. The non-typological familiarity between individuals of the new networked collectivity accompanies freedom of participation, in order to inspire the responsibility of one's choices and the openness of the network itself.

All these features emerge within the hostile environment of ferocious predatory capitalism. By definition, they confront it. Of course, they are not a consistent and complete alternative societal model. We can describe real societal models only after their instauration and we don't know yet if a single new societal model will appear or many.

At present, we know that the seeds of a free public space and time have emerged, which are the preconditions of direct democracy. We will refer to two examples from our own experience in mid-crisis Greece. The factory of VIO.ME. in Thessaloniki (which produced industrial metal components) was occupied by workers after the management declared bankruptcy. More accurately, the factory itself did not go bankrupt, but other enterprises owned by the same management did, and the closure of the factory was a way for the management to retain its profit. However, the workers themselves occupied the factory and started an experiment of self-management that is an example of how a public space-market can be formed. VIO.ME. workers chose to create a network together with the solidarity movement that rose instead of re-entering the system of capital economy, initially due to the lack of capital. Inevitably, they had to adjust their production to the new ideas regarding the content of production and the quality of the product. They turned to producing house cleansers of general use in a small scale, making sure that their product is ecologically friendly and the procedure of its production clean and non-polluting. The initial rudimentary public space of occupants and consumers gradually broadened to the degree that many households in Greece are using the cleansers of VIO.ME. with great satisfaction, without necessarily being activists. In the case of VIO.ME., we see clearly the new significations of our time:

1. A common ground.

2. A product that is also a proposition toward society and the individual.

3. The creation of a public space-market for transaction, interaction, and communication.

4. An exit from the mainstream economy and a quest for free public time.

5. Seeds of direct democracy present in the egalitarian and inclusive manner of decision-making, self-management, and execution.

The only thing missing from the occupied VIO.ME. factory is self-education and research, which flourished in the occupied factories of Argentina following the country's 2001 economic crisis. Institutions of self-education are a necessary step toward autonomy.

The occupation of the Greek State Television and Radio Broadcasting corporation (ERT) by fired employees is another example. When, in the summer of 2012 the extreme-right Samaras-Venizelos government decided to close the national television network and replaced it with another of their liking, the majority of journalists, technicians, and employees who were fired proceeded to occupy radio and TV stations across the country and, along with many fellow citizens standing in solidarity, began broadcasting culturally richer and deeper content which lasted for nearly two years before the "left" government of Tsipras restored those who were fired, without changing anything from the previous establishment (to the point that they appointed a new management that had nothing to do with the workers' struggle of the previous years). However, the occupied ERT, self-managed by directly democratic general assemblies of workers and listeners alike, was a unique example of an occupied broadcast platform on the national level and beyond. It is prime proof of how wide, free, public, and social space and time can provide the most valid certification and evaluation. For instance, dozens of local radio stations across Greece produced the best programming Greeks had heard and created a real public radio with meaningful and thorough journalism and critique. A pluralist radio with socially valuable news, that owed nothing to the state or to private capital, but which witnessed the psychical transformation of the producers themselves when they were liberated from the chain of command. Every individual radio producer felt accountable to the public, to society, and not to conservative or progressive managerial authorities. These efforts could have become successful examples of self-institution and self-management in Greece if the people had not placed their trust in the SYRIZA government, which quickly disappointed them by restoring the previous, hierarchical management model. Unsurprisingly, both the quality and the ratings of the broadcasts of the reinstated state ERT are in free fall, losing the public's interest while conforming to the managers' will. We do not mean to suggest that such examples will deterministically and automatically spread until the instauration of direct democracy. However, we cannot but see the seeds of free public space multiplying along with the emergence of new significations of solidarity, freedom, and autonomy. At the same time, the Occupy movement proclaimed direct democracy, without any hegemonic analysis predicting it.

If we examine the function and operation of contemporary communities in their limited but open free public spatiality and temporality, we will see direct democracy outlined. The decisive difference from the past is that contemporary networked communities are created by emancipated individuals and are formulated by individual propositions collectively projected. A network of autonomous individuals that resist delegation is the political "subject" of direct democracy, but so is also every autonomous physical subject. The emergence of a new human mentality that can reclaim both private and public temporality will suffice to create those conditions for individuals to deliberate on common decision-making in all domains of social life toward societal self-governance. This public deliberation cannot happen in any field other than public space and public time; it is for this reason that these human creations are the preconditions of the instauration of direct democracy globally.

Meanwhile, concurrently with the creation and broadening of these new social imaginary significations, we have observed the gradual minimization, petrification, and perhaps even the eventual extinction of traditional general political movements, namely movements that have a concrete political program or anti-program (e.g., the socialist movement, the Marxist movement, the anarchist movement). These political activities have been replaced by specific political movements, like those that defend and reclaim land, those against climate change and industrial pollution, those that fight for clean and free energy, those protecting rivers and water flows; their activities have unfolded and widened over the last thirty to forty years. The question posed by analysts over this period is which political imaginary line could connect all of them, which new political movement will occur or how are these movements going to rise to power. However, the signification of these specific movements is manifested in the institution of new social functions that are not restricted to the defense of class or social rights but move forward to refer to an alternative organization of human living. The new political movement that will express the rise of the project of personal and collective autonomy cannot be anything else but the social activities inspired by that same project.

There are some points among those aforementioned that can allow us to formulate ideas regarding the political aims and amplification of human creations that stem from the emergence of new liberating significations and meanings. These are:

1. A limited economy, subjugated to other sectors of human social activities that does not produce political power, which is produced only through the decisions and actions of directly democratic assemblies.

2. An actually free market, an *agora*, in the sense of a free public space of transaction and communication—and not in the vulgar modern sense where capital flows between "buyers" and "sellers" who aspire to fleece one another according to the rules of bargaining power, brute force, or luck—can operate as an incubator for an expanded free public space and a political formation of individuals with the ability to self-manage everything that falls under their jurisdiction.

3. Education, knowledge, self-education, and free research are essential functions of free public space and integrated parts of the productive procedure and its propositions toward the individual and society.

The world of the internet offers numerous possibilities for knowledge and self-education, provided it is not co-opted into a platform dedicated to the amplification of power. Free schools of self-education, reproducing both the responsibility of knowledge and the knowledge of responsibility, creating through constant reinstitution forms of education capable of inspiring individuals who can cope with the complexity of contemporary reality, something that mainstream and official education fails to provide.

As regards production, research and constant self-education ensure the quality and open certification of produced goods, which, combined with the transparent exposition of the whole productive process, within free public space make the mainstream's closed and centralized certification look absurd.

4. During this open educational process, individual inspirations and projects can flourish, around which collective groups of manufacturers, researchers and producers can develop. The individual project, the inspiration of every person, gives the signal for the formation of a group based on cooperation and personal creativity with the purpose of enriching and enlarging collective actions. This creativity cannot be measured in terms of the labor market but in terms of social validity. We do not refer to tenant work or work based on time or labor hours, but creative work, a work-proposition to society, work that is offered for the cause of free and equal co-existence of all. This project may be individual in the initial conception but is collective in reference to the social history of ideas, invention, and wider completion, superseding the artificial division between the individual and their collectivity. This new open collective identity is incarnated in the self-governed individual, replacing the isolated private time and the state-controlled public time with a new synthesis of private and public temporality on the basis of freedom and autonomy within direct democracy.

5. Nothing can happen by networked communities which are enclosed. It is necessary to rid ourselves of the ideological fixations on commercialization and move forward to an egalitarian conception of commerce as an essential social function of transaction in terms of solidarity and overall self-sufficiency instead of profit growth and aggressive expansion.

6. By overcoming commercialization, by moving toward an egalitarian commerce, we render the monetary issue as a technical and utilitarian problem. Many times, social networks exhaust themselves in an attempt to standardize alternative currencies or have problems of exchangeability with official currencies or ways to incorporate them into state or private financial activities. However, this is not a direction toward autonomy. These are more probably remnants of attitudes of social trust toward the old finance model, the significations of which, we have argued, are now collapsing. Monetary decisions, and the technology used to execute them, are not in themselves enough to determine the content of human activity, individual or collective. Cryptocurrencies, such as Bitcoin and others with "cryptoeconomic incentives" that bake the ghost of *homo economicus* into the code, are similarly insufficient on their own. Indeed, it is exactly the role of money, as the only means of value attribution, which has made it a noose around society's neck. If we attribute social value to the product or the service, instead of the financial value, currency in itself is just a convention, a tool of exchange. Any social networked collectivity could ensure currency exchangeability to goods and services without accumulating surplus value, if not motivated by profit.

7. Skill, craftsmanship, invention, and any other manifestation of human creativity, including its products, cannot be monopolized as they are today by the grant of patents that translates into financial capital. The

inventor or the creator, of course, deserves public acknowledgment and recognition, even glory, at times. However, the product of their ingenuity, which builds upon social-historical innovation, should belong to everybody and newly found techniques and ideas should spread across the whole of society through the educational process and institutions. The abolition of patents at every level of production, creation, and consumption is a necessary precondition for a limited economy within a free public space to exist.

8. Science and research can develop, when unhindered by financial restrictions or demands, oriented to the new social needs set by all in a democratic and egalitarian manner. New ideas, significations, and meaning can emerge freely within the constant and deliberate reinstitution of society that is direct democracy.

Today we can revive neither the solidarity nor the federalism of the past. We must redefine both solidarity and federalism as the project of autonomy through the instauration and expansion of free public space and free public time, upon the common ground and beyond it, toward a new, liberated, global reality.

NOTES

Chapter 1

1. The "Great Acceleration" is the latest period in the proposed "Anthropocene" geological time scale which, by some estimates, stretches back 12,000 to 15,000 years to the Agricultural Revolution.
2. Steffen et al. (2015).
3. Intergovernmental Panel on Climate Change (2018).
4. Bulletin Staff (2019).
5. Lartey (2018).
6. BBC (2020).
7. Buchanan et al. (2020).
8. MacFarquhar (2020).
9. Kusmer (2020).
10. Davies, Pegg, and Lawrence (2020).
11. Porter (2020). Indeed, neoliberal privatization and cuts to the national healthcare system produced such bad results that it inspired millions of people, led by a 100-year-old veteran, to donate £32 million to support the nurses. See BBC (2020).
12. Although similar, but brief and fragmented, instances can be pointed to such as those in Samos, Argos, Corinth, and Syracuse who entered "isopolity" agreements with Athens. See Cartledge 2016, Chapter 9.
13. Jameson (2003).
14. Also cited in Straume 2011.
15. GlobalScan (2011).
16. Pew Research Center (2014).
17. Gallup (2018).
18. Gallup (2020).
19. YouGov (2016).

20 For example, water (83 percent), electricity (77 percent), gas (77 percent) and railways (76 percent), see "Jeremy Corbyn's Nationalisation Plans Are Music to Ears of Public."

21 Smith, Jacobs, and McCarthy (2017).

22 Ramsay (2019).

23 Cadwalladr, Graham-Harrison, and Townsend (2018).

24 Sharman (2018).

25 Cadwalladr (2018).

26 *The Alt-Right Playbook: How to Radicalize a Normie* (2019).

27 Tech Transparency Project (2020).

28 La Botz (2019).

29 See Note 19.

30 Ibid.

31 PA Media (2020).

32 EURACTIV with Reuters (2020).

33 For the United States, see Crear-Perry and McAfee (2020). For the UK, see Hundal (2020).

34 Vogel, Rutenberg, and Lerer (2020).

35 DSA, "About US."

36 Pollin (2018). For a direct rebuttal to Pollin, see Kallis (2019). See also, Ocasio-Cortez (2019).

37 Rehman (2019).

38 Hickel (2019).

39 Murray (2020).

40 Leake et al. (2020).

41 Referring to his work on capital, Marx writes "it is the ultimate aim of this work, to lay bare the economic law of motion of modern society—it can neither clear by bold leaps, nor remove by legal enactments, the obstacles offered by the successive phases of its normal development.... To prevent possible misunderstanding, ... here individuals are dealt with only in so far as they are the personifications of economic categories, embodiments of particular class relations and class-interests. My standpoint, from which the evolution of the economic formation of society is viewed as a process of natural history, can less than any other make the individual responsible for relations whose creature he socially remains, however much he may subjectively raise himself above them," in Marx (1867: 7).

Chapter 2

1. Spannos (2014).
2. "London Paper Asserts C.I.A. Engineered the Coup in Greece" (1973).
3. Blum (2014).
4. Currier (2015).
5. Spannos (2016).
6. Moyo (2019).
7. See Castoriadis (1997: 287–8) for an explanation of this translation.
8. Peter Wagner's theory of multiple trajectories of modernity suggests consideration of basic *problématiques* that all human societies need to address such as epistemological, political, and economic dimensions, respectively: (a) what knowledge a societal self-understanding is seen to rest upon; (b) how to determine and organize the rules for the life in common; and (c) how to satisfy the basic material needs for societal reproduction.

Chapter 3

1. Diamandouros was Greece's National Ombudsman from 1998 to 2003, before becoming the European Union's Ombudsman from 2003 to 2013.
2. Diamandouros (2013) provided an invaluable summary of both the "cultural dualism" thesis and the broader debate.
3. A terminology that we adopt for the rest of this book, however, with the added broader scope that we refer to the crisis of dominant social imaginary significations to reproduce themselves, particularly as they relate to the significations of capitalism.
4. OECD.stat (2000–2018).
5. Lowen (2015).
6. Economists such as Paul Krugman, James K. Galbraith, Thomas Piketty, and Joseph Stiglitz supported the "No" vote. Some, such as Krugman, highlighted examples such as Argentina, which recovered from its debt default. See also, the forceful argument for default in Roos, J. E. (2019), *Why Not Default: The Political Economy of Sovereign Debt*, Princeton University Press: New Jersey.

Chapter 4

1. The version of the Truman Doctrine announced by President Harry Truman on July 12, 1948 included special references to Greece and Turkey.
2. To make the distinction clear between the group and journal, where Socialisme ou Barbarie remains in a non-italic typeface we are referring to the group. Where *Socialisme ou Barbarie* is italicized we are referring to the journal.
3. Along with Claude Lefort, as part of Chaulieu-Montal tendency.
4. Pannekoek (1953).
5. Pallis wrote and translated under the pseudonyms Maurice Brinton and Martin Grainger.
6. Suzi Adams (2011: 2) argues that Castoriadis's break with Marxism signifies an ontological turn toward the connection between autonomy and creation.
7. An interesting biographical fact: Castoriadis was married to Piera Aulagnier (from 1968 to 1984), a student of Lacan's, who played a significant role in post-Lacanian psychoanalysis and co-founded the *Organisation psychanalytique de langue française*.

Chapter 5

1. Such is the answer provided by Buddhist philosophy.
2. The term had been used, in a different manner, as Castoriadis acknowledges, in algebra books, such as in Serre (1965) as well as in Bourbaki (1970).
3. Castoriadis discusses at length the notion of biological *autopoiesis*, introduced by Humberto Maturana and Francisco Varela, which considers the emergence and evolution of life as the self-creation of the living being. However, Castoriadis distinguishes his own notion of autonomy as self-determination attributed solely to human subjectivity from Varela's notion of biological autonomy, which he prefers to call "representational-cognitive closure."
4. Aristotle, *Physics*, 4.11.219b-220a.
5. Rancière (2019).

Chapter 6

1. To be clear, we use these references as exemplary and general terms, to cover the whole barbarism of the death camp networks in Europe and the nuclear bombardment of Japan.
2. With the obvious exceptions of the kingdoms of England and France that had already been proto-nations which, along with the Spanish and British colonies overseas, provided the matrix for the concept of the nation state.

Chapter 7

1 Yellow Vests (2018).

Chapter 9

1 Heidegger (1966).
2 The effect when attempts to censor information fail and the attempted censorship itself causes the information to be disseminated more widely.
3 Vincent (2011).
4 Rapier (2018).
5 Gencer et al. (2018).
6 The FairCoop.
7 Ohlheiser (2020).

Chapter 10

1 Ringstrom (2015).
2 Wood, Graham et al. (2019).
3 Miyakis, Pefanis et al. (2011).
4 Hoffman (1996).

Chapter 11

1 See the works of Vandana Shiva for multiple examples.
2 SZ/ICIJ (2016).
3 "The Peliti Network."
4 Athens Wood School.

REFERENCES

Adams, S. (2011), *Castoriadis's Ontology: Being and Creation*, New York: Fordham University Press.

The Alt-Right Playbook: How to Radicalize a Normie (2019) [video], Innuendo Studios, YouTube. Available online: https://www.youtube.com/watch?v=P55t6eryY3g (accessed May 5, 2020).

Arendt, H. (1963), *Eichmann in Jerusalem: A Report on the Banality of Evil*, New York: Viking Press.

Arnason, J. P. (2014), "Social Imaginary Significations," in Suzi Adams (ed.), *Cornelius Castoriadis: Key Concepts*, London: Bloomsbury.

Athens Wood School. Available online: http://athenswoodschool.blogspot.com (accessed May 29, 2019).

Bastani, A. (2019), *Fully Automated Luxury Communism*, London: Verso.

BBC (2020a), "Captain Tom Moore's NHS Appeal Tops £32m on 100th Birthday," April 30. Available online: https://www.bbc.co.uk/news/uk-england-beds-bucks-herts-52472132 (accessed April 30, 2020).

BBC (2020b), "George Floyd Death: Ex-officer Charged with Murder in Minneapolis," May 30. Available online: https://www.bbc.co.uk/news/world-us-canada-52854025 (accessed June 2, 2020).

Bhambra, G. K., Gebrial, D., and Nişancıoğlu, K., eds. (2018), *Decolonising the University*, London: Pluto Press.

Blum, W. (2014), 'Overthrowing Other People's Governments: The Master List." Available online: https://williamblum.org/essays/read/overthrowing-other-peoples-governments-the-master-list (accessed May 9, 2020).

Bookchin, M. (2002), "The Communalist Project," *Harbringer*, 3(1).

Bourbaki, N. (1971), *Algébre*, Paris: Hermann.

Bray, M. (2017), *Antifa: The Anti-Fascist Handbook*, Brooklyn: Melville House Publishing.

Brinton, M. (1968), "Paris: May 1968," London: Solidarity, 30. Available online: https://www.marxists.org/archive/brinton/1968/06/may-68.htm (accessed May 26, 2019).

Buchanan, L., Bui, Q., and Patel, J. K. (2020), "Black Lives Matter May Be the Largest Movement in U.S. History," July 3. Available online: https://www.nytimes.com/interactive/2020/07/03/us/george-floyd-protests-crowd-size.html (accessed July 29, 2020).

Bulletin Staff (2019), "Welcome to 'The New Abnormal'," *Bulletin of the Atomic Scientists*. Available online: https://thebulletin.org/doomsday-clock (accessed December 31, 2019).

Cadwalladr, C. (2018), "'I made Steve Bannon's psychological warfare tool': Meet the Data War Whistleblower," Guardian, March 18. Available online: https://www.theguardian.com/news/2018/mar/17/data-war-whistleblower-christopher-wylie-faceook-nix-bannon-trump (accessed May 25, 2019).

Cadwalladr, C., Graham-Harrison, E., and Townsend, M. (2018), "Brexit Insider Claims Vote Leave Team May Have Breached Spending Limits," *Guardian*, March 24. Available online: https://www.theguardian.com/politics/2018/mar/24/brexit-whistleblower-cambridge-analytica-beleave-vote-leave-shahmir-sanni (accessed May 25, 2019).

Cartledge, P. (2009), *Ancient Greece: A History in Eleven Cities*, New York: Oxford University Press.

Cartledge, P. (2016), *Democracy: A Life*, Oxford: Oxford University Press.

Castoriadis, C. (1957), "Workers' Councils and the Economics of a Self-Managed Society," originally in French as "*Sur le contenu du socialisme II*," translated Pallis, C. (1972), London: Solidarity. Available online: https://www.marxists.org/archive/castoriadis/1972/workers-councils.htm (accessed May 26, 2019).

Castoriadis, C. (1984), *Crossroads in the Labyrinth*, trans. M. H. Ryle and K. Soper, Cambridge: MIT Press.

Castoriadis, C. (1987), *The Imaginary Institution of Society*, trans. Kathleen Blamey, Cambridge: Polity Press.

Castoriadis, C. (1991), *Philosophy, Politics, Autonomy*, trans. D. A. Curtis, Oxford: Oxford University Press.

Castoriadis, C. (1993), "The Greek and the Modern Political Imaginary," *Salmagundi*, 100: 102–29.

Castoriadis, C. (1996 [1992]), "The Athenian Democracy: False and True Questions," in P. Lévêque and P. Vidal-Naquet, *Cleisthenes the Athenian: An Essay on the Representation of Space and Time in Greek Political Thought from the End of the Sixth Century to the Death of PLATO*, trans. David Ames Curtis, New York: Humanities Press International.

Castoriadis, C. (1997a), *The Castoriadis Reader*, ed. David Ames Curtis, London: Blackwell.

Castoriadis, C. (1997b), *World In Fragments: Writings on Politics, Society, Psychoanalysis, and the Imagination*, ed. and trans. David Ames Curtis. Stanford: Stanford University Press.

Castoriadis, C. (1997c), "Anthropology, Philosophy, Politics," *Thesis Eleven*, 49: 114.

Castoriadis, C. (2000), *Oi omilies stin Ellada (Speeches in Greece)*, Athens: Ypsilon.

Castoriadis, C. (2002), *On Plato's Statesman*, trans. David Ames Curtis. Stanford: Stanford University Press.

Castoriadis, C. (2003), *The Rising Tide of Insignificancy*, translated from the French and edited anonymously as a public service. http://www.notbored.org/RTI.pdf. Electronic publication date: December 4, 2003.

Castoriadis, C. (2005), *Figures of the Thinkable including Passion and Knowledge*, translated from the French and edited anonymously as a public service. http://www.notbored.org/FTPK.pdf. Electronic publication date: February 2005.

Castoriadis, C. (2007), *Figures of the Thinkable*, Stanford: Stanford University Press.

Castoriadis, C. (2008), *Fait e à faire. Les Carrefours du labyrinthe*, Paris: Points.

Castoriadis, C. (2010), *A Society Adrift: More Interviews and Discussions on The Rising Tide of Insignificancy, Including Revolutionary Perspectives Today*, translated from the French and edited anonymously as a public service. http://www.notbored.org/ASA.pdf. Electronic publication date: October 2010.

Castoriadis, C. (2014), "Obituary for A[gis] Stinas," in V. Karalis (ed.), *Cornelius Castoriadis and Radical Democracy*, Leiden: Brill.

Cohn, N. (1957), The Pursuit of the Millennium: *Revolutionary Millenarians and Mystical Anarchists of the Middle Ages*, Oxford: Oxford University Press.

Crear-Perry, J. and McAfee, M. (2020), "To Protect Black Americans from the Worst Impacts of COVID-19, Release Comprehensive Racial Data," *Scientific American*, April 24. Available online: https://blogs.scientificamerican.com/voices/to-protect-black-americans-from-the-worst-impacts-of-covid-19-release-comprehensive-racial-data (May 5, 2020).

Currier, C. (2015), "The Kill Chain," *The Intercept*, October 15. Available online: https://theintercept.com/drone-papers/the-kill-chain (accessed May 9, 2020).

Davies, Harry, Pegg, David, and Lawrence, Felicity (2020), "Revealed: Value of UK Pandemic Stockpile Fell by 40% in Six Years," *Guardian*, April 12. Available online: https://www.theguardian.com/world/2020/apr/12/revealed-value-of-uk-pandemic-stockpile-fell-by-40-in-six-years (accessed April 28, 2020).

Diamandouros, N. (1994), *Cultural Dualism and Political Change in Postauthoritarian Greece Madrid* by Nikiforos Diamandouros, Instituto Juan March de Estudios e Investigaciones, Centro de Estudios Avanzados en Ciencias Sociales.

Diamandouros, N. (2013), "Cultural Dualism Revisited," in A. Triandafyllidou, R. Gropas, and H. Kouki (eds.), *The Greek Crisis and European Modernity*, Basingstoke, UK: Palgrave Macmillan.

Diamond, J. (2005), *Collapse: How Societies Choose to Fail or Succeed*, New York: Viking Press.

Dominey, P. F., Hoen, M., Blanc, J. M., and Lelekov-Boissard, T. (2003), "Neurological Basis of Language and Sequential Cognition: Evidence from Simulation, Aphasia, and ERP Studies." *Brain and language*, 86(2): 207–25.

Dosse, F. (2014), *Castoriadis. Une vie*, excerpts translated by Chris Spannos for this text, Paris: La Découverte.

DSA, "About US." Available online: https://www.dsausa.org/about-us/what-is-democratic-socialism (accessed May 25, 2019).

Dupuy, J. (2000), *The Mechanization of the Mind: On the Origins of Cognitive Science*, trans. M. B. DeBevoise. Princeton, NJ: Princeton University Press.

EURACTIV with Reuters (2020), "Merkel Open to Big EU Recovery Fund, But Says More Clarity Needed First," *EURACTIV*, April 24. Available online: https://www.euractiv.com/section/economy-jobs/news/merkel-open-to-big-eu-recovery-fund-but-says-more-clarity-needed-first (accessed May 3, 2020).

The FairCoop. Available online: https://fair.coop/en (accessed December 28, 2019).

Fukuyama, F. (2002), *The End of History and the Last Man*, New York: Free Press.

Gallup (2018), "Democrats More Positive about Socialism Than Capitalism." Available online: https://news.gallup.com/poll/240725/democrats-positive-socialism-capitalism.aspx (accessed May 25, 2019).

Gallup (2020), "U.S. Support for More Government Inches Up, but Not for Socialism." Available online: https://news.gallup.com/poll/268295/support-government-inches-not-socialism.aspx (accessed April 28, 2020).

Gencer, A. E., Basu, S., Eyal, I., Renesse, R., and Sirer, E. G. (2018), "Decentralization in Bitcoin and Ethereum," *Hacking Distributed*, January 15. Available online: http://hackingdistributed.com/2018/01/15/decentralization-bitcoin-ethereum (accessed May 28, 2019).

GlobalScan (2011), "Sharp Drop in American Enthusiasm for Free Market, Poll Shows." Available online: https://globescan.com/sharp-drop-in-american-enthusiasm-for-free-market-poll-shows (accessed May 25, 2019).

Gödel, K. (1931), "Über formal unentscheidbare Sätze der Principia Mathematica und verwandter Systeme, I." "Monatshefte für Mathematik und Physik" 38: 173–198. Available online: https://doi.org/10.1007/BF01700692 (accessed July 29, 2020)

Hastings-King, S. (2014), *Looking for the Proletariat: Socialisme Ou Barbarie and the Problem of Worker Writing*, London: Brill.

Heidegger, M. (1966), "Only a God Can Save Us," *Der Spiegel*, May 1.

Hickel, J. (2019), "Is It Possible to Achieve a Good Life for All Within Planetary Boundaries?", *Third World Quarterly*, 40(1): 18–35. Available online: https://www.tandfonline.com/doi/abs/10.1080/01436597.2018.1535895?journalCode=ctwq20 (accessed May 3, 2020).

Hobsbawm, E. (1995), *Age of Extremes The Short Twentieth Century, 1914-1991*, London: Abucus Books.

Hoffman, D. (1996), "Yeltsin's 'Ruthless' Bureaucrat," *Washington Post*, November 22. Available online: https://www.washingtonpost.com/archive/politics/1996/11/22/yeltsins-ruthless-bureaucrat/d8236b02-fa5e-4777-b29a-97cd72d63913/?noredirect=on&utm_term=.f4a58574bcee (accessed May 28, 2019).

Hundal, S. (2020), "Why Are a Third of UK COVID-19 Patients Ethnic Minority," openDemocracy, April 11. Available online: https://www.opendemocracy.net/en/opendemocracyuk/why-are-third-uk-covid-19-patients-ethnic-minority (accessed May 5, 2020).

Intergovernmental Panel on Climate Change (2018), "Global Warming of 1.5°C." Available online: https://www.ipcc.ch/site/assets/uploads/sites/2/2018/07/SR15_SPM_version_stand_alone_LR.pdf (accessed May 25, 2019).

Jameson, F. (2003), "Future City," *New Left Review*, 21. Available online: https://newleftreview.org/issues/II21/articles/fredric-jameson-future-city (accessed December 31, 2019).

"Jeremy Corbyn's Nationalisation Plans Are Music to Ears of Public," *Guardian*, October 1, 2018. Available online: https://www.theguardian.com/business/2017/oct/01/jeremy-corbyn-nationalisation-plans-voters-tired-free-markets (accessed May 25, 2019).

Kallis, G. (2019), "A Green New Deal Must Not Be Tied to Economic Growth," *Truthout*, March 10. Available online: https://truthout.org/articles/a-green-new-deal-must-not-be-tied-to-economic-growth (accessed May 25, 2019).

Karagiannis, N., and Wagner, P. (2013), "The Liberty of the Moderns Compared to the Liberty of the Ancients," in J. P. Arnason, K. A. Raaflaub, and P. Wagner (eds.), *The Greek Polis and the Invention of Democracy*, Chichester, West Sussex, UK: Wiley-Blackwell: 371–83.

Klein, N. (2007), *The Shock Doctrine: The Rise of Disaster Capitalism*, New York: Metropolitan Books/Henry Holt.

Klimis, S. (2014), 'Tragedy,' in Suzi Adams (ed.), *Cornelius Castoriadis: Key Concepts*, London: Bloomsbury.

Klooger, J. (2014), "Ensemblistic Identitary Logic (Ensidic Logic)," in Suzi Adams (ed.), *Cornelius Castoriadis: Key Concepts*, London: Bloomsbury.

Kuhn, T. (1962), *The Structure of Scientific Revolution*, Chicago: University of Chicago Press.

Kusmer, A. (2020), "Mutual Aid Groups Respond to Double Threat of Coronavirus and Climate Change," *PRI*, April 13. Available online: https://www.pri.org/stories/2020-04-13/mutual-aid-groups-respond-double-threat-coronavirus-and-climate-change (accessed May 3, 2020).

La Botz, D. (2019), "DSA Two Years Later: Where Are We At? Where Are We Headed?," *Medium*, January 4. Available online: https://medium.com/@danlabotz/dsa-two-years-later-where-are-we-at-where-are-we-headed-3d3912bb8736 (accessed May 25).

Lartey, J. (2018), "Oppression in America: 'To root this out we need a movement against racist policies'," *Guardian*, June 6. Available online: https://www.theguardian.com/us-news/2018/jun/06/everyday-racism-in-america-how-to-fix-it (accessed May 5, 2020).

Latouche, S. (1993), *In the Wake of the Affluent Society: An Exploration of Post-Development*, London: Zed Books.

Latouche, S. (2009), *Farewell to Growth*, Cambridge: Polity Press.

Leake, J., Shipman, T., Wright, O., and Lay, K. (2020), "Coronavirus: 100,000 Dead If UK Eases Lockdown Too Fast, Scientists Warn," *The Times*, May 10. Available online: https://www.thetimes.co.uk/article/coronavirus-100-000-dead-if-uk-eases-lockdown-too-fast-scientists-warn-rqqbf956g (accessed May 11, 2020).

Lenin, V. I. (1918), "The Immediate Tasks of the Soviet Government," *Pravda*, 83. Available online: https://www.marxists.org/archive/lenin/works/1918/mar/x03.htm (accessed May 27, 2019).

Lévêque, P. and Vidal-Naquet, P. (1996), *Cleisthenes the Athenian: An Essay on the Representation of Space and Time in Greek Political Thought from the End of the Sixth Century to the Death of Plato*, trans. David Ames Curtis, New York: Humanities Press International.

'London Paper Asserts C.I. A. Engineered the Coup in Greece' (1973). *New York Times*. July 1. Available online: https://www.nytimes.com/1973/07/01/archives/london-paper-asserts-c-i-a-engineered-the-coup-in-greece-sent-to.html (accessed May 98, 2020).

Lowen, M. (2015), "Greek Debt Crisis: What Was the Point of the Referendum?," *BBC*, July 11. Available online: https://www.bbc.co.uk/news/world-europe-33492387 (accessed May 26, 2019).

MacFarquhar, N. (2020), "Many Claim Extremists Are Sparking Protest Violence. But Which Extremists?," *New York Times*, May 31, 2020. Available online: https://www.nytimes.com/2020/05/31/us/george-floyd-protests-white-supremacists-antifa.html (accessed June 2, 2020).

Mann, C. C. (2011), *1493: Uncovering the New World Columbus Created*, New York: Alfred A. Knoff.

Marker, C. (1989), "The Owl's Legacy (L'Héritage de la chouette)," Icarus Films.

Marx, K. (1867), "Preface to the First German Edition," in *Capital A Critique of Political Economy Volume I*, Moscow: Progress Publishers.

Mason, P. (2016), *Post Capitalism: A Guide to Our Future*, UK: Penguin.

Mauss, M. (2002), *The Gift*, London: Routledge

Merleau-Ponty, M. (2007), *The Merleau-Ponty Reader*, ed. T. Toadvine and L. Lawlor, Northwestern University Press.

Mirowski, P. (1999), *More Heat than Light: Economics as Social Physics, Physics as Nature's Economics*, New York: Cambridge University Press.

Mouzakitis, A. (2014), "Creation *ex nihilo*," in Suzi Adams (ed.), *Cornelius Castoriadis: Key Concepts*, London: Bloomsbury.

Moyo, D. (2019), "Make Voting Mandatory in the U.S.," *New York Times*, October 15. Available online: https://www.nytimes.com/2019/10/15/opinion/united-states-voting-mandatory.html (accessed May 9, 2020).

Pannekoek, A., (1953), "Letter 1" and other letters, *Viewpoint*. Available online: https://www.viewpointmag.com/2011/10/25/letter-1-pannekoek-to-castoriadis (accessed December 30, 2019).

Mumford, L. (1934), *Technics and Civilization*, New York: Harcourt Brace and World.

Murray, M. (2020), "In New Poll, 60 Percent Support Keeping Stay-at-home Restrictions to Fight Coronavirus," *NBC News*, April 19. Available online: https://www.nbcnews.com/politics/meet-the-press/poll-six-10-support-keeping-stay-home-restrictions-fight-coronavirus-n1187011 (accessed May 5, 2020).

Negri, A. (1999), *Insurgencies: Constituent Power and the Modern State*, Minneapolis, MN: University of Minnesota Press.

Ober, J. (1996), *The Athenian Revolution*, Princeton, NJ: Princeton University Press.

Ober, J. (2017), *Demopolis: Democracy before Liberalism in Theory and Practice*, Cambridge: Cambridge University Press.

Ocasio-Cortez, A. (2019), "Recognizing the Duty of the Federal Government to Create a Green New Deal," submitted to the US House of Representatives 116th Congress, 1st Session, February. Available online: https://www.congress.gov/bill/116th-congress/house-resolution/109/text (accessed May 25, 2019).

O'Connell, M. (2017), *To be a Machine: Adventures Among Cyborgs, Utopians, Hackers, and the Futurists Solving the Modest Problem of Death*, London: Granta.

OECD.stat, "Average Annual Hours Actually Worked per Worker," data from 2000 to 2018. Available online: https://stats.oecd.org/Index.aspx?DataSetCode=ANHRS# (accessed May 26, 2019).

Ohlheiser, A. (2020), "How Covid-19 Conspiracy Theorists Are Exploiting YouTube Culture," *MIT Technology Review*, May 7. Available online: https://www.technologyreview.com/2020/05/07/1001252/youtube-covid-conspiracy-theories (accessed May 10, 2020).

PA Media (2020), "There Is Such a Thing as Society, Says Boris Johnson from Bunker," *Guardian*, March 29. Available online: https://www.theguardian.com/politics/2020/mar/29/20000-nhs-staff-return-to-service-johnson-says-from-coronavirus-isolation (accessed May 3, 2020).

Paul, H.K. (2014), "A Failure of Imagination: Human Rights Through Neoliberalism, The Economic Crisis, And Austerity Policy," in Deric Shannon (ed.), *The End of the World As We Know It?*, Oakland: AK Press.

"The Peliti Network." Available online: http://peliti.gr (accessed May 28, 2019).

Pew Research Center (2014), "Emerging and Developing Economies Much More Optimistic than Rich Countries about the Future." Available online: https://www.pewglobal.org/2014/10/09/emerging-and-developing-economies-much-more-optimistic-than-rich-countries-about-the-future (accessed May 25, 2019).

Polanyi, K. (1944), *The Great Transformation*, New York: Farrar & Rinehart.

Pollin, R. (2018), "De-Growth vs a Green New Deal," *New Left Review*, 112. Available online: https://newleftreview.org/issues/II112/articles/robert-pollin-de-growth-vs-a-green-new-deal (accessed May 25, 2019).

Porter, T. (2020), "3 Nurses in the UK Forced to Wear Trash Bags Instead of Real Protective Gear Have Tested Positive for the Coronavirus," *Business Insider*, April 9. Available online: https://www.businessinsider.com/coronavirus-uk-nurses-forced-to-wear-bin-bags-test-positive-2020-4?r=US&IR=T (accessed April 30, 2020).

Rapier, G. (2018), "Bitcoin Could Use More Energy Than Argentina This Year," *Business Insider*, January 10. Available online: https://markets.businessinsider.com/currencies/news/bitcoin-mining-could-use-more-energy-than-electric-cars-this-year-morgan-stanley-2018-1-1012823094 (accessed May 28, 2019).

Ramsay, A. (2019), "Boris Johnson Made Politics Awful, Then Asked People to Vote It Away," openDemocracy, December 22. Available online: https://www.opendemocracy.net/en/opendemocracyuk/boris-johnson-made-politics-awful-then-asked-people-vote-it-away (accessed January 3, 2020).

Ranciére, J. (2017), *A Coffee with Jacques Ranciére beneath the Acropolis*, Athens: Babylonia.

Rancière, J. (2019), "On the *Gilets Jaunes* Protests," *Verso*, February 12. Available online: https://www.versobooks.com/blogs/4237-jacques-ranciere-on-the-gilets-jaunes-protests (accessed May 26, 2019).

Rawls, J. (1971), *A Theory of Justice*, Cambridge, MA: Harvard University Press.

Rehman, A. (2019), "The 'green new deal' Supported by Ocasio-Cortez and Corbyn Is Just a New Form of Colonialism," *Independent*, May 4. Available online: https://www.independent.co.uk/voices/green-new-deal-alexandria-ocasio-cortez-corbyn-colonialism-climate-change-a8899876.html (accessed May 26, 2019).

Renton, D. (2019), *The New Authoritarians: Convergence on the Right*, London: Pluto Press.

Ricoeur, P. (1985), *Time and Narrative*, trans. Kathleen McLaughlin and David Pellauer, Chicago: The University of Chicago Press.

Ringstrom, A. (2015), "IKEA to Invest Up to 3 Billion Euros in New Shopping Centres," Reuters, April 15. Available online: https://uk.reuters.com/article/uk-ikea-shoppingcentres/ikea-to-invest-up-to-3-billion-euros-in-new-shopping-centres-idUKKBN0N61LN20150415 (accessed November 23, 2019).

Ross, K. (2018), "A coffee with Kristin Ross," Athens: *Babylonia*.

Serre, J.-P. (2008), *Les Algebras and Lie Groups*, Berlin Heidelberg: Springer.

Sharman, J. (2018), "Steve Bannon Intended to Use Cambridge Analytica to Suppress Black Vote in 2016 and Promote 'culture war', Says Whistleblower," *Independent*, May 17. Available online: https://www.independent.co.uk/news/world/americas/us-politics/steve-bannon-cambridge-analytica-2016-election-black-vote-trump-culture-war-a8355396.html (accessed on May 25, 2019).

Shiva, V. (2005), *Earth Democracy: Justice, Sustainability and Peace*, London: South End Press.

Smith, D., Jacobs, B., and McCarthy, T. (2017), "Sean Spicer Apologizes for 'even Hitler didn't use chemical weapons' Gaffe," *Guardian*, April 11. Available online: https://www.theguardian.com/us-news/2017/apr/11/sean-spicer-hitler-chemical-weapons-holocaust-assad (accessed May 25, 2019).

Smith, J.C.A (2014), "Capitalism," in Suzi Adams (ed.), *Cornelius Castoriadis: Key Concepts*, London: Bloomsbury.

Spannos, C. (2014), "Bread, Education, Freedom: 41 Years after the Greek Junta," *teleSUR*, November 17. Available online: https://www.telesurenglish.net/analysis/Bread-Education-Freedom-41-Years-After-the-Greek-Junta-20141117-0014.html (accessed May 2, 2020).

Spannos, C. (2016), "Mass Surveillance and 'Smart Totalitarianism,'" *ROAR Magazine*, Winter (4). Available online: https://roarmag.org/magazine/mass-surveillance-smart-totalitarianism (accessed May 9, 2020).

Spiros, M., Angelos, P., Athanassios, T. (2011), "The Challenges of Antimicrobial Drug Resistance in Greece," *Clinical Infectious Diseases*, 53(2): 177–184. Available online: https://doi.org/10.1093/cid/cir323 (accessed August 23, 2020).

Srnicek, N. and Williams, A. (2016), *Inventing the Future*, London: Verso.

Steffen, W., Broadgate, W., Deutsch, L., Gaffney, O., and Ludwig, C. (2015), "The Trajectory of the Anthropocene: The Great Acceleration," *The Anthropocene Review*, 2(1): 81–98.

Straume, I. (2014), "Democracy," in Suzi Adams (ed.), *Cornelius Castoriadis: Key Concepts*, London: Bloomsbury.

Straume, I. S. and Humphrey, J. F. (2011) *Depoliticization: The Political Imaginary of Global Capitalism*, Nordic and Baltic regions: NSU Press.

SZ/ICIJ (2016), "The Panama Papers: Exposing the Rogue Offshore Finance Industry," *Süddeutsche Zeitung and International Consortium of Investigative Journalists*. Available online: https://www.icij.org/investigations/panama-papers (accessed November 30, 2019).

Tech Transparency Project (2020), "Extremists Are Using Facebook to Organize for Civil War Amid Coronavirus," Campaign for Accountability, April 22. Available online: https://www.techtransparencyproject.org/articles/extremists-are-using-facebook-to-organize-for-civil-war-amid-coronavirus (accessed April 28, 2020).

Todorov, T. (1987), *The Conquest of America*, New York: Harper.

Tovar-Restrepo, M. (2012), *Castoriadis, Foucault, and Autonomy: New Approaches to Subjectivity, Society, and Social Change*, London: Continuum Studies in Continental Philosophy.

Triantafyllidou, A., Gropas, R. and Kouki H. (2013), "Introduction: Is Greece a Modern European Country?" in Anna Triandafyllidou, Ruby Gropas, and Hara Kouki (eds.), *The Greek Crisis and European Modernity*, UK: Palgrave Macmillan.

Vincent, D. (2011), "China Used Prisoners in Lucrative Internet Gaming Work," *The Guardian*, May 25. Available online: https://www.theguardian.com/world/2011/may/25/china-prisoners-internet-gaming-scam (accessed November 21, 2019).

Vogel, K., Rutenberg, J., and Lerer, L. (2020), "The Quiet Hand of Conservative Groups in the Anti-Lockdown Protests," April 21, *New York Times*. Available online: https://www.nytimes.com/2020/04/21/us/politics/coronavirus-protests-trump.html (May 5, 2020).

Wagner, P. (2007), "Imperial Modernism and European World-Making," in Nathalie Karagiannis and Peter Wagner (eds.), *Varieties of World-Making: Beyond Globalization*, Liverpool: Liverpool University Press.

Wagner, P. (2010), "Multiple Trajectories of Modernity: Why Social Theory Needs Historical Sociology," *Thesis Eleven*, 100: 53–60.

Wallerstein, I. and Balibar, E. (1988) *Race, Nation, Class, Ambiguous Identities*, London: Verso.

Whitmarsh, T. and Thomson, S., eds. (2013), *The Romance between Greece and the East*, New York: Cambridge University Press.

Wiener, N. (1948), *Cybernetics, or Control and Communication in the Animal and the Machine*, Paris: Hermann & Cie.

Wittgenstein, L. (1974), *Tractatus Logico-Philosophicus*, London: Routledge.

Wood, A., Graham, M. et al. (2019), "Networked But Commodified: Digital Labour in the Remote Gig Economy," *New Internationalist*, February 28. Available online: https://newint.org/features/2019/02/28/networked-commodified-digital-labour-remote-gig-economy (accessed May 28, 2019).

Yellow Vests (2018), "Call from the Yellow Vests of Commercy to Set Up Popular Assemblies," *Internationalist Commune*, November. Available online: https://internationalistcommune.com/yellow-vests-commercy/ (accessed May 27, 2019).

YouGov (2016), "Socialism and Capitalism Results." Available online: https://yougov.co.uk/opi/surveys/results#/survey/94978480-d625-11e5-a405-005056900127 (accessed May 25, 2019).

CONTRIBUTORS

Alexandros Schismenos was born in Athens, Greece, 1978. He holds a Ph.D. in Philosophy and has authored four books in Greek and several articles regarding social autonomy and political philosophy. He has participated in social and ecological movements since the late 1990s.

Nikos Ioannou was born in Agrinio, Greece, 1964. He practices and teaches carpentry. He is the co-author of two books in Greek and several articles regarding contemporary politics. He has been a social and ecological activist since the late 1970s.

Chris Spannos was born in Los Angeles, California, United States, 1976. He has been researching and writing about social movements and autonomy for more than two decades. He was founder and editor of *The New Significance* from 2010 to 2014, a web magazine covering social change in the twenty-first century. He hosted Imaginary Lines, a media analysis program, until May 2015.

INDEX

abolished 127
abolishing 163, 178
abolition 43, 127, 134, 203
abyss 64, 76, 121
Achelous 157
activist 34, 54, 126
activists 4, 197
Adams, Suzi 208 n.5 (Ch. 4)
Afghanistan 34
Africa 16, 23, 104, 160, 161, 163, 169, 183
agents 34, 60, 111
agora 79, 115, 187, 200
agriculture 16, 18, 47, 160, 183, 193, 194
alienation 20, 25, 31, 132, 157, 165, 180
Allende, Salvador 17
alteration 25, 81, 131, 135, 149
alterity 67, 68, 75, 140
alt-right 12
America, Latin 5, 23, 158, 161, 163, 183, 190, 191
America, United States of 7, 10, 11, 14–16, 32–6, 43, 44, 54, 55, 93, 98, 99, 102, 109, 129, 158, 174, 192
American Revolution 106
Amvrakikos 156
anarchist 96, 127, 133, 199
anarchy 96
Anasazi 129
anonymous 59, 104, 138
Anthropocene, *see* Great Acceleration
anthropological/anthropologist 19, 66, 96, 121, 122, 157, 158, 171, 183
antifascist 57
Antigone 29, 30
apathy, voter 36, 105
Arabia, Saudi 13
Arab Spring 6, 104, 145

Arendt, Hannah 106
Aristotle 71, 122
Arnason, Johann 7, 9, 31
art 181
artificial intelligence 28, 201
artistic 102, 111, 113
Asia 77, 144, 158–61, 169, 183
Asian 163, 165
assembly 28, 79, 111, 112, 114, 119, 124, *see also ecclesia*
Athenian/Athenians 24, 28, 29, 31, 32, 37, 43, 156
Athens 8, 22, 24, 25, 27, 29, 33, 37, 38, 46, 52, 53, 92, 99, 101–3, 112, 117, 119, 181, 188, 194, 195
Atlantic 90
atom 47, 155
atomized 173
Augustine, St. 71
Aulagnier, Piera 208 n.6 (Ch. 4)
Auschwitz 86
authoritarian/authoritarianism 5, 13, 16, 32–4, 42, 44, 87, 92, 98, 105, 109, 121, 132, 135, 148, 169
authority 53, 58–61, 64, 76, 77, 78, 80, 87, 89, 91, 92, 95, 96, 100, 101, 103, 106, 110, 112, 114–17, 119–23, 126, 128, 130–4, 136, 142, 146, 147, 168, 176
automation 17
autonomy/autonomous 3, 6–10, 12, 14, 20–4, 26–9, 31, 39, 46, 47, 51, 56–8, 60–3, 79–82, 92, 101, 105, 109, 110, 113, 114, 116, 117, 119, 121, 123, 124, 130, 134, 135, 137, 139, 151, 172, 175–80, 184, 186, 192, 198–203
autopoiesis 208 n.3 (Ch. 5)
avant-garde 100
Aztec 78

INDEX

Bachelard, Gaston 108
Balkans 93
Bannon, Steve 12, 13
barbarism 3, 20, 21, 45
becoming 66, 68, 87, 124, 135, 141, 162, 174
being 3, 6, 7, 9, 12, 21, 25, 29, 43, 57, 60–71, 82, 106, 107, 110, 123, 126, 129, 132, 135, 137, 139–42, 155, 158, 190
being-for-itself 69–71, 129
beings 12, 25, 28, 47, 60, 67, 68, 70, 74, 121, 123, 138, 155
Belgium 173
Bergson, Henri 68
Berlin 55
bio-chronical 70
biodiversity 10, 15, 16, 19
biology/biological 70, 90, 122, 123, 142
bio-political 95
birth 10, 27, 42, 64, 65, 70, 76, 86, 166, 171, 177, 186, 188, 190, 194
Bitcoin 144, 145, 202
Black Lives Matter 5, 35
blockchain 139, 144, 148
Boggs, Grace Lee 54
Bolshevik 120
Bookchin, Murray 109, 126, 127, 131
Bourbaki, Nikolas 206 n.2 (Ch. 5)
bourgeois 90
Brazil 13, 169
Brexit 11, 13, 170
Britain 10, 32, 34, 87, 98, 170
British 11, 15, 34, 53
bureaucracy/bureaucratic 33, 54, 55, 86, 87, 92, 95, 100, 118, 155, 164, 165, 173, 184, 186
Burroughs, William 163
Byzantium/Byzantine 42, 90

calculation 10, 45, 138, 139, 141, 155, 157, 179
calendars 73–5, 77, 78, 95, 96, 107, 130, 133
Cambridge Analytica 13, 147
Cape Town 16

capital 17, 22, 55, 88, 91–4, 96, 98–100, 109, 114, 130–2, 156–8, 160–4, 166–9, 172, 180, 183, 184, 186–9, 192–4, 197, 198, 200, 202
capitalism 7–11, 14, 15, 17–23, 26, 39, 40, 42, 45, 47, 55, 56, 85, 90, 93–5, 98, 124, 130, 137, 144, 145, 155, 156, 159–67, 169–73, 177–80, 182, 183, 191, 192, 197
capitalists 8, 17, 19, 20, 33, 43, 45, 56, 64, 80, 86, 94–6, 103, 105, 115, 129, 155–8, 162, 164–8, 171, 175, 178, 180, 181, 184–8, 195
Cardan, Paul 58, *see also* Castoriadis, Cornelius; Chaulieu, Pierre
Cartesian 138
Castille 90
Castoriadis, Cornelius 3, 4, 6, 7, 9, 11, 12, 18, 20–2, 24–33, 37–40, 47, 51–62, 64–76, 79–82, 87, 89, 91, 92, 94, 95, 106, 108, 110, 114, 127–9, 135, 138, 139, 150, 156, 164, 171, 172, 176, 178, 179, 182, 183, *see also* Cardan, Paul; Chaulieu, Pierre
catastrophe 4, 29, 43, 76, 157, 169
causal/causality 7, 78
Central Intelligence Agency (CIA) 34, 36
centralized/centralization 119, 145, 201
chaos/chaotic 29, 39, 43, 64, 65, 69–71, 76, 129, 142, 147
Chaulieu, Pierre 58, *see also* Cardan, Paul; Castoriadis, Cornelius
Chile/Chilean 5, 17, 34, 97
China 10, 23, 34, 98, 144, 147, 148, 155, 159, 163–6, 168, 169, 173
Chinese 7, 161, 165, 168, 169
Chomsky, Noam 167
Christianity/Christian 33, 39, 66, 78, 100
church 13, 42
Churchill, Winston 53
cinema 162, 181
citizens 11, 28, 32, 33, 36, 58, 60, 61, 79, 80, 92, 115, 130, 163, 193, 198
citizenship 38
civilian 92, 102

civilization 41, 42, 85, 90, 93, 129, 161, 182, 185
civil rights 97, 118
civil war 14, 34, 43, 52, 170
class 37, 53, 54, 56, 92, 105, 116, 161, 171, 172, 200
classical 24, 27, 79, 92, 106
Cleisthenes 27
climate change 4, 16, 19, 20, 170, 200
Clinton, Hillary 35
Cogito (I think) 39
cognition 70, 138
cognitive 19, 60, 70, 130, 138, 143
Cohn, Norman 100
Cold War 4, 23, 33, 44, 52, 86, 161, 167
collective/collectivity 3, 4, 6, 9, 22, 24, 26–8, 30, 31, 37, 47, 54, 60–2, 72, 73, 77–9, 81, 88, 91, 94, 96, 99, 102, 103, 106, 107, 112–15, 119, 124–6, 132, 134, 138, 146, 173–5, 177, 178, 183–90, 195, 196, 199–202
Colón Cristóbal 90
colonialism/colonial 16, 41, 77
Columbian Exchange, the 90
Commercy 124, 125
common good 184
common ground 111, 118, 187–90, 197, 203
commons 162, 163, 187
common sense 32, 190
communal 96, 103, 112, 124, 134, 143, 184, 185, 191
commune 106, 109, 119, 120, 134
communist 14, 34, 36, 52–4, 72, 118, 167, 168
communitarian 183, 184, 186, 188, 191, 193
computans, homo 156, 171
computation 18
conscious/consciousness 12, 16, 21, 60, 71, 73, 74, 86, 94, 108, 109, 114, 133, 138, 139, 141, 146, 148, 179, 186
conservative 5, 11, 15, 16, 55, 86, 102, 199
constitution/constitute/constituent 9, 45, 46, 57–61, 69, 72, 73, 76, 78, 91, 92, 97, 106, 109, 111, 115, 116, 119, 120, 131, 140–2, 146, 164, 176, 191
consumerism 18, 95, 96, 163, 166, 167, 172, 181
consumption 8, 18, 47, 95, 99, 158, 159, 165–7, 172–4, 176, 179, 184, 189, 194, 203
Corbyn, Jeremy 206 n.20
Corfu 103
Coronavirus 4, 5, 10, 14, 15, 147, *see also* Covid-19
Covid-19 4, 5, 15, 16, 19, *see also* Coronavirus
creation 4, 9, 12, 19–22, 25–30, 43, 58, 59, 67, 68, 70, 73, 77, 79, 81, 82, 88, 89, 91, 94, 118, 121, 122, 125, 127, 134, 135, 138–43, 145, 150, 168, 176–9, 183, 186, 189, 193, 196, 197, 199, 200, 203
creativity/creative 11, 22, 29, 30, 52, 59, 62, 67–9, 77, 79, 81, 101, 113, 123, 124, 128, 132, 136, 139, 143, 176, 177, 201, 202
Creon 29, 30
crisis 34, 42, 45–7, 56, 61, 83, 85–8, 98, 100, 102, 104, 105, 161, 182, 186, 192–4, 197, 198
cryptocurrency 144, 202
crypto economic incentives 202
culture 12, 23, 25, 27, 31, 42, 44, 45, 72, 96, 106, 157, 162, 165, 177, 181–4
cum nihilo 68
Curtis, David Ames 27, 33
cybernetic 137–40
cyberspace 23, 140–3, 146–9
cyborg 142

Dakota 5, 35
data 13, 28, 45, 95, 150, 160, 166
death 4, 53, 63, 64, 65, 70, 76–8, 142, 182
Debord, Guy 54
December (1944) 53
December (2008) 89, 99–101, 104, 105
decentralization 145, 148
decisive moment 3, 4, 6, 19, 20, 21, 39, 47, 62, 82, 87, 109, 138, 148, 176
de-corporealization 141, 149

INDEX

de-growth 18, 195
delegates 106, 125
deliberation 6, 28, 31, 79, 80, 99, 101, 102, 111, 118, 122, 128, 135, 149, 151, 166, 176, 190, 195, 199
democracy 3, 6, 13, 16, 17, 20, 22–7, 29–34, 36–9, 41–4, 46, 54, 57, 58, 60, 61, 79, 85, 101–3, 105, 106, 109–15, 118–20, 122–4, 135, 137, 146, 150, 151, 153, 167, 168, 176, 177, 179, 184, 185, 190, 191, 195, 197–9, 201, 203
democratic 5, 6, 8, 14, 15–17, 19, 24, 27, 28, 30–3, 35, 36, 39, 41, 42, 58, 61, 80, 89, 92, 99, 103, 105, 106, 109, 111, 112, 114–17, 119, 125–7, 134, 135, 151, 167, 183, 184, 185
demos 27, 28
depoliticization 20, 87
Descartes, Rene 39
de-signification 86, 159, 177
diachronicity 104, 143
dialectics 56, 149
Diamandouros, Nikoforos 42–5, 207 n.1 (Ch. 3)
Diamond, Jared 129
dictatorial/dictatorship 42–4, 78, 104, 130, 168
digital 13, 14, 35, 88, 95, 137, 139–51, 166, 174, 177
directors 56, 164, 178
distributed consensus 148
distributed filesharing 148
divine 29, 30, 60, 92, 122
doctrine 18, 33, 34, 104
dogmas 124, 159, 161, 178
dogmatism/dogmatic 55, 56, 67, 110
Dominican Republic 90
Doomsday Clock 4
Dosse, François 51–3
doxa 32
dream 73, 193
dualism 41–3, 45
Dunayevskaya, Raya 54
Dupuy, Jean-Pierre 138
duration 70, 80, 102, 107, 150, 156, 157, 181

East/Eastern 5, 8, 34, 41, 55, 77, 104, 144, 145, 158, 161, 163, 167, 169
Easter Island 129
ecclesia 79
ecology/ecological 6, 18, 20, 22, 90, 102, 116, 120, 129, 144, 145, 157, 179, 193, 195, 197
economist 59, 158, 160, 180
economy/economic 5, 7–11, 14, 15, 17–19, 21–3, 35, 36, 39–42, 44, 45, 55, 56, 58, 61, 79, 88, 90, 91, 93, 94, 99, 102–4, 113, 117, 123, 126, 130, 143–5, 151, 153, 155, 156, 158–64, 166–73, 175, 177, 178, 180, 182, 184, 188–90, 192–8, 200, 202, 203
education 25, 37, 47, 52, 59, 65, 73, 92, 93, 95, 98, 99, 109, 113, 117, 129, 135, 150, 159, 163, 186, 195, 196, 198, 200, 201, 203
efficiency/efficient 16, 178, 184, 185, 191
ego 60, 73, 141
Egypt/Egyptians 5, 34, 97
eidos 91
election 13, 37, 102, 115, 174
Eliot, T. S. 63
elite 15, 36, 81, 87, 90, 92, 128, 132, 168, 169, 171, 190
emancipated/emancipation/ emancipatory 20, 26, 101, 106, 113, 172, 196, 199
employee/employment 81, 104, 159, 170, 194, 198
"End of history," the 3, 100
England 15
English 32, 51
enigma 63
Enlightenment 3, 17, 41–5, 91, 98, 100, 121, 122
ensemblistic-identitary 62, 64–7, 69, 127, 140, 149, 151
enterprises 90, 158, 189, 192, 194, 197
entropy 70, 141
environment/environmental 10, 21, 26, 36, 47, 68, 70, 112, 122, 129, 132, 139, 141, 143, 147, 149, 160, 169, 174, 180, 182, 190, 194, 197

Epirus   103
epistemology/epistemological   72, 138, 140, 141, 207 n.8 (Ch. 2)
equalitarian/egalitarian   60, 103, 184, 194, 198, 202, 203
equality   105, 109, 112, 113, 116, 121–3, 179, 184, 185, 187
eternal/eternity   9, 15, 25, 39, 42, 45, 63, 66, 68, 72, 75, 76, 77, 80, 128, 130, 131, 135, 155
ethics   60, 148
ethnic   92, 100, 181
Eurocentric   22, 41, 42
Europe   6, 7, 22, 23, 51, 53, 99, 101, 127, 158, 163–5, 167, 181, 182
European   7, 10, 15, 34, 42–6, 86, 90, 91, 110, 158, 161, 163, 165–7, 169, 170, 174, 181, 195
European Central Bank   44, 46, *see also* Troika
European Commission   46
European Union (EU)   7, 13, 15, 42, 44, 170, 171, 207 n.1 (Ch. 3)
Exarcheia   99, 194
executants   56, 164, 178
execution   35, 89, 97, 114, 178
existential   4, 63, 64, 71, 76, 116, 134
ex nihilo   21, 68
exploitation   13, 55, 95, 97, 103, 121, 129, 130, 162, 164
extraction   18, 103, 157
extremism/extremist   5, 13, 34

faith   170, 172
faithful, the   113
fake news   36, 138
family   12, 37, 47, 52, 64, 79, 92, 93, 179, 193
far-right   11–14, 34, 102, 171
fascism   3, 11
fascist   11–13, 17, 85, 97
February Revolution   120
Federal Bureau of Investigation (FBI)   35
feudal   22, 91, 93
finance/financial   10, 15, 18, 26, 45, 47, 55, 98, 104, 130, 145, 157, 158, 160–3, 167, 169–74, 178, 180–2, 184–6, 189, 192–6, 202, 203
Floyd, George   5
France   53, 54, 57, 81, 89, 125, 173
Frankfurt   171
freedom/free   3, 6, 10, 14, 15, 20, 27, 29, 35, 38, 41, 42, 60, 66, 79, 80, 81, 88, 91, 92, 94, 95, 100–2, 105, 106, 109, 111–24, 126, 132–4, 136, 137, 141, 142, 145–8, 151, 161, 167, 168, 177, 180, 184–8, 190, 192–201, 203
French   3, 51, 54, 55, 58, 77, 106, 171
French Revolution   77, 106
Freud, Sigmund   36, 59, 71, 73
Fukuyama, Francis   3
future   4, 10, 20, 27, 60, 66, 74–6, 78, 80–2, 101, 102, 105, 113, 116, 118, 123, 131, 135, 143, 151, 155, 168, 170, 182, 183, 186, 193

general assemblies   125, 198
German   90, 113, 171
Germany   34, 86, 173, 194
global/globalization   81, 87–90, 94–9, 101, 103–5, 108, 110, 111, 119, 123, 124, 129–31, 136, 139, 140, 143, 144, 146, 147, 149, 151, 155, 158–71, 173, 175, 177, 178, 180–5, 190–4, 199, 203
god   22, 25, 28, 29, 60, 63, 113, 121, 123
Gödel, Kurt   66
Golden Dawn Party   97, 98
Google   147, 174
government/governance/governmental   123, 125, 131, 132, 134, 147, 159, 162, 165, 167–9, 179, 184, 191, 192, 198, 199, 201
Great Acceleration   4, 205 n.1 (Ch. 1)
Greece   3, 8, 13, 22, 23, 26, 31, 33, 34, 40–7, 52, 53, 60, 63, 79, 89, 92, 97, 99, 101, 103, 104, 111, 112, 117, 155–8, 161, 163, 173, 176, 188, 193, 197–9
Greek   3, 7, 8, 22, 23, 28, 31–4, 39, 41–7, 52, 53, 61, 89, 92, 98, 99, 101–3, 110, 113, 158, 159, 162, 163, 165, 171, 181, 198
Green New Deal   15, 17, 18, 178

growth   3, 7, 8, 17–21, 27, 47, 56, 93, 99, 105, 126, 129, 137, 151, 155–63, 165–70, 175–8, 180, 184, 186, 188, 189, 192, 194, 195, 202

hacker   142, 148
Halkidiki   103, 165
Hardt, Michael   110, 115
Hastings-King, Stephen   19, 51, 55, 57
health/healthcare   5, 10, 11, 15, 16, 19, 36, 47, 98, 163, 205 n.11
Heidegger, Martin   86, 137, 138
Hendrix, Jimmy   181
heteronomous   7, 8, 20–3, 25, 26, 34, 35, 39, 45, 62, 76, 77, 80, 85, 104, 114, 122, 127–32, 135, 155
heteronomy   6, 8, 22, 25, 28, 45, 47, 60, 61, 66, 74, 75, 77, 79, 123, 126, 129, 135, 145, 146, 176, 180
Hickel, Jason   19
hierarchy/hierarchies   89, 98, 104, 109, 111, 128, 130
Hippocratic   75
Hiroshima   86
Hitler, Adolf   13
Hobsbawm, Eric   86
holocaust   13
homo computans   156, 171, *see also homo economicus*; *homo oeconomicus*
homo economicus   202
homo oeconomicus   156
Hong Kong   5, 97, 171
horizon/horizontal   6, 7, 27, 61, 64, 68, 74, 76, 101–3, 109, 115, 116, 123, 139, 149, 184, 196
hubris   29, 30, 38
humanism   121, 138
Hungary   55

id   71, 74
ideology/ideological   4, 6, 10–17, 21, 32, 35, 43, 45, 77, 97, 110, 120, 124, 137, 138, 144, 146, 148, 169, 172, 176, 182, 202
imaginary   6–9, 11, 12, 17–23, 25, 26, 31–5, 37, 39–44, 47, 57–62, 64, 67–9, 71–5, 77–9, 85–7, 89, 92–4, 96, 97, 104, 105, 109, 114, 119–24, 126–9, 131–6, 140, 142, 143, 145, 146, 148–50, 155, 156, 164, 166, 167, 173, 174, 176, 179, 180, 184–6, 192, 199, 200
imagination   9, 12, 17, 19, 21, 22, 59, 70, 71, 73, 74, 101, 129, 149
immigrant   11, 12, 88, 163, 165, 169, 170, 173
immortal/immortality   38, 39, 63, 71, 75, 77
imperialism   16, 41, 90, 170
indeterminacy/indeterminate   12, 39, 62, 69, 80, 81, 128
India   6, 10, 13, 159, 183, 190, 191
indigenous   5, 35, 88, 90, 92, 97, 166
individualism   57, 174
individuality   66, 145, 146, 174
Industrial Revolution   11, 91
industry/industrial   11, 15, 20, 57, 91, 93, 95, 96, 98, 105, 158, 159, 161, 162, 165, 166, 168, 169, 181, 182, 191, 192, 194, 197, 200
inequality   16, 55, 97, 108, 185
infinity/infinite   63, 69, 76, 88, 142, 144, 146, 147, 149, 150
information   4, 36, 96, 103, 104, 111, 130, 138, 140, 142, 143, 147–51, 209 n.2 (Ch. 9)
in nihilo   68
insignificance   20, 85, 87, 105
instituted   7, 19, 24, 25, 30, 47, 60–2, 64, 72, 74, 80, 81, 89, 91, 96, 106, 122, 127, 128, 131, 132, 134, 135, 142, 156, 163, 165, 183, 184, 188
instituting   24, 25, 29, 45, 47, 58, 61, 62, 81, 91, 101, 109, 111, 119, 124, 127, 128, 131, 132, 146, 176
institution   6, 9, 12, 16, 23, 25–7, 29, 30, 32–4, 37, 43, 44, 57, 58, 60, 62, 65, 68, 69, 72, 76–8, 80, 85, 88–92, 95, 98, 99, 101, 102, 106, 109, 111–15, 117–20, 122, 123, 127, 128, 130–5, 137, 142, 146, 151, 155, 161, 167, 173, 178, 179, 184, 186, 188, 190, 198–203

International Monetary Fund (IMF) 44, 46, 102, *see also* Troika
internet 14, 96, 104, 136, 137–43, 145–9, 160, 176, 177, 201
intersubjective 60
Ioannina 103, 112
Iran 34, 181
Iraq 5, 34, 36, 98
Islamic 45, 109, 119
Isopolity 205 n.12 (Ch.1)
Istanbul 52, 181
Italian 90
Italy 173

James, C. L. R. 54
Jameson, Fredric 9
Japan 194
Japanese 181
Jews 13
Johannesburg 181
Johnson, Boris 11, 15, 85, 87
Johnson–Forest Tendency 54
Joplin, Janice 181
judicial 35, 188
jurisdiction/jurisdictional 30, 91, 97, 111, 112, 119, 187, 200
justice 29, 81, 89, 98, 116, 118, 123, 145
justification 78, 114, 138, 180, 195

kairos 6, 75, 82
Kant, Immanuel 114
Karagiannis, Nathalie 27, 31, 37
Keratea 103
Klein, Naomi 104, 161, 167, 168
Klimis, Sophie 29, 30
Korea, South 10
Kouki, Hara 44, 45
kratos 89
Krugman, Paul 207 n.6
kulturkritik 86
Kurdish 109
Kurdish Revolution 109

labor 36, 46, 55, 56, 64, 80, 91, 95, 104, 106, 132, 159–61, 164, 165, 168–73, 177, 194, 201
Labour Party 11, 14

Lacan, Jacques 59, 208 n.6 (Ch. 4)
La Isabela 90
Lambrakis, Grigoris 34
language 7, 9, 43, 59, 69, 72, 73, 127, 128, 148
langue (*phatis*) 128
Latouche, Serge 194, 195
Latour, Bruno 138
law 9, 20, 22, 25, 26, 28–31, 37, 39, 46, 52, 55, 56, 60, 61, 66, 68, 81, 92, 93, 97, 113, 120, 122, 123, 125, 126, 131, 135, 145, 162, 170, 179, 206 n.41
lawless 182
leaning on (*Anlehnung*) 75, 109
Lebanon 5
Lefkimmi 103
Lefort, Claude 54, 208 n.2 (Ch. 4)
leftist 11, 34, 54, 96
Legein 69, 127, 128
legislation/legislator/legislative 30, 89, 91, 97, 121
Lenin, V. I. 120
Leninism 57
Lennon, John 181
Le Pen, Marine 171
Lévêque, Pierre 27
Liberal 3, 32–4, 36, 40, 43, 44, 46, 87, 89, 137, 164, 176
Liberalism 11, 27, 32, 36
liberty 97, 122, 123, 168
Library of Congress 150
living being 68, 70, 208 n.3 (Ch. 5)
lockdown 14
logic 12, 18, 27, 64–7, 69, 123, 128, 179, 188
logical 18, 67, 123, 132
London/Londoner 57, 88, 171
London Solidarity 57
lot/lottery 28, 32, 102, 115
Lyotard, Jean-François 54

machines 91, 138, 142, 186
magma/magmatic 52, 57, 62, 64, 68, 69, 74, 93, 96, 117, 118, 130, 136, 141, 148
Mann, Charles C. 90
Marker, Chris 43

INDEX

market   3, 4, 15, 17, 28, 39, 42, 45, 46, 56, 79, 91, 94, 95, 97, 115, 137, 144, 147, 155, 158–63, 166, 168–71, 177, 181, 184–97, 200, 201
Marx, Karl   20, 22, 54, 55, 56, 85, 100, 206 n.41
Marxism/Marxist   19, 20, 55–8, 86, 100, 110, 115, 116, 122, 126, 133, 199, 208 n.5 (Ch. 4)
masses   20, 120, 146, 164, 174
mastery   7, 10, 17, 18, 21, 26, 27, 39, 47, 67, 137, 142, 155, 170, 176
materialism   55, 56
Maturana, Humberto   208 n.3 (Ch. 5)
May 1968   54, 57
May, Theresa   15
Mayan   129
means of production   55, 56, 91, 94
media   13, 36, 45, 95, 97, 104, 145, 147, 158
medieval   60, 61, 93, 94, 100, 127
Melos   38
memorandum   102, 169, 171
Merleau-Ponty, Maurice   138, 151
metaphysical   56, 60, 63, 66, 77, 79, 113, 115, 122, 123, 131, 132, 146
metaphysics   93, 100, 106, 110, 113, 114, 121, 124, 141
Mexico   8, 11, 54, 88
Middle Ages   33, 90
Minneapolis   5
minor   60, 79
mode of being   7, 60, 69, 123
modernity   18, 22, 26, 39, 41, 42, 45, 78, 86, 100, 180, 207 n.8
monarchy   43, 60, 87
monetary   44, 46, 93, 202
money   38, 64, 104, 143, 144, 156, 158, 160, 161, 189, 195, 202
monopoly/monopolize   55, 89, 91, 117, 122, 131, 164, 191, 202
Mont Pelerin Society   158
mortality   4, 38, 39, 63, 76, 77, 79, 80, 135, 136, 142
Moscow   171, 181
Mumford, Lewis   95
Muslim   11, 35

myth/mythical   29, 92–4, 127, 165, 166, 167, 171, 181, 184, 189

national   5, 11, 15, 42–4, 53, 54, 78, 91–4, 98, 112, 113, 123, 164, 165, 170, 171, 179, 180, 198, 205 n.11
nationalism   16, 42, 93, 98
nationalist   52, 85
nationalization   14, 15, 93
nation state   86, 92–4, 97, 98, 112, 119, 161, 162, 164, 168, 170, 180, 208 n.2 (Ch. 6)
nature   7, 8, 16, 21, 39, 56, 67, 69, 74, 109, 123, 142, 143, 161, 163, 176, 185, 195
Nazi   11, 34, 53, 86, 97, 98, 121, 174
Negri, Antonio   110, 115, 116, 119
neoliberal   14, 45, 90, 96, 129, 158, 160, 161, 167, 168, 189, 191, 205 n.11
neoliberalism   5, 10, 17, 39, 86, 104, 156, 158, 163, 164, 194, 195
network   9, 12, 13, 25, 42, 58, 85, 88, 98, 103–6, 111, 112, 119, 123–6, 130, 138, 143, 146, 149, 158, 176, 177, 178, 183–5, 187–91, 193–9, 202, 208 n.1 (Ch. 6)
New Democracy Party (ND)   102
Nietzsche, Friedrich   86
nomos   28, 92
North Atlantic Treaty Organization (NATO)   34
Notre-Dame-des-Landes   107
Nuit Debout   106, 107

obedience/obey   8, 29, 120
Ober, Josiah   24, 25, 27, 31
Ocasio-Cortez, Alexandria   14, 206 n.36
Occupy   6, 9, 10, 31, 41, 81, 89, 101–4, 106, 110, 111, 119, 146, 193, 198, 199
oikos   79
oil   35, 103
oligarchical   60, 92
oligarchy   33, 34, 40, 44, 46, 87, 89, 102, 124, 164, 176
ontological   7, 14, 29, 43, 57, 62–5, 67–70, 75, 76, 81, 82, 116, 122, 123, 129, 137–41, 146, 176, 208 n.5 (Ch. 4)

ontology   12, 17–19, 22, 24, 27, 39, 57, 61, 62, 64, 65, 72, 81, 121, 126
oppression   4, 5, 16, 20, 54, 56, 103, 111, 121, 124, 136, 161, 169
orthodox/orthodoxy   15, 42, 55, 56
Other, the   59, 130, 142
Otherness   64, 68, 75
Oxi (the "No" vote)   46

paideia   37, 38
Pallis, Christopher Agamemnon   57, 208 n.4 (Ch. 4)
Pan Hellenic Socialist Party (PASOK)   102
Pannekoek, Anton   54
Papadopoulos, George   34
Papandreou, George   171
paradigm   25, 86, 91, 95, 96, 124, 138, 162, 164, 165
paradox/paradoxical   29, 41, 51, 56, 118, 133, 140
Paris/Parisian   52, 53, 61, 87, 88, 101, 106, 120
parliament/parliamentary   43, 98, 102
Parmenides   66
participation   5, 37, 38, 53, 116, 118, 120, 146, 196
Peloponnesian War   29, 38
Pericles   37, 38
philosophical   6, 8, 32, 47, 51, 55, 56, 65, 66, 78, 80, 86, 123
philosophy   3, 6, 22, 27, 40, 44, 51, 52, 55–8, 60, 62, 63, 65, 66, 79, 81, 89, 91, 106, 113, 114, 133, 134, 137, 138, 176
Physics, the   71
Pinochet, Augusto   17
Plato/platonic   32–4, 39, 66, 122, 141
pluralism   88, 122, 198
poietic   62, 67, 128
Poland   55
Polanyi, Karl   91
police   5, 35, 97, 99, 101, 102, 104, 108, 111, 162, 165
polis   32, 33, 92
political   4, 6, 7, 10–14, 16, 22, 24, 27, 29–32, 34, 36–8, 41–6, 51–4, 56, 58, 60–2, 64, 76, 79, 80, 85, 87, 89–95, 98–102, 104–28, 130–6, 146, 147, 149, 163, 164, 166, 167, 169, 170, 173, 174, 176–9, 182, 184, 186–8, 190, 196, 199, 200, 207 n.8 (Ch. 2)
politics   22, 27, 30, 32, 37, 38, 46, 49, 51, 52, 56, 83, 95, 98, 102, 107, 113, 114, 123, 127, 133–5, 146, 150, 168
Pollin, Robert   17, 206 n.36
power   6, 11, 12, 26, 29–31, 33–6, 38, 42, 43, 46, 52, 55, 56, 58, 60, 62, 76, 79, 87, 89, 91–3, 96, 98, 99, 102–4, 108–11, 114–20, 123, 124, 126–9, 131–4, 136, 162, 168, 170, 172, 173, 176, 187, 189, 200, 201
Prague   88
praxis   26, 54, 56, 81, 82, 105, 113, 114, 124, 135
private   23, 37, 79, 80, 91, 92, 94–6, 98, 100, 114, 115, 123, 132, 133, 135, 136, 141, 142, 144, 149, 156, 158, 159, 162, 164, 167–70, 173, 174, 180, 184, 187–90, 192, 198, 199, 201, 202
production   8, 9, 18, 20, 30, 47, 55, 56, 64, 86, 91, 94–6, 101, 104, 105, 113, 120, 155, 158–61, 164–6, 169–73, 181, 185–7, 190, 191, 193, 194, 196, 197, 201, 203
productive   55, 158, 161, 164, 165, 166, 185, 191, 194, 200, 201
progress   8, 21, 27, 39, 41, 44, 55, 58, 139, 193
progressive   15, 25, 177, 199
project   3, 6, 7, 9, 10, 14, 17, 18, 20, 21–4, 26, 27, 30, 31, 39, 42–5, 47, 51, 60, 61, 63, 77, 79, 81, 92, 96, 99, 102, 105, 107, 109, 110, 116, 119, 121, 126, 127, 130, 134, 137, 139, 146, 149, 168, 175, 177, 179, 180, 183, 185, 186, 195, 196, 199–201, 203
proletariat/proletarian   107, 113
pseudo-economies   144
pseudo-historical   93
pseudonym   53, 58, 208 n.4 (Ch. 4)
pseudo-rational   26
psyche   19, 59, 60, 65, 70, 71–4, 76
psychedelic   96

psychoanalysis   22, 36, 59, 75, 139, 208 n.6 (Ch. 4)
psychological   130, 149
public   5, 6, 8, 10, 14–16, 19, 22, 23, 26, 30, 31, 33, 36, 37, 43, 46, 47, 55, 58, 60, 64, 66, 72, 73, 76, 79–81, 86, 88, 95, 96, 98–102, 104–6, 108, 109, 111, 112, 114, 115, 117–19, 122–5, 127, 128, 131–6, 145–51, 159, 162–4, 171, 173, 174, 176, 178, 180, 184–90, 192–201, 203

radical   11, 12, 15, 17, 19–22, 39, 54, 58, 59, 61, 62, 68, 72–4, 81, 86, 96, 102, 105, 106, 110, 113, 114, 116–18, 124, 126, 127, 129, 132–4, 178–80, 184, 195
radically   95, 96, 139, 143, 187
Rancière, Jacques   81, 106, 108, 113
rational/rationality/rationalize   7, 9, 10, 17, 18, 21, 26, 27, 33, 37, 39, 41, 42, 44, 45, 47, 56, 58, 61, 67, 85, 137, 142, 155, 170, 176, 182
rationalism/rationalistic   56, 65, 66, 93, 121
Reagan, Ronald   158
reality   25, 55, 57–9, 61, 64–9, 71, 74, 75, 78, 87, 93, 110, 116, 117, 121–3, 125, 128, 135, 136, 137, 139–41, 143, 145–8, 158, 161, 163, 164, 167, 173, 179–81, 183, 190, 192, 194, 195, 201, 203
rebel/rebellion   5, 21, 97, 99, 100, 101, 104, 106, 113, 124
rebellious   96, 136, 181
reflect/reflection/reflective   76, 95, 113, 114, 122, 126, 127, 140, 141, 143, 146, 149, 150, 195
reform   27, 42, 43, 45, 46, 81
refugee   169, 173
regime   5, 24, 25, 32, 34, 43, 54, 86, 89, 100, 122, 127, 130, 145, 161, 167–9, 181, 182, 188
religion   9, 17, 41, 86, 98, 123
representation   8, 23, 30–2, 35, 68, 69, 71, 74, 77, 78, 79, 87, 106, 111, 115, 124, 125, 129, 131, 141, 142, 148–50, 174, 186, 187
representative   22, 24, 26, 31, 32, 36, 43, 44, 85, 93, 111, 124, 125, 148, 156, 157, 173, 174

revolution   11, 21, 60, 61, 77, 86, 89, 91, 93, 106, 108, 109, 120, 127, 134, 137, 140, 179, 205 n.1
revolutionary   22, 23, 27, 29, 52, 53–6, 96, 100, 109, 110, 114, 116, 118, 124, 136, 176, 179
Rojava   89, 109, 112, 183
Roman   33, 63
Ross, Kristin   107
Russell's Paradox   118
Russia/Russian   98, 120, 169

Samaras, Antonis   171, 198
Sanders, Bernie   14
scapegoat   11, 17, 21, 148
Schmitt, Carl   86, 121
science   11, 17, 57, 63, 169, 203
scientific   19, 41, 56, 138
scientist   4, 138
Scorsese, Martin   169
Seattle   88
Second World War   4, 23, 33, 34, 44, 86, 138, 172
self-conscious   86, 114, 186
self-creation   12, 24–6, 208 n.3
self-destruction   4, 30, 86, 168, 182
self-determination   140, 208 n.3 (Ch. 5)
self-governance   26–8, 32, 60, 111, 119, 123, 125, 179, 199
self-government   24, 27, 58, 80, 109, 179, 184
self-limit/self-limitation   6, 18, 27, 29, 38, 178
self-management   54, 55, 179, 192, 197–9
significance   31, 74, 81, 89, 97, 101, 140, 141, 145–7, 170, 177
signification   6–12, 14, 18–21, 23, 25, 35, 37, 40, 42, 45, 47, 56–9, 61, 62, 64, 66, 69, 71–7, 80, 85–7, 89, 93, 98, 99, 101, 104, 105, 109, 117, 120–2, 127–36, 138–40, 145, 147, 149–51, 155, 156, 159, 162–4, 166, 167, 169, 173, 174, 176–80, 183–6, 189–93, 195–7, 199, 200, 202, 203, 207 n.3 (Ch. 3)
slavery   16, 123

230   INDEX

social-historical   7, 11–13, 20, 21, 23, 25, 26, 39, 42, 47, 54, 57, 61, 62, 64, 66, 69, 72, 77, 78, 82, 85, 88, 89, 93, 95, 96, 101, 103, 105, 109, 111, 113, 115–17, 121–4, 127, 132, 135–7, 139–45, 148, 149, 157, 172, 176, 177, 180, 183, 186, 189
socialism   11, 14, 15, 17, 19, 54–7
Socialisme ou Barbarie (the group and journal)   54, 57
socialist   14, 15, 17, 19, 33, 57, 86, 94, 102, 178, 199
sociological   8, 77, 96, 116, 118, 138
sociology/sociologist   52, 138
solidarity   53, 57, 94, 97, 100, 103, 105, 111, 112, 116, 121, 123, 124, 136, 177, 178, 184, 185, 187, 195, 197–9, 202, 203
sophist   121
Soviet Union   54, 55, 167
Stalinism/Stalinist   53, 54
state, the   5, 12, 13, 15, 23, 24, 26, 28, 32, 34, 35, 37, 43, 45, 46, 54–6, 58, 85, 86, 88–105, 109, 112–19, 122, 123, 126, 128, 130–4, 136, 137, 145–8, 158, 161–5, 167–70, 176, 178, 180, 183–9, 191, 193, 194, 198, 199, 201, 202, 208 n.2 (Ch. 6)
Statesman   33, 87
Straume, Ingerid   9, 18, 24
subjective   62, 71–7, 96, 143
subjectivity   60, 66, 70, 72, 74, 77, 105, 114, 126, 134, 138–41, 145, 149, 208 n.3 (Ch. 5)
Sugar Man   181
symbol/symbolic/symbolize   4, 58, 59, 72, 74, 77, 78, 85, 86, 88, 95–7, 104, 107, 128, 140, 149, 159, 165, 166, 168, 180

tax   11, 15, 81, 188–90
taxation   92, 188–90
technique   69, 92, 94–8, 127, 130, 145, 147, 181, 189, 203
technology   13, 35, 138, 139, 144, 176, 202

temporality   8, 27, 45, 63–5, 70, 72–9, 85, 88, 89, 93–6, 99, 100, 102–9, 112, 117, 123, 124, 128, 130, 132, 135, 136, 143, 172, 180, 188, 194–6, 199, 201
teukhein   69, 127, 128
Thatcher, Margaret   9, 15, 158
Thessaloniki   34, 88, 112, 117, 197
time   3, 5, 6, 8, 11, 12, 14, 16, 18, 22, 26, 27, 33, 36, 43, 47, 49, 57, 62–82, 85, 86, 88–91, 93, 95, 96, 98–102, 104–8, 111–14, 116–18, 122, 125, 128–37, 139, 141–3, 146, 149–51, 156, 157, 159, 162, 165, 167, 168, 172–4, 176, 177, 179, 180, 183–7, 189, 190, 192, 193, 195–9, 201–3, 205 n.1
totalitarian/totalitarianism   32, 33, 116, 117, 121, 123, 133, 164, 165
Tovar-Restrepo, Marcela   51, 52
tragedy   28–30, 46
transhumanist movement   139, 142
Troika   46
Trotsky, Leon   54
Trotskyism   53, 54, 57
Trump, Donald   11–16, 35, 85, 87, 147–9, 174, 193
Tsipras, Alexis   46, 171, 198

UK (United Kingdom)   5, 11, 13–16, 57, 87
United States, *see* America, United States of

Valera, Francisco   208 n.3 (Ch. 5)
Vassilikos, Vassilis   43
Venice   90
Venizelos, Eleftherios   43
Venizelos, Evangelos   198
Vidal-Naquet, Pierre   27
Vietnam   10
VIO.ME (factory)   197, 198

Wagner, Peter   13, 27, 31, 37, 39, 44, 47, 85, 155, 207 n.8 (Ch. 2)
Web3 technologies   148
Weller, Ken   57

West, the   3, 4, 9, 11, 13, 20, 22, 31, 32, 34, 35, 38, 39, 41, 42, 43, 44, 47, 53, 55, 56, 161, 176, 191, *see also* Western
Western   3, 6, 16, 18, 22, 26, 31–4, 38–44, 52, 62, 65, 85–7, 90–6, 99, 103–5, 121, 129, 130, 146, 155, 157, 159, 161, 165, 167, 169, 170, 179, 181, 183, 185, 191–3
White House   12, 16, 35
WikiLeaks   145
women   5, 11, 37, 38, 95, 109, 179

workers   15, 53–8, 61, 95, 106, 114, 116, 120, 156, 158–60, 165, 169–73, 179, 197, 198

xenophobia   6, 85

Yellow Vests   81, 112, 124, 125, 145, 146
Yeltsin, Boris   168, 169

Zapatistas   88, 145, 183
Zone to Defend (ZAD)   107

www.ingramcontent.com/pod-product-compliance
Lightning Source LLC
Chambersburg PA
CBHW072230290426
44111CB00012B/2035